THE BEST SHORT PLAYS *1979*

Chilton Book Company

RADNOR, PENNSYLVANIA

THE
BEST
SHORT
PLAYS 1979

edited and with an introduction by

STANLEY RICHARDS

Best Short Plays Series

Copyright © 1979 by Stanley Richards
All Rights Reserved
Published in Radnor, Pennsylvania, by Chilton Book Company
and simultaneously in Don Mills, Ontario, Canada,
by Thomas Nelson & Sons, Ltd.

Library of Congress Catalog Card No. 38-8006
ISBN 0-8019-6719-8
ISSN 0067-6284

Manufactured in the United States of America

1 2 3 4 5 6 7 8 9 0   8 7 6 5 4 3 2 1 0 9

for Gertrude Samuels

BOOKS AND PLAYS BY STANLEY RICHARDS

ANTHOLOGIES:

The Best Short Plays, issued annually, 1968–1978
Great Musicals of the American Theatre: Volume One
Great Musicals of the American Theatre: Volume Two
America on Stage: Ten Great Plays of American History
The Tony Winners
Best Plays of the Sixties
Twenty One-Act Plays
Best Mystery and Suspense Plays of the Modern Theatre
10 Classic Mystery and Suspense Plays of the Modern Theatre
Great Rock Musicals
Modern Short Comedies from Broadway and London
Best Short Plays of the World Theatre: 1968–1973
Best Short Plays of the World Theatre: 1958–1967
Canada on Stage

PLAYS:

Through a Glass, Darkly
August Heat
Sun Deck
Tunnel of Love
Journey to Bahia
O Distant Land
Mood Piece
Mr. Bell's Creation
The Proud Age
Once to Every Boy
Half-Hour, Please
Know Your Neighbor
Gin and Bitterness
The Hills of Bataan
District of Columbia

CONTENTS

INTRODUCTION

As editor of *The Best Short Short Plays* series, I have come in for a fair share of questioning about recent trends in the field of the short drama. But since all of the plays contained in this volume were selected long before the writing of these words, it would be more logical to consider this introduction as a retrospective rather than a prophecy.

In contemplating the twelve plays herein, one notices a striking trend, if you will, toward restoring humanity to the theatre. Each of the works is riveted to some facet of present-day living, whether it be anxiety, insecurity, love and disillusionment, isolation, the struggle for survival in inhospitable climates, or the reflection of death. Even in the two light comedies, Alan Ayckbourn's *Ernie's Incredible Illucinations* and Frank D. Gilroy's *The Next Contestant*, there is beneath the comic exterior a strong underlying grip on reality.

There is also in these plays a welcome return to an emphasis on the effective use of words. Words always have been the wellspring from which all else flows in the theatre, but, somehow, beginning perhaps in the early 1960s, the stage took some curious turns. Words suddenly became mere adjuncts or superfluities in favor of obfuscation, stupendous stage effects, far-out celebrations, and heady theatricalism in the experimental, avant-garde, and absurdist theatre. As Mordecai Gorelik, the noted scene designer, playwright, author and educator, wrote in an enlightening magazine piece, *Theatre vs. Drama:* "It is impossible to believe that the future belongs to theatrical technique alone, with 'words' excluded or permanently reduced to grunts, screams and gibberish. The playwright is not merely an artisan in dialog; his script is the chart of an action which ascends, crisis by crisis, toward 'a spire of meaning'—a movement called by the Greeks *anagnorisis*, the journey from the unknown to the known. This journey, in the theatre, is attended by all the colorful resources of staging: acting, setting, costumes, lighting and sound effects, music and dance, in ways which clarify and intensify the meaning of the playscript, making it ever more persuasive and comprehensible—if it is a sane entertainment to begin with."

In a similar vein, critic Walter Kerr wrote in *The New York Times*: "Our theatre has struggled on, producing newer, stranger forms year after year, producing fewer new mature playwrights as those same years wore on. . . . What is very clear is that words, those strangely charged constructs by means of which a sustained intellectual intensity is generated, are not only the original tool of the theatre; they are the remaining tool of the theatre, the one means the stage has of coping with—maybe even whipping—the competition of film and television."

That the stage is very much alive again and thriving throughout the nation cannot be disputed. According to *Variety*, during the 1977–78 season the country's professional theatre—on Broadway and on the road—grossed $210 million, the largest recorded sum in the nation's playgoing history. Although figures for Off-Broadway, regional, community, educational, stock, and amateur theatre were unobtainable, it may be safe to assume that they, too, benefited from the nationwide rekindling of interest in and enthusiasm for the pleasures of the stage.

Now, what are the "trends" for 1980—?

STANLEY RICHARDS
New York, NY

John Bishop

CABIN 12

John Bishop

John Bishop makes his debut in *The Best Short Plays* series with *Cabin 12,* a powerful and affecting play that examines the tension and grief of a father and son who have come to a strange town to arrange for the burial of their son and brother, a young truck driver who has been killed in a highway accident.

Performed by the Circle Repertory Company in New York City in 1978 on a double bill with Lanford Wilson's *Brontosaurus,* the drama was described in the press as "grippingly done and beautifully written . . . *Cabin 12* is as good a short play as you'll see in a long time."

Mr. Bishop is a graduate of Carnegie-Mellon University. He acted for three years, then turned his talents to directing, staging musicals in Dallas for five summers and, later, for the Pittsburgh Civic Light Opera Company. The author made his Broadway debut as a playwright in 1977 with *The Trip Back Down.* Starring John Cullum, the presentation won wide acclaim and Mr. Bishop was hailed as "a talented new playwright with a voice that rings true."

Cabin 12 appears in an anthology for the first time in *The Best Short Plays 1979.*

Characters:

BOB MCCULLOUGH
HAROLD MCCULLOUGH
THE GIRL
THE MAN

Time:

The present.

Place:

A motel cabin in western Virginia.

The action takes place in front of and inside a motel cabin in western Virginia. The motel is rather old, probably built during the post-war travel boom of the late forties and reflects an earlier style of motel—individual cabins with steel lawn chairs in front of each door and all varieties of weeds and vines crawling the outside walls. When the lights come up we see two steel chairs downstage indicating the front of the motel room. Just upstage of these chairs, the inside of the cabin is indicated by two beds, a bureau, a nightstand and a clothing rack. There is a telephone on the nightstand and on the bureau a TV set, a blotter and a plastic tray with ice bucket and drinking glasses wrapped in paper envelopes.

The stage is empty but we can hear country-western music playing as if from the cabin next door. After a moment two men enter and cross to the cabin. They pantomime opening the door and enter the room. The first man is Bob McCullough, about thirty-six, stockily built he looks like the powerful high school guard he once was. He is wearing a conservative suit and tie. The second man is Bob's father, Harold McCullough. He is in his early sixties, also heavy set, with the strong forearms of a man who has spent all his years as a factory laborer. He is wearing a jacket and vest, white shirt and tie with dark trousers. He is a little drunk.

Bob throws an overnight case onto a bed and crossing to the bureau empties his pockets of cash and keys. Then he crosses to a bed and sits

*down just staring in front of him. After a moment he loosens his
necktie.*
*Harold is carrying an athletic bag which he puts on the bureau,
opens and takes out a bottle of Seagram's. He tears the paper off a
glass and pours a large drink. After he throws the paper out in the
bathroom, he hangs up his jacket, puts the bag down next to the TV
set.*

BOB: Easy, Dad.

HAROLD: What?

BOB: The drink.

HAROLD: This ain't a drink. A drink has water and ice in it.

BOB: I guess we should call Mom. (*But he doesn't reach for
the phone. He rubs his neck and shoulders and face to ease the exhaustion he feels. Harold crosses to a chair below the bureau and sits
sipping his drink*)

HAROLD: You were quite a while with the State Police.

BOB: Yeah.

HAROLD: (*After a pause*) Well, was it like they first told us
and all?

BOB: Pretty much.

HAROLD: (*After another pause*) What's this room costing us?
I didn't notice.

BOB: Twelve.

HAROLD: Not so bad. Though maybe they're lucky to get
it. I don't suppose anybody stops here. Except some tourists
who can't find nothing else. What anybody sees in the South
beats me. Carl Hemsley is all the time coming down here on
vacation. Well, not here exactly, but South. I never could
figure out why he'd want to. There's nothing here. You didn't
see the town . . . nothing . . . a paper box factory and that's
it. I can't figure out what Scott was doing here. Off the Inter-
state.

BOB: Tired probably. Tired and bored. (*The country-
western music has been playing under all this dialogue. Now it stops a
moment and a new record begins. Bob turns and shouts at the direction the music comes from*) Turn the goddamn radio down!

HAROLD: It's not a radio. It's a record player. They keep
playing the same songs.

BOB: It's a goddamn, half-ass, lame-brain, red-neck radio station . . .

HAROLD: (*Pointing to the bottle*) Have a drink.

BOB: . . . with only two records. Fix me one, will you? I'm gonna call Mom. (*Harold goes to the bureau to pour Bob a drink. Bob crosses to phone stand and picks up the telephone*) I want to call long distance . . . uh . . . McCullough. Room 12 . . . area code 419-552-6133 . . . yeah, charge it to the room here.

HAROLD: (*Holding up Bob's glass*) Water?

(*Bob nods and Harold goes into the bathroom with water pitcher*)

BOB: (*On phone*) . . . Mom! . . . Yeah. Fine. Dad's fine. (*During phone call, Harold hands drink to Bob, then takes cord from TV and tries to find an outlet*) And everything has been taken care of. We drove all night and got here about ten this morning. We've just now got a chance to check into a motel and call you . . . well, this has been our first chance to call, Mom, we've had so damn much to do. We're going to get some sleep tonight and drive back home tomorrow . . . yes . . . how are you, Mom? You all right? Is Jean with you? . . . Good . . . Well, I wasn't at the hospital. Dad was . . . (*Harold re-enters from the bathroom and brings the drink down to Bob. Bob takes the receiver from his mouth and cups his hand over it, speaking to his father*) She wants to know if he was burned.

HAROLD: What the hell's she got to know that for!

BOB: (*On phone again*) Well . . . ah . . . not . . . Mom, not much. He was . . . they figure he was . . . dead before that.

HAROLD: Hit the windshield.

BOB: It was probably instant . . . okay . . . yes . . . (*Again, Bob takes the phone from his ear and cups it in his hand as he speaks to his father*) She wants to know about the body.

HAROLD: (*Looking for matches in his pockets, crosses to jacket to get matches*) Fuck her.

BOB: (*Looks at Harold a moment and then goes back to the phone*) Dad took care of all the arrangements, Mom . . . I'm sure he remembered. Finfrocks. Right. Listen, let me talk to Jean a minute . . . (*Sits on bed. A pause while Bob waits, sipping his drink*) Hi! How are you? . . . Girls okay? . . . Okay, well I'll be back tomorrow. Listen, has anyone talked to Kathy? Is she with her folks or what? . . . Yeah? Good. Well, I'll see you tomorrow. Okay? . . . What? (*Bob lays the phone on the bed and rises speaking to Harold*) Mom's back on. She wants to talk to you. (*He walks around, finally sits on the dresser*)

HAROLD: (*Crossing and picking up the phone*) Hello, Grace . . . Finfrocks. Yeah, I remembered . . . I don't recall right now . . . goddamn it I just don't recall! I'll be home tomorrow. We can talk about it then. Tonight I'm just going to get drunk . . . *tomorrow,* Grace . . . goodbye, Grace. (*He stands still a beat after he hangs up, staring into space*) What the hell does that mean?

BOB: What?

HAROLD: (*Referring to the country-western tune now playing from next door*) C.C. Rider?

BOB: I don't know, Dad. Did you send the body back to Finfrocks for burial like Mom wants?

HAROLD: Ummm.

BOB: It's important to her.

HAROLD: It's all too big a deal. The boy is dead. My son is dead. That's it. That says it all. Everything else is bullshit. The services . . . bullshit! The minister talking about somebody it don't sound like you ever knew . . . bullshit. None of it for Scotty. Why do it?

BOB: (*Repeating tonelessly*) It's important to her.

HAROLD: I'm going outside a bit. (*Crosses into doorway with his drink. Bob crosses to bed, gets bag and puts it in bathroom. The country-western music stops and after a moment a Girl enters in a bathing suit, carrying a towel. She crosses the stage and as she nears Harold he speaks*) Hello.

GIRL: (*Stops a moment, surprised*) Hi!

(*Man is closing door*)

HAROLD: Going for a swim?

(*Man enters from the direction the Girl entered. He is tall, lanky, but hard muscled. He also wears a bathing suit and carries a towel. The Girl is a bit bewildered by Harold's friendliness*)

GIRL: (*Stops*) Yeah. Want to join us?

HAROLD: Well, it's certainly a nice warm evening for it.

GIRL: Yeah, it sure is. (*Glances back at the Man who comes to her side. He gives Harold a truculent look*) Be dark soon, though.

MAN: (*To Girl*) C'mon let's go.

HAROLD: Enjoy yourselves. (*The Man gives Harold a cold stare and the couple exit. Bob has come out of the bathroom and as they leave he opens the cabin door and crosses down to his father. Harold takes a long drink*) Would you believe that was *her* playing that shit-kicking music? (*Looking at the sky*) Nice night. (*Pointing out*) Are those the Appalachians, Bob?

BOB: I guess so.

HAROLD: The foothills more likely, huh?

BOB: Yeah.

HAROLD: Look like they're covered in blue smoke, (*Sits in chair*) Scotty told me about the mountains. Wanted me to ride along with him one time. But my kidneys aren't young enough to go bouncing around in a tractor trailer. (*He pauses. Bob crosses to other chair and sits*) The mountains are pretty. The rest of it they can keep. (*Pause*) Don't care much for the people either. They're supposed to be friendly. I didn't find them so. Did you?

BOB: Only if you're spending money.

HAROLD: (*Laughs*) Yeah. At the hospital . . . Christ! I could have made all the arrangements in half the time if they'd of spoke English. I couldn't understand a word anyone was saying. Till I found a doctor from up North.

BOB: You should have heard the sheriff. A fucking nitwit.

HAROLD: You know when I left you at that city building, or whatever it was, this morning, I got lost right off. The first guy I asked for directions of just sent me around in a circle. So I ask this guy holding up a lamppost in front of a dry cleaners. "Waal," he says, "If'n I was you . . ." and I says "Listen, Mac, you ain't me so just tell me if this street goes to the hospital or not." (*He shakes his head*) Ignorant. Just plain damn ignorant. Like I said I coulda been done in half the time at that hospital. (*A pause*) I suppose that's why it took you so long, too?

BOB: Yeah.

HAROLD: You sure spent alot of time there. All afternoon. Who all did you talk to? State troopers, sheriff . . . who else?

BOB: That's about it. (*Pause*) There was a guy there from Overland.

HAROLD: Yeah?

BOB: Little fucker with glasses. He was there when we first pulled up. Did you see him?

HAROLD: No.

BOB: He had brought down the manifest, and some guy from the insurance company to take care of that end of it. The truck and all.

HAROLD: Insurance?

BOB: For the company. On the truck and cargo. I got a chance, though, to ask him what the company covered Scott for. It turns out that it depends on the kind of health plan he had and his shares in the credit union. I'll have to go over to Kathy's when we get back and see if she's got some papers on it.

HAROLD: Well, I think he had some personal insurance. I sure urged him to get it.

BOB: Three thousand. Double indemnity.

HAROLD: That's all he had.

BOB: Yeah. Ain't worth a shit.

HAROLD: I'll get us another drink. (*He starts into the cabin. Stops and turns to Bob*) What about Kathy? Did you tell her you'd call?

BOB: Yeah. I suppose I'll have to. (*Rises and puts his head into his hands, wearily*)

HAROLD: (*At dresser as he pours the drinks*) She'll probably be with her folks, don't you think? I can imagine what old man McKee will say to her. He never did like Scott's drivin' a truck. (*Crosses room to outside*) I guess there was traffic coming the other way, right?

BOB: Huh?

HAROLD: In the other lane. So that Scotty had to cut for the shoulder.

(*Harold hands Bob a drink*)

BOB: I don't know. I guess so.

HAROLD: The troopers didn't say?

BOB: (*Flaring*) For Christ's sake, Dad! If you wanted to know about it, why didn't you stick around and ask?

HAROLD: I had to get over to the hospital and make those

arrangements, didn't I? Besides I couldn't this afternoon, Bob, I just couldn't.

BOB: (*Turning to Harold. Sorry that he blew up*) There could have been a car that didn't stop. No way of knowing.

HAROLD: Or else why would Scotty have gone into the shoulder . . . into the trees. Right?

BOB: I guess so, Dad.

HAROLD: I mean that's the thing I don't understand. Why Scotty went into the trees. He was too good a driver. Too fast, you know? His reflexes were too fast. I just can't understand it. It isn't at all like . . .

BOB: Let it alone, why don't you! He's dead. That's it, Dad. There's nothing to understand.

HAROLD: Then why were *you* trying to? All day over there with those policemen. All day.

BOB: There were things had to be done there, Dad.

(*Both men are quiet again for a moment*)

HAROLD: (*Sits*) Do you remember that Siamese cat your Aunt Sara had? It had a funny name . . . what was it? Sounded like a Chinese queer.

BOB: I don't remember.

HAROLD: Well, one day when Scotty was about fourteen he caught that cat just as it started to leap. Wham! Like that. He caught it. Scotty was that quick. (*Pause*) That was the most surprised goddamn cat I ever saw.

BOB: I guess after a long drive your reflexes are slower. (*Sits*) He'd been driving since Williamsport. And God knows how far he planned on getting. Matter of fact it's one of the things the insurance people got their asses in an uproar about. He was driving illegal hours.

HAROLD: Hell, don't all of them? Don't all them truckers? Seems to me they have to . . . in order to earn a decent living. (*He pauses*) The goddamn insurance company probably owns the goddamn truck company anyhow. (*Again he pauses*) You're probably right. He was worn out, poor kid. Pushing that rig all those hours. In these hills. When it happened he was just too tired to give a damn.

BOB: I don't know how you'd ever get that tired.

HAROLD: Everybody isn't as strong as you, Bob. You never understand that, do you? You just move straight ahead, always don't you? And expect everybody else is doing the same. But they aren't, Bob. Not everybody is strong that way. You should remember that.

BOB: Yeah? Well, I'm thirty-six years old, Dad. You can stop worrying about me.

HAROLD: I stopped worrying about you a long time ago, Bob.

BOB: It sounds like it.

HAROLD: I never worried about you. I worried sometimes about the people around you. (*They hear noise from pool. Harold moves downstage*) A man wants to see his sons happy. Wants to see them find some kind of peace in life. Some kind of quiet.

BOB: There ain't too much quiet to be had when you're trying to support a family.

HAROLD: I guess I know that.

BOB: Yes, I guess you do. It's just I'm not into alot of talking right now, Dad.

HAROLD: I'm only trying to figure a few things out is all, Bob. About Scott. (*After a moment*) I never wanted to interfere much when you were kids, you know? I always felt you should work things out yourselves. My Dad never let me alone and Christ, I got sick of that. But now . . . I wonder . . . Scotty seemed so goddamned lost these past few years. Things didn't go well for him. He was . . . disappointed alot and . . .

BOB: Scott was always disappointed about one thing or another, Dad.

HAROLD: Well, what was it? Something I did? I don't know what to think. He came over last week and he looked so tired, so down. He said he was going to see you. He called you from our house. Did he come over?

BOB: Yeah.

HAROLD: Well, what was the trouble?

BOB: Nothing. Nothing, really, Dad.

HAROLD: Was he having trouble with his marriage?

BOB: No more than anybody else.

HAROLD: Well, what was it? What was happening to him?

BOB: Nothing. Just dumb things. He . . . just dumb things.

HAROLD: What? (*Bob doesn't answer. He turns away. After a moment Harold continues*) This truck driving, that was just temporary I feel sure. The best part for him was the country. The scenery. He always liked things like that, didn't he? Nature. (*Sits*)

BOB: Yes.

HAROLD: Remember the little plants he was always trying to grow when he was a kid? He worked so hard on them. And at first he always wanted me to see how much they'd grown . . . until he saw I didn't care.

BOB: Aloe.

HAROLD: What?

BOB: They were aloe plants.

HAROLD: All the time I wasn't with him . . . because I had to work or I just didn't want to be home. I talked to him once on the phone, from a bar, because Grace said he'd been crying. And I asked him what he wanted and he said "I wanted you . . . that's what." I'll tell you, Bob, the mistakes you make as a parent, they . . . they hang on. You always think, if I hadn't done that or this . . .

BOB: (*Rising abruptly and crossing to the cabin*) I'm going to call Kathy. (*He goes into cabin and stands by the phone. Harold remains seated seemingly studying his drink. Bob picks up phone and speaks into it*) This is Bob McCullough in room 12. I want to call . . . (*He fishes a card out of his wallet and reads from it*) Person to person to Mrs. Kathy McCullough. Area code 419. The number is 552-6497.

(*Harold rises and crosses into the room and picks up the ice bucket from dresser*)

HAROLD: Gonna get some ice. (*He exits*)

BOB: (*On phone*) Hello . . . yes . . . was that your mother who answered? . . . Well, I'm glad you're over there. How are you? . . . I would have called you sooner but we just got into a motel . . . everything is taken care of. Dad arranged for . . . ahh . . . arranged for the . . ahhh Finfrocks to handle the funeral and . . . what? Well, it was like they said, an accident

. . . a farmer stopped his pick-up in front of Scott's truck. Stopped suddenly to make a turn into a dirt road. And Scott couldn't . . . couldn't . . . had to swerve and jackknifed . . . Kathy? Kathy, you still on? . . . It was an . . . he died instantly . . . an accident . . . of course . . . it was an accident . . . what are you talking about, Kathy? Of course they're sure. Everyone's sure. (*To himself*) Christ! . . . No, no one else was hurt . . . yes . . . yes . . . and Kathy . . . all right, sure, Kathy. I'll talk to you then . . . goodbye.

> (*Harold has returned at some point during the phone call and taken a seat outside the cabin with his drink. Bob hangs up the phone, rubs his face wearily and then crosses to the cabin door and pantomimes opening it. Harold half turns to him*)

HAROLD: (*Rises and looks through windows, then returns to seat*) Come on out. Gonna be dark real soon. How's Kathy?

BOB: Sounded very tired. (*Pause*) She asked if anyone *else* was hurt.

HAROLD: She with her folks? (*Pause*)

BOB: (*In his own thoughts*) What? (*Pause*) Yes. (*Sits in chair*)

HAROLD: (*A moment's pause*) I always thought she and Scott were a strange couple. But she loved him, I guess. She said Scotty was too delicate to be a truck driver. Delicate! One of the best football players Mansfield High ever had! Women use the strangest goddamn words. (*Leaning to bottle*) Wanna drink?

BOB: In a minute.

HAROLD: You know what I've been thinking about? What this evening reminds me of? Softball. You know? We always played at this time. Early evening . . . after work. It even smells the same now. The grass . . . the dirt. Everybody, all the different sections of the factory coming out to play softball. And the team was written right here. (*He draws a line across his chest*) Tool and die . . . punch shop . . . line "B" assembly. Some of the guys with the grease from their machines still on their hands and faces . . . you could never really get it all off. And wearing their team shirts and beat-up old baseball shoes. Those as could afford cleats, anyhow. Some good ballplayers, too. Good ones. Tommy Henrich's brother he played for the Warehouse gang. Jimmy Henrich. (*The couple we saw earlier going to the pool now return, crossing stage toward their cabin*) How was the water?

GIRL: Real fine. You ought to try it.

MAN: C'mon.

BOB: (*Coldly*) Do us a favor and keep your record player turned down.

MAN: (*Takes a long look at Bob and says toughly*) Don't worry about it, ol' buddy.

GIRL: (*Obviously used to her partner's ways, she quickly moves to his side and urges him into the cabin*) C'mon, honey.

(*Bob rises quickly, staring at the Man*)

HAROLD: (*Standing, facing Bob*) You remember Jimmy Henrich, Bob? Everything he hit was a line drive . . . ZABAAM! I saw him once turn a third baseman around with a line shot. The guy had come rushing in for a bunt . . . WHAP! (*He takes a violent baseball swing*) Christ, he could hit! They say he may have been even better than his brother. You don't know who Tommy Henrich was, do you?

BOB: A Yankee, wasn't he?

HAROLD: Yep. He sure was. (*Doing a pitching motion*). Who was it you and Scott played for?

BOB: Miller Electric.

HAROLD: Green and gold uniforms, wasn't it?

BOB: (*Rises and starts for cabin door*) I think so.

HAROLD: You know at first I was a little ashamed of you.

BOB: (*Stops*) What?

HAROLD: The way you held the bat. You know? Way up on the handle. I thought it looked kinda . . . funny . . . at first. There was all the rest of the boys swinging away like Mickey Mantle and then you'd come up and just sort of stand there and hold your bat out with a little tiny swing, (*He demonstrates*) . . . and "blop" the ball would drop out just behind the in-field somewhere.

BOB: That's the way you hit a softball, Dad.

HAROLD: I realized that. I said it was just at first I felt that way. You got to admit it isn't the most exciting thing to watch. A big guy like you up there just kind of blopping at the ball.

(*They both smile*)

BOB: I got on base.

HAROLD: Umm. (*He drinks and thinks a moment*) Who was that third baseman you had? The guy you and Scott hung around with for a while. Remember? He was always over at the house till I thought he didn't have a home of his own.

BOB: You mean Dave Schnug?

HAROLD: That's him. His father owned a dry cleaners.

BOB: No, that was Billy Sowach.

HAROLD: Oh. Do you ever see any of those boys anymore?

BOB: Just around town. You know.

HAROLD: What position did the Sowach kid play?

BOB: He didn't play softball with us. He was on the football team. An end.

HAROLD: Those were good days for you boys. (*After a pause*) Remember Scotty at shortstop?

BOB: He was something else.

HAROLD: Christ he was fast! Remember how fast he was? His reflexes, too. Fast. Quick. He was the only boy in the history of Mansfield ever to get a hit off the King and His Court. Remember?

BOB: Two hits.

HAROLD: Two hits. Right. Two hits. (*A pause*) Well, he sure deserved more than what he got.

BOB: (*Sits in chair*) We all do, Dad.

HAROLD: (*Pause*) He wanted to be a farmer. That's a funny thing. (*Bends to ground*) I came *from* a farm. Couldn't wait to get off of it. Couldn't get off it fast enough. He wanted to go back to one. And the last time I saw Scotty, I thought of my Dad . . . Warren . . . Scott was standing in our backyard, just after dinner a couple of Sundays ago and he leaned down to pick up a blade of grass and stick it in his mouth. I saw him through the window and just the way the sun hit him . . . a kind of reddish glow across his hair and shoulders . . . it made him look like my dad. The way dad used to stand outside in the evening and sometimes bend down and taste the dirt. For iron, is what I believe they tasted it for. And when I saw Scotty reach down for that grass I got the two mixed up in my mind for a moment. For just a moment he was my dad out there. (*Tears have begun to come into his eyes and he sniffs to hold them back. He rises quickly and faces Bob*) I wonder what he was thinking when it happened? (*Since Bob does not answer him he turns to him*) On the highway yesterday. I wonder what was on his mind? (*After a moment*) You don't care, do you?

BOB: I just don't want to talk about it anymore.

HAROLD: You know, I can't figure you. I just can't figure you. Because someone is dead you don't just shut them off.

BOB: I haven't.

HAROLD: (*Moves still closer to Bob, almost face to face*) You sure as hell have. Or is it just me? Maybe that's it. You don't want to talk about Scott with me. God knows you spent a hell of alot of time talking about him with everyone else today.

BOB: We've been over this.

HAROLD: You're talking to the police, you're talking to the sheriff, the highway boys, the coroner. But you won't talk with me.

BOB: (*Rising*) This is bullshit! (*He crosses and enters cabin. Puts glass on dresser*)

HAROLD: (*Follows Bob*) No. You listen to me. You listen. I want to know why you can't talk to me.

BOB: There's no point. The fact is he's dead. That's bad enough right there. What the hell he was thinking don't matter a damn anymore.

HAROLD: Matters to me. To me. He was my son and everything about his death matters to me.

BOB: (*Yelling*) He died over there on that highway. In an ambulance on the way to the hospital. In a goddamn traffic accident just like a hundred people do every day. It can happen to anyone. Just like that! There is no reason. Nothing.

HAROLD: Then what in the hell were you looking for today?

BOB: (*Sits on bed*) Nothing. Nothing . . .

HAROLD: (*Crosses between beds, pacing*) We drove by where it happened on the way here this afternoon, didn't we?

BOB: I'm not sure. (*Suddenly from next door we hear again country-western music playing rather loudly. Bob turns toward the sound and shouts*) Knock it off!

HAROLD: (*Still pacing, ignoring the music*) You're not sure? Oh, for Christ's sake! Of course you're sure. We drove right by it. It wasn't on our way but you drove right by where it happened. You even slowed down. I'm not dumb. I can gather facts same as you. I know what you were doing. So what are you giving me all this crap for?

BOB: That goddamn music is driving me crazy.

HAROLD: Why did we drive by there, Bob? (*Bob doesn't answer*) Why?

BOB: What the fuck difference does it make?

HAROLD: What is it you're thinking?

BOB: I'm not thinking nothing. Not a goddamn thing.

HAROLD: (*Faces Bob*) You are. I say you are.

BOB: Shit!

HAROLD: (*Pause*) He so admired you. There is a picture where Scotty is sitting on your Mom's lap and she's trying to feed him. He must only be about six months old. And there you are. You've just come into the kitchen and Scotty is ignoring his food, smiling this big joyful smile at you. That's the way he always was about you. He thought you were . . .

BOB: (*Blowing up, almost incoherent*) Well, all that didn't work out! Just didn't work out. So let's drop it.

HAROLD: What do you mean, didn't work out?

BOB: (*Crossing to the wall where the music is coming from*) Goddamn it, I said knock it off! (*In response the music is turned up full volume*) Goddamn it! (*He runs out the door and to the next cabin*)

HAROLD: Bob!

(*He goes after Bob who is pounding on the other cabin door. It opens and the Man appears, very angry also*)

MAN: What the hell is wrong with you?

BOB: Listen buddy, I asked you to keep that goddamn music down . . .

MAN: You want something done you don't go pounding on the walls.

BOB: Just keep the fucking music down.

MAN: Who are you? You own this place? (*He turns to go back into the room*) Go fuck yourself.

(*Bob grabs him and pulls him out of the cabin door. Harold jumps into the melee and the three of them wrestle, tearing the Man's shirt off as they claw at each other. Harold finally gets a hold on Bob and pulls him back. As he does, the Man hits Bob in the face. Bob explodes from Harold's grip and hits the Man two powerful blows. Man crumples to his knees. Harold grabs Bob again, this time wrestling him across the stage to their cabin*)

HAROLD: Stay here, dammit! Stay here. (*Harold crosses to the Girl who is helping the Man to his feet*)

GIRL: Oh my God! My God! We'll call the police. (*Kneels beside Man*)

HAROLD: No. No police. We don't need the police. Here . . . (*Taking out his wallet*) Here's some money. At least fifty dollars. Maybe more. Take it. Take him to a doctor if you want. Buy a new shirt. Here, take the money. I'm sorry. (*The Girl takes the money. Harold stands back as she helps the Man into the cabin*) No police, okay? I'm sorry. I think he'll be all right. Just too much happening here. You understand? And he got between. I'm sorry. (*The couple exit. Harold moves toward Bob who waves him away. The phone rings in the cabin. Harold starts toward it, then changes his mind and lets it ring. He stands facing Bob and watching him. Bob has been hunched in the chair, finally his head comes up and he draws a deep breath. He begins to flex his hands*) Well, you sure got that music turned off. A guy turns his record player up too high and he gets his teeth loosened. A farmer stops his truck too soon and my son is dead. (*Pause*) When you were little you used to hold your breath until you'd pass out and fall over, banging your head on the floor in the process. And you could never figure out . . . never, why life shouldn't be exactly what you wanted it to be. (*Pause*) You can beat the shit out of the whole motel, Bob, but it ain't gonna help. (*A beat*) He killed himself, didn't he?

BOB: I don't know.

HAROLD: Come on, son.

BOB: I don't know, goddamn it! I don't want to think about it.

HAROLD: Well, you better, cause I can't see no one else around here to punch—unless you want to start on me. Or we can go down the road here to a bar and find some other guys for you to . . .

BOB: (*Viciously*) I hope the next time that farmer stops his shit wagon on the highway he gets himself spattered all over some trucker's grill.

(*Harold, jarred by his son's vehemence, speaks almost to himself*)

HAROLD: Jesus . . . what happened to us? (*He walks slowly to a chair and sits*) Once Scotty locked himself in the bathroom, by mistake. It was when he was seven years old and we were going to a movie that afternoon. I had to take the goddamn door off the hinges to get him out and I was so damn mad at him that as soon as the door came off and I saw him standing in there, tiny and scared . . . his cheeks all wet from crying, I stepped forward and hit him. I hit him in the face . . . Jesus! I couldn't look at him for months after that . . . no never . . . never could I look at him without remembering.

BOB: (*Pause*) Scott said he was worth more dead than alive.

HAROLD: When did he say that?

BOB: When he came over to see me.

HAROLD: Yes.

BOB: When he came over to *talk* to me. (*He speaks very low, the words just audible*) We sat out in back and he said to me that he thought it was finished with him. He couldn't see anything ever changing for him. He could never be . . . never have . . . all the things he'd wanted. He felt tired all the time he said. It was all he could do to leave your house. He wanted more than anything just to go upstairs into his old room and go to sleep. And he said he thought he was going to die. He and I never talked much, Dad. We couldn't somehow. And then that evening, all this coming out . . . and I said nothing, Dad. Nothing. I just kept looking at him and this dumb thought . . . just words really like on a piece of white paper in my mind. "This is a brother. This is a brother." Just those words, nothing else. It was like I couldn't think. I couldn't help. And I couldn't do nothing, and I don't know why that was. (*He rises and crosses to look offstage as he talks*) When we started down here this morning. After they called us about the accident. Just after I picked you up I remembered something and I been thinking about it all day. It's when I was a senior and we were playing . . . Massillion, I think it was. It was raining and cold. A cloud of steam or mist or something lay over our heads just under the lights. We could hardly see the stands. The rain stopped in the fourth quarter. We were covered with mud by then. No score. Nobody doing anything much. Just beating the shit out of each other, waiting for something to break it. We were running an off-tackle. A simple off-tackle, and I was past the line looking for somebody to hit. And I remember wondering why the whistle hadn't blown. There was the safety men ahead of me and I thought that probably I hadn't heard the whistle. That the play was over, but that what the hell I'd take him on anyhow. And I did. A good shot and I went right through him and under him, rolling in the mud. Then I looked up and there was *Scott!* Carrying the ball in the crook of his wrist like he always did when he was clear. There he was, pounding past me . . . he'd broken out and he was running . . . running like a goddamn pony. My God, he looked beautiful. There wasn't no one gonna catch him that night. I stood up and I yelled at his back. "Run," I yelled. And I started to laugh. I was so fucking proud. And tears. I was crying . . . I don't know . . . all the tough, slogging bullshit of that game just let go. And something else as I watched my brother going down that field. I was crazy. Standing there roaring and laughing and crying. Shaking my fist watching my brother . . . my brother! Run you son of a bitch! Run you beautiful mother-fucker! RUN! (*He pauses a long moment then turns back toward Harold*) I wanted to go to him. Hug him. I could have. The rest of the team was all around him in the end zone. But I didn't. I just put down my head and I walked off the field.

(*Pause. He crosses into room for drink at dresser and realizes that booze is outside*)

HAROLD: It got all fucked up. It just got all fucked up.

(*Phone rings. Bob crosses and answers it*)

BOB: Hello . . . well, this is his son, Bob McCullough . . . yeah . . . that's right . . . well, you'd better take that up with the hospital, hadn't you? . . . Not right now. You say you talked to the hospital and . . . yeah, yeah . . . look, why don't you go home. And we'll take this up in the morning. O.K.? He's not coming to the phone tonight, Mr. Jackson. Just leave things till morning, all right? . . . Goodbye.

(*Bob hangs up the phone slowly and stands thinking. Harold rises and crosses into the cabin with booze and puts it on dresser*)

HAROLD: Was that your Mom again?

BOB: No. It was a Mr. Jackson. (*Harold does not react to the name*) The mortician here.

HAROLD: (*Pouring himself a drink*) Oh.

BOB: The one you made the arrangements with this afternoon.

HAROLD: (*Holding up bottle*) Drink?

BOB: You *did* talk to him?

HAROLD: Yes.

BOB: Before you went to the hospital?

HAROLD: I think so . . . let's see. I dropped you off with the highway patrol then I went to the hospital . . . no, I drove to this Jackson's place but he was closed wasn't open yet so . . .

BOB: Where is Scott's body, Dad?

(*The look between the two men holds a moment. Then Harold puts down his glass and nods*)

HAROLD: Here. In the car.

BOB: (*Almost a whisper*) What? (*Harold crosses to the bed and sits*) Jesus Christ!

HAROLD: And I plan to bury him tonight somewhere up in those hills out there.

BOB: (*Still stunned*) Christ!

HAROLD: Don't you see, son? He doesn't need Finfrocks and more of the bullshit that didn't work for him anyway. He doesn't need a lot of people crowding around talking crap about what he might have been. He doesn't need that.

BOB: Jesus, Dad . . .

HAROLD: And I want to do it quietly. He should go quietly after all this.

BOB: What have you done . . . the hospital . . . the police . . .

HAROLD: It's all taken care of. Money here. A lie there. People don't really care. It's not their business anyhow. It's my son. (*He rises and crosses to the clothing rack taking off his vest and tie*) Now I want to get some sleep. A nap. And go up in the hills after midnight.

BOB: Dad there are rules. Laws. Certain ways of doing things.

HAROLD: (*A sharp laugh*) Yeah, I know. I been doing them. All my life. And Scotty was *trying* to do 'em. That's how he ended up dead. He paid too fucking much attention to them. It counted for too much with him. And nobody ever told him it don't amount to nothing. Nothing. (*Pause*) You must be very tired. We need some rest, both of us. (*Chuckling*) You were the only kid ever was, who didn't want a light on anywhere at night. Pitch black before you'd go to sleep. Remember?

BOB: Mom wants a funeral, Dad.

HAROLD: (*Gently*) Yes, I know she does. I've thought of that. And I'm sorry. But it's all bullshit. A grave so big by so big . . . and seven black cars . . . and forty-five bunches of flowers and people whispering things at you. That's all bullshit and noise to me. Noise. Scott lived his life with that noise. So have you. So have I. I still hear the presses, you know that, Bob? They clang and roar right there. (*He puts a finger to a spot in back of his ear*) That factory is built into my head. I smell sheet metal and grease no matter where I am. I'll smell it at the funeral no matter how many goddamn flowers they have there. And all it does is to remind me . . . remind me of all the fucking time I've wasted. All the time trying to make it mean something. I'm tired of doing that, Bob. I'm tired of being ripped and torn and pushed. I want some quiet. I want to bury my son my way. I want to dig his grave myself. I want to lower the body in myself. And I want to spread the first shovel of dirt over his face . . . myself. And I'm going to, Bob, I'm going to.

(*Harold exits into the bathroom. Bob sits, head in hands for a moment. Then he rises . . . crosses to the cabin door and steps outside. He stands a moment . . . then calls, softly . . .*)

BOB: Scotty . . . ? (*Then grief hits him like a body blow. Gasping . . . crying, he doubles over. He fights for control through the sobs. After a moment he straightens up. He turns and goes back inside the cabin and sits on the bed. He digs into his overnight case and takes out a travel alarm. He winds it, sets it and puts it on the nightstand. He then lies down on the bed, facing up, staring at the ceiling, arms behind his head. Harold comes out of the bathroom. He stands a moment and smiles at Bob. He sees the clock and moves for it. As he takes it Bob's hand comes over quickly and encloses his father's hand on the clock. Harold looks at Bob. His shirt is out and unbuttoned*) I've set it for one A.M. That should give us time enough.

HAROLD: I saw a road this afternoon. Leads up into the mountains. We can take it.

BOB: O.K.

HAROLD: We'll find some trees . . . a quiet place. Where the sun comes first in the morning.

BOB: Yes.

HAROLD: Yes. Thank you, Bob. (*He crosses to the bureau to his athletic bag and takes out a toothbrush and paste. He starts for the bathroom and comes back to above where Bob lies. He puts out a hand and lays it lightly on Bob's head*) I'll have the lights out in a minute, son.

(*He exits into the bathroom. Bob lies staring at the ceiling as the lights fade*)

Alan Ayckbourn

ERNIE'S INCREDIBLE ILLUCINATIONS

Alan Ayckbourn

One of Great Britain's most popular writers of comedies, Alan Ayckbourn was born in London on April 12, 1939. He was educated at Haileybury and went straight into the theatre after leaving school, working as an actor and stage manager for several provincial theatres. He subsequently joined the Library Theatre at Scarborough as an actor and there began writing plays. To this day, he maintains his association with the theatre, serving as Director of Productions.

A prolific playwright, Mr. Ayckbourn has had more than a dozen West End productions since his initial London entry *Mr. Whatnot* at the Arts Theatre, London, in 1964. In 1975 five of his comedies were running concurrently, something of a record for a modern dramatist. Now an international figure, his plays have been translated into twenty-four languages and are performed all over the world.

Among his most popular works are *Relatively Speaking; How the Other Half Loves* (his first play to reach Broadway, 1971); *Absurd Person Singular* (which regaled New York audiences for 592 performances, 1974); the trilogy, *The Norman Conquests* (a Broadway hit in 1975); *Absent Friends; Just Between Ourselves* (winner of the Best New Play Award presented by the London *Evening Standard,* 1977); and *Bedroom Farce* (a long-running National Theatre presentation, scheduled for Broadway in 1979).

Ernie's Incredible Illucinations is published for the first time in the United States in *The Best Short Plays 1979.*

Characters:

ERNIE
MUM
DAD
RECEPTIONIST
DOCTOR
OFFICER
AUNTIE MAY
1ST BARKER
2ND BARKER
3RD BARKER
4TH BARKER
REFEREE
TIMEKEEPER
MAN
KID SARACEN
EDDIE EDWARDS
WOMAN
2ND MAN
LADY
ATTENDANT
TRAMP
GIRL LIBRARIAN
LADY LIBRARIAN
PATIENTS, SOLDIERS, CROWDS, BOXERS, etc.

Scene:

At one side of the stage—a doctor's waiting room. It is filled with an assortment of miserable-looking patients, coughing, wheezing, sneezing and moaning. Amongst them sit Mr. and Mrs. Fraser (Mum and Dad) and their son Ernie.

ERNIE: (*To audience, after a second*) If you ever want to feel ill—just go and spend a happy half-hour in a doctor's waiting room. If you're not ill when you get there, you will be when you leave.

(A man enters, having seen the doctor. He is moaning. He crosses the waiting room and goes out. The other patients look at him and sorrowfully shake their heads.

The Receptionist enters)

RECEPTIONIST: Mr. and Mrs. Fraser . . . *(Mum and Dad rise)* Doctor will see you now.

MUM: Thank you. Come on, Ernie.

(Mum and Dad and Ernie follow the Receptionist across the stage to the Doctor who sits behind a table)

MUM: 'Morning, Doctor.

(Receptionist leaves)

DOCTOR: Ah. Ah. Mr. and Mrs. Fraser. Is that it?

MUM: That's right. I'm Mrs. Fraser . . . and this is my husband, Mr. Fraser . . . and this is our son . . . Ernie.

DOCTOR: Ah yes. Ernie. I've been hearing all sorts of things about you, young Ernie. Now, what have you been up to, eh?

DAD: Illucinations.

DOCTOR: I beg your pardon?

DAD: Illucinations.

DOCTOR: Oh, yes illuci—quite, yes.

MUM: What my husband means, Doctor, is that Ernie has been creating these illusions.

DOCTOR: Ah.

MUM: Well, they're more than illusions, really.

DAD: I'll say.

DOCTOR: Beg pardon?

DAD: I'll say.

MUM: He's been causing that much trouble. At school, at home, everywhere he goes. I mean we can't go on like this. His Dad's not as strong as he was, are you, Albert?

DAD: No.

DOCTOR: What?

DAD: No.

DOCTOR: Perhaps it would be better if you told me a little more about it. When did you first notice this . . . ?

MUM: Ah well . . .

DAD: Ah.

MUM: Now then . . .

DAD: Now . . .

MUM: He'd have been . . . well, it'd have been about . . . near enough . . . er . . .

DOCTOR: Go on.

(*Ernie steps forward. During his speech Mum and Dad remain seated. The Doctor moves to the side of the stage, produces a notebook and makes notes on what follows*)

ERNIE: It started with these daydreams. You know, the sort everybody gets. Where you suddenly score a hat trick in the last five minutes of the Cup Final or you bowl out the West Indies for ten runs . . . or saving your granny from a blazing helicopter, all that sort of rubbish.

It was one wet Saturday afternoon and me and my Mum and my Dad were all sitting about in the happy home having one of those exciting afternoon rave-ups we usually have in our house.

(*Ernie sits at the table in the Doctor's chair and starts to read a book. Mum has started knitting and Dad just sits, gazing ahead of him. A long silence*)

ERNIE: It was all go in our house.

(*Pause*)

MUM: I thought you'd be at the match today, Albert.

DAD: Not today.

MUM: Not often you miss a game.

DAD: They're playing away.

MUM: Oh.

DAD: In Birmingham. I'm damned if I'm going to Birmingham. Even for United.

ERNIE: Meanwhile . . . while this exciting discussion was in progress, I was reading this book about the French wartime resistance workers and of the dangers they faced . . . often arrested in their homes. I started wondering what would happen if a squad of soldiers turned up at our front door, having been tipped off about the secret radio transmitter hidden in our cistern . . . when suddenly . . .

(*The tramp of feet, and a squad of soldiers comes marching on and up to their front door*)

OFFICER: *Halte!* (*He bangs on the door*)

(*Pause*)

DAD: That the door?

MUM: What?

DAD: The door.

MUM: Was it?

OFFICER: Open zis door. Open the door! (*He knocks again*)

MUM: Oh, that'll be the milkman wanting his money. He always comes round about now. Albert, have you got ten bob . . . ?

DAD: (*Fumbling in his pockets*) Ah . . .

OFFICER: (*Shouting*) Open zis door immediately. Or I shall order my men to break it down. (*He bangs on the door again*)

MUM: Just a minute. Coming.

DAD: Should have one somewhere . . .

OFFICER: We know you're in there, English spy! Come out with your hands up . . .

MUM: What's he shouting about? Oh, I'd better ask him for three pints next week, if Auntie May's coming . . .

OFFICER: Zis is your last chance . . . (*He knocks again*)

MUM: Oh, shut up . . .

(*The Officer signals his men. Two of them step back, brace their shoulders and prepare to charge the door*)

MUM: I'm coming . . . I'm coming.

ERNIE: I shouldn't go out there, Mum . . .

MUM: What?

ERNIE: I said don't go out there . . .

MUM: What—

ERNIE: It's not the milkman. It's a squad of enemy soldiers . . .

MUM: Who?

ERNIE: They've come for me . . .

MUM: Who has?

ERNIE: The soldiers. They've found out about the radio transmitter . . .

MUM: What radio?

DAD: Hey, here, that's a point. Have you paid our telly licence yet, Ethel? It might be the detector van.

MUM: Oh, sit down, Albert. Stop worrying. It's just Ernie. Shut up, Ernie.

ERNIE: But Mum . . .

DAD: I think I'll take the telly upstairs. Just in case . . .
(The soldiers charge at the door. A loud crash)

ERNIE: Don't go out, Mum.

MUM: Shut up.

DAD: *(Struggling with the set)* Just take it upstairs.

ERNIE: Don't go.

MUM: I can't leave him out there. The way he's going he'll have the door off its hinges in a minute . . . *(She moves to the door)*

DAD: Mind your backs. Out of my way . . .

ERNIE: Mum . . .

(Mum opens the door just as the two soldiers are charging for the second time. They shoot past her, straight into the hall, collide with Dad and land in a heap with him. Dad manages to hold the TV set above his head and save it from breaking)

MUM: Hey . . .

DAD: Oy!

(The Officer and the other soldiers enter. Ernie crouches behind the table)

OFFICER: Ah-ha! The house is surrounded.

MUM: Who are you?

OFFICER: Put up your hands. My men will search the house.

DAD: *(Feebly)* Hey . . .

OFFICER: *(Shouting up the stairs)* We know you're hiding in here, you can't get away . . .

DAD: Hey . . . *hey* . . . HEY!

OFFICER: Ah-ha. What have we here?

DAD: Oh. It's the telly. The neighbour's telly. Not mine.

OFFICER: Ah-ha.

DAD: Just fixing it for him, you see . . .

OFFICER: Outside.

DAD: Eh?

OFFICER: You will come with me.

DAD: What, in this? I'm not going out in this rain.

OFFICER: Outside or I shoot.

DAD: Here . . .

MUM: Albert . . .

ERNIE: Hold it. Drop those guns!

OFFICER: Ah, so . . . (*He raises his gun*)

ERNIE: Da-da-da-da-da-da-da-da-da-da-da.

(*The soldiers collapse and are strewn all over the hall. Mum screams. Then a silence*)

MUM: Oh, Ernie. What have you done?

ERNIE: Sorry, Mum.

DAD: Oh, lad . . .

MUM: Are they—dead?

DAD: Yes.

(*Mum screams again*)

DAD: Steady, steady. This needs thinking about.

MUM: What about the neighbours?

DAD: Could create a bit of gossip, this could.

MUM: What about the carpet? Look at it.

DAD: Hasn't done that much good.

MUM: What'll we do with them?

DAD: Needs a bit of thinking about.

(*Ernie steps forward. As he speaks and during the next section, Dad and Mum carry off the bodies*)

ERNIE: Well, Mum and Dad decided that the best thing to do was to pretend it hadn't happened. That was usually the way they coped with all emergencies . . .

(*Doctor steps forward*)

MUM: (*Struggling with a body*) We waited till it got dark, you see . . .

DOCTOR: Yes? And then . . . ?

DAD: We dumped 'em.

DOCTOR: I beg your pardon?

DAD: We dumped 'em. Took 'em out and dumped 'em.

DOCTOR: Dumped them? Where, for heaven's sake?

DAD: Oh . . . bus shelters . . . park benches . . .

MUM: Corporation car park.

DAD: Left one in the all-night cafeteria.

MUM: And one in the Garden of Rest.

DAD: Caused a bit of a rumpus.

DOCTOR: I'm not surprised.

MUM: We had the police round our way for days—trying to sort it out . . .

DAD: They never did get to the bottom of it, though.

DOCTOR: Extraordinary. And then?

ERNIE: (*Stepping forward*) And then—Auntie May arrived to stay. I liked my Auntie May.

(*Auntie May enters. Doctor steps back again*)

AUNTIE: 'Ullo, Ernie lad. Have a sweetie.

ERNIE: Ta, Auntie. And Auntie May took me to the fair.

(*The stage is filled with jostling people, Barkers and fairground music*)

1ST BARKER: Yes, indeed, the world's tallest man! He's so tall, madam, his breakfast is still sliding down him at tea time. Come along now, sir. Come inside now . . .

2ND BARKER: (*Simultaneously*) Ladies and Gentlemen. I am prepared to guarantee that you will never again, during your lifetimes, see anything as unbelievably amazing as the Incredible Porcupine Woman. See her quills and get your thrills. Direct from the unexplored South American Jungle . . .

3RD BARKER: Try your luck . . . come along, madam . . . leave your husband there, dear, he'll still be there when you come back . . . tell you what—if he isn't I can sell you a replacement . . . five shots for sixpence . . . knock 'em all down and pick up what you like . . .

ERNIE: Can I have a go on that, Auntie?

AUNTIE: Not now, Ernie.

ERNIE: Oh, go on, Auntie May.

AUNTIE: I want a cup of tea.

ERNIE: Have an ice cream.

AUNTIE: I've had three. I can't have any more. It'll bring on my condition . . .

ERNIE: What condition, Auntie?

AUNTIE: Never you mind what. But I should never have had that candy floss as well. I'll suffer for it.

4TH BARKER: Just about to start, Ladies and Gentlemen. A heavyweight boxing bout, featuring the one and only unofficial challenger for the heavyweight championship of the world—Kid Saracen. The Kid will be fighting this afternoon, for the very first time, a demonstration contest against the new sensation from Tyneside, Eddie "Grinder" Edwards. In addition, Ladies and Gentlemen, the Kid is offering fifty pounds—yes, fifty pounds—to any challenger who manages to last three three-minute rounds . . .

ERNIE: Oh, come on, Auntie. Let's go in and watch.

AUNTIE: What is it?

ERNIE: Boxing.

AUNTIE: Boxing? I'm not watching any boxing. I don't mind wrestling but I'm not watching boxing. It's bloodthirsty.

ERNIE: Auntie . . .

AUNTIE: Nasty stuff, boxing . . .

4TH BARKER: Come along, lady. Bring in the young gentleman. Let him see the action . . .

AUNTIE: Oh, no . . .

4TH BARKER: Come along. Two is it?

ERNIE: Yes, please. Two.

4TH BARKER: Thank you, son.

AUNTIE: Eh?

ERNIE: This way, Auntie.

(*Before Auntie May can protest, she and Ernie are inside the boxing booth. The crowd have formed a square around the ring in which stand Kid Saracen, Eddie Edwards and the Referee*)

REFEREE: Ladies and Gentlemen, introducing on my right, the ex-unofficial challenger for the World Heavyweight Championship—Kid Saracen . . . (*Boos from the crowd*) And on my left the challenger from Newcastle upon Tyne . . . Eddie Edwards . . . (*Crowd cheers. To boxers*) Right, I want a good clean fight, lads. No low blows and when I say break, stop boxing right away. Good luck.

TIMEKEEPER: Seconds out—

(*The bell rings. The crowd cheers as the boxers size each other up. They mostly cheer on Eddie—"Come on, Eddie," "Murder him, Eddie," etc. Boxers swap a few punches*)

AUNTIE: Oooh. I can't look.

(*The man next to her starts cheering*)

MAN: Flatten him, Eddie.

(*Auntie peers out from behind her hands in time to see the Kid clout Eddie fairly hard*)

AUNTIE: Hey, you stop that!

MAN: Get at him, Eddie . . .

AUNTIE: Yes, that's right, get at him.

MAN: Hit him.

AUNTIE: Knock him down.

MAN: Smash him.

AUNTIE: Batter him. (*She starts to wave her arms about in support of Eddie, throwing punches at the air*)

MAN: That's it, missis. You show 'em.

AUNTIE: I would, I would.

MAN: Give 'em a run for their money, would you?

AUNTIE: I'm not that old . . .

MAN: Eddie!

AUNTIE: Come on, Eddie!

ERNIE: Eddie!

(*In the ring Kid throws a terrific blow which brings Eddie to his knees*)

REFEREE: One . . . two . . . three . . .

MAN: Get up, Eddie . . .

AUNTIE: Get up . . . get up . . .

REFEREE: . . . four . . .

(*Eddie rises and blunders round the ring. The Kid knocks him clean out. The Referee counts him out. Crowd boos wildly. The Kid walks smugly round the ring, his hands raised above his head in triumph*)

AUNTIE: You brute!

MAN: Boo. Dirty fight . . .

AUNTIE: Bully . . .

REFEREE: (*Quietening the crowd*) And now—Ladies and Gentlemen, the Kid wishes to issue a challenge to any person here who would like to try his skill at lasting three rounds . . . any person here. Come along now . . . anybody care to try . . .

(*Muttering from the crowd*)

AUNTIE: (*To the Man*) Go on, then.

MAN: Who, me?

AUNTIE: What are you frightened of, then?

MAN: I'm frightened of him . . .

REFEREE: Come along now. We're not asking you to do it for nothing. We're offering fifty pounds . . . fifty pounds, gentlemen . . .

AUNTIE: Go on. Fifty quid.

MAN: I'd need that to pay the hospital bill . . .

AUNTIE: Go on . . .

MAN: It's all right for you, lady . . . just standing there telling other people to go and get their noses broken.

AUNTIE: All right, then. I'll go in myself. Excuse me . . . (*She starts to push through the crowd towards the ring*)

MAN: Hey . . .

ERNIE: Auntie, where are you going?

AUNTIE: Out of my way . . .

MAN: Hey, stop her . . . she's off her nut . . .

ERNIE: Auntie!

AUNTIE: (*Hailing the Referee*) Hey, you . . .

REFEREE: Hallo, lady, what can we do for you? Come to challenge him, have you?

(*Laughter from the crowd*)

AUNTIE: That's right. Help me in.

REFEREE: Just a minute, lady, you've come the wrong way for the jumble sale, this is a boxing ring . . .

AUNTIE: I know what it is. Wipe that silly smile off your face. Come on then, rings out of your seconds . . .

(*Crowd cheers*)

REFEREE: Just a minute. Just a minute. What do you think you're playing at . . . ?

AUNTIE: You said anyone could have a go, didn't you?

WOMAN: That's right. Give her a go, then.

REFEREE: (*Getting worried*) Now, listen . . .

KID SARACEN: Go home. There's a nice old lady . . .

(*Crowd boos*)

AUNTIE: You cheeky ha'porth.

2ND MAN: Hit him, Grandma!

(*Crowd shouts agreement*)

REFEREE: Tell you what, folks. Let's give the old lady ten shillings for being a good sport . . .

AUNTIE: I don't want your ten bob . . . Come on.

WOMAN: Get the gloves on, Granny.

AUNTIE: I don't need gloves. My hands have seen hard work. I was scrubbing floors before he was thought of . . .

WOMAN: That's right, love.

ERNIE: (*Stepping forward*) And then suddenly I got this idea. Maybe Auntie May could be the new heavyweight champion of the world . . .

(*The bell rings. Auntie May comes bouncing out of her corner flinging punches at the Kid who looks startled. Crowd cheers*)

AUNTIE: Let's have you.

KID SARACEN: Hey, come off it!

(*Referee tries vainly to pull Auntie back but she dances out of reach*)

KID SARACEN: Somebody chuck her out.

(*Kid turns to appeal to the crowd. Auntie punches him in the back*)

AUNTIE: Gotcher.

KID SARACEN: Ow!

(*Auntie bombards the Kid with punches*)

ERNIE: (*Commentator style*) And Auntie May moves in again and catches the Kid with a left and a right to the body and there's a right cross to the head—and that really hurt him—and it looks from here as if the champ is in real trouble . . . as this amazing sixty-eight-year-old challenger follows up with a series of sharp left jabs . . . one, two, three, four jabs . . . (*The Kid is reeling back*) And then, bang, a right hook and he's down . . . (*Kid goes down on his knees. Crowd cheers*)

AUNTIE: (*To Referee*) Go on. Start counting.

CROWD: One—two—three—four—five—six . . .

(*The Kid gets up again*)

ERNIE: And the Kid's on his feet but he's no idea where he is . . . and there's that tremendous right uppercut . . . and he's down again . . .

(*Crowd counts him out. Auntie dances round the ring with glee. The crowd bursts into the ring and Auntie is lifted on to their*

shoulders. They go out singing "For she's a jolly good fellow."
Referee and the Kid are left)

REFEREE: Come on. Get up—Champ.

KID SARACEN: Ooooh. (*He staggers to his feet*)

(*Kid goes out supported by the Referee. Ernie, Dad, Mum and the*
Doctor are left)

DOCTOR: (*Still writing, excitedly*) Absolutely incredible!

MUM: Terrible it was. It took it out of her, you know. She
was laid up all Sunday.

DAD: And we had all those fellows round from the
Amateur Boxing Association trying to sign her up to fight for
the Combined Services.

MUM: So I told his Dad on the Monday, seeing as it was
half term, "Take him somewhere where he won't get into
trouble," I said. "Take him somewhere quiet."

DAD: So I took him down to the library.

(*Doctor retires to the side of the stage again. Dad, Mum and Ernie*
exit.

The scene becomes the Public Library. It is very quiet. Various
people tip-toe about. At one end sits an intellectual-looking Lady
with glasses, reading; at the other, an old Tramp eating his
sandwiches from a piece of newspaper. One or two others. A uni-
formed Attendant walks up and down importantly. The Lady with
glasses looks up at the lights. She frowns)

LADY: Excuse me . . .

ATTENDANT: Sssshhh!

LADY: Sorry. (*Mouthing silently*) The light's gone.

ATTENDANT: (*Mouthing*) What?

LADY: (*Whispering*) I said the light's gone over here.

ATTENDANT: (*Whispering*) What?

LADY: New bulb.

ATTENDANT: (*Shakes his head not understanding*)

LADY: (*Loudly*) UP THERE! YOU NEED A NEW
BULB—IT'S GONE. I CAN'T SEE.

PEOPLE: Ssshhhh!

ATTENDANT: (*Whispering*) Right.

LADY: (*Whispering*) Thank you.

(*Attendant tip-toes out as Dad and Ernie tip-toe in*)

DAD: (*To Ernie*) Sssshhhh!

(*Ernie nods. They tip-toe and sit*)

ERNIE: (*To audience*) I didn't really think much of this idea of my Mum's . . .

PEOPLE: Ssssshhhh!

ERNIE: (*Whispering*) I didn't really think much of this idea of my Mum's. It was a bit like sitting in a graveyard only not as exciting. The trouble is, in library reading rooms some bloke's pinched all the best magazines already and you're left with dynamic things like *The Pig Breeder's Monthly Gazette* and suchlike. I'd got stuck with *The Bell Ringer's Quarterly*. Which wasn't one of my hobbies. Nobody else seemed to be enjoying themselves either. Except the bloke eating his sandwiches in the corner. I reckoned he wasn't a tramp at all, but a secret agent heavily disguised, waiting to pass on some secret documents to his contact who he was to meet in the library and who was at this very moment lying dead in the Reference Section, a knife in his ribs. Realising this, the tramp decides to pick on the most trustworthy-looking party in the room . . . My Dad!

(*The Tramp gets up stealthily and moves over to Dad. As he passes him he knocks his magazine out of his hand*)

DAD: Hey!

TRAMP: Beg pardon, Mister. (*He bends to pick up the magazine and hands it back to Dad. As he does so he thrusts his newspaper parcel into Dad's hands*) Sssshhhh. Take this. Quickly. They're watching me. Guard it with your life.

DAD: Eh?

(*Tramp hurries away. A sinister man in a mackintosh gets up and follows him out*)

DAD: Who the heck was that?

ERNIE: Dunno, Dad.

DAD: (*Examining the parcel*) What's all this, then?

ERNIE: Dunno.

DAD: I don't want his sandwiches. Spoil my dinner. (*As he unwraps the parcel*) Hey!

ERNIE: What is it?

DAD: Looks like a lot of old blueprints and things. Funny. This anything to do with you?

ERNIE: (*Innocently*) No, Dad.

(*Attendant enters with a stepladder. He places it under the light. A Girl Librarian who has entered with him steadies the steps. Attendant produces a bulb from his pocket and starts to climb the steps*)

ERNIE: (*Who has been watching him*) And now, as Captain Williams nears the summit of this, the third highest mountain in the world, never before climbed by man . . . (*Wind noises start*) He pauses for a moment through sheer exhaustion . . .

(*Attendant feeling the effects of the wind clings to the ladder for dear life. It sways slightly*)

ATTENDANT: (*Shouting down to the Girl Librarian*) More slack. I need more slack on the rope . . .

GIRL LIBRARIAN: (*Shouting up to him*) More slack . . . Are you all right?

ATTENDANT: I—think—I can . . . make it.

GIRL LIBRARIAN: Be careful. The rock looks treacherous just above you.

ATTENDANT: It's all right. It's—quite safe—if I . . . just aaaaaahhh! (*He slips and holds on with one hand*)

LADY: Captain! What's happened?

ATTENDANT: Damn it! I think I've broken my leg . . .

LADY: Oh, no!

GIRL LIBRARIAN: How are we going to get him down?

(*Dad rises*)

ERNIE: And here comes Major Fraser, ace daredevil mountaineer, to the rescue.

DAD: Give me a number three clambering iron and a hydraulic drill lever, will you? I'm going up.

GIRL LIBRARIAN: Oh no, Major.

DAD: It's the only way.

LADY: Don't be a fool, Major.

DAD: Someone's got to go. Give me plenty of line . . . (*He starts to climb*)

GIRL LIBRARIAN: Good luck.

LADY: Good luck.

(*A sequence in which Dad clambers up the ladder buffeted by the wind*)

DAD: Can you hold on?

ATTENDANT: Not—much—longer.

DAD: Try, man, try. Not much longer . . .

LADY: Keep going, man.

(*Dad reaches the Attendant. People cheer. The two men slowly descend the ladder*)

ERNIE: And here comes the gallant Major Fraser, bringing the injured Captain Williams to safety . . .

(*Dad and Attendant reach the floor. More cheers and applause from the onlookers. The Attendant is still supported by Dad with one arm round his neck. General shaking of hands. Wind noise stops*)

ATTENDANT: (*Coming back to reality, suddenly*) Hey, hey! What's going on here? (*To Dad*) What do you think you're doing?

DAD: Oh.

ATTENDANT: Let go of me.

DAD: Sorry I—

ATTENDANT: Never known anything like it. This is a public building, you know . . .

DAD: Ernie . . .

ERNIE: Yes, Dad.

DAD: Did you start this?

ERNIE: (*Innocent*) Me, Dad?

DAD: Now listen, lad—

(*Lady Librarian enters screaming*)

LADY LIBRARIAN: Oh, Mr. Oats, Mr. Oats . . .

ATTENDANT: What's the matter, girl? What's the matter?

LADY LIBRARIAN: There's a man in the Reference Section.

ATTENDANT: Well?

LADY LIBRARIAN: He's dead.

LADY: Dead?

LADY LIBRARIAN: Yes. I think he's been killed. There's a knife sticking in his ribs . . .

(*Girl Librarian screams. Attendant hurries out followed by the others, leaving Ernie and Dad*)

DAD: Ernie!

ERNIE: Sorry, Dad.

(*Doctor moves in. Mum joins them*)

DOCTOR: Incredible.

DAD: Embarrassing.

DOCTOR: Yes, yes.

(*The scene is now back to where it was at the beginning, with the four in the Doctor's room on one side and the waiting room full of patients on the other*)

MUM: Can you do anything, Doctor?

DOCTOR: Mmmm. Not much, I'm afraid.

MUM: No?

DOCTOR: You see, it's not really up to me at all. It's up to you. An interesting case. Very. In my twenty years as a general practitioner I've never heard anything quite like it. You see, this is a classic example of group hallucinations . . .

DAD: Illucinations, yes.

DOCTOR: Starting with your son and finishing with you all being affected . . .

MUM: All?

DOCTOR: All of you. You must understand that all this has happened only in your minds.

DAD: Just a minute. Are you suggesting we're all off our onions?

DOCTOR: Off your . . . ?

DAD: You know. Round the thing. Up the whatsit.

DOCTOR: No . . .

DAD: My missis as well?

DOCTOR: No. No.

DAD: Then watch it.

DOCTOR: I was just explaining . . .

DAD: You don't need. It's Ernie here, that's all. He imagines things and they happen.

DOCTOR: Oh, come now. I can't really accept that.

DAD: Why not?

DOCTOR: It's —impossible. He may *imagine* things—

DAD: He does.

DOCTOR: But they don't *really* happen. They *appear* to, that's all.

DAD: Is that so?

DOCTOR: Of course.

(*Slight pause*)

DAD: Ernie.

ERNIE: Yes, Dad.

DAD: Imagine something. We'll see who's nutty.

ERNIE: What, Dad?

DAD: Anything, son, anything. Just to show the Doctor.

MUM: Nothing nasty, Ernie. Something peaceful . . .

DAD: How about a brass band? I like brass bands.

MUM: Oh, dear. Couldn't it be something quieter? Like—a mountain stream or something . . .

DAD: Don't be daft, Ethel. The Doctor doesn't want a waterfall pouring through his surgery. Go on, lad. A brass band.

ERNIE: Right, Dad. (*He concentrates*)

(*A pause*)

DOCTOR: Well?

DAD: Give him a chance.

(*A pause*)

MUM: Come on, Ernie. (*Pause*) He's usually very good at it, Doctor.

DAD: Come on, lad.

ERNIE: It's difficult, Dad, I can't picture them.

DOCTOR: Yes, well I'm afraid I can't afford any more time just now, Mr. and Mrs. Fraser. I do have a surgery full of people waiting to see me . . . (*Calls*) Miss Bates! . . . so you will understand I really must get on.

RECEPTIONIST: (*Enters*) Yes, Doctor.

DOCTOR: The next patient, please, Miss Bates.

RECEPTIONIST: (*Going*) Yes, Doctor.

DOCTOR: (*Getting up and pacing up and down as he speaks*) What I suggest we do is, I'll arrange an appointment with a specialist and . . . he'll be able to give you a better diagnosis . . . (*His steps become more and more march-like*) than I will. I'm quite sure that—a—few—sessions—with a trained—psychiatrist—will—be—quite—sufficient—to—put—everything—right—right—left—right—left—left—left—right—left . . .
(*The Doctor marches to the door of his room, does a smart about turn and marches round his desk. He is followed by the patients from the*

waiting room, some limping, some marching and all playing, or as if playing, brass instruments) L-e-e-e-ft . . . Wheel . . .

(*After a triumphal circuit of the room everyone marches out following the Doctor who has assumed the rôle of drum major*)

ERNIE: (*Just before he leaves*) It looks as though the Doctor suffers from illucinations as well. I hope you don't get 'em. Ta-ta.

(*He marches out jauntily, following the band*)

Curtain

Lanford Wilson

BRONTOSAURUS

Lanford Wilson

When Lanford Wilson's *Brontosaurus* originally opened as the inaugural production of the Circle Repertory Company's experimental late-night series, it was received with general acclaim in the Manhattan press. Mel Gussow of the *New York Times* described it as "pungent and incisive . . . a giant of a one-act play" while Marilyn Stasio wrote in *Cue* magazine that "*Brontosaurus* is a close encounter of the human kind. It bristles with wonderfully witty dialogue and piercing insights." Rob Baker of the New York *Daily News* was equally enthusiastic, concluding his review with the observation that "*Brontosaurus* proves once again that Lanford Wilson is probably our greatest functioning American playwright."

The popularity of this dramatic portrait of a middle-aging antiques dealer confronted by the callowness of youth, prompted the theatre's management to schedule it for a regular engagement along with John Bishop's *Cabin 12,* which appears earlier in this volume.

Lanford Wilson was born in Lebanon, Missouri, in 1937, and was educated at San Diego State College and the University of Chicago, where he started writing plays. He inaugurated his professional career at the now defunct Caffe Cino in Greenwich Village. After having had ten productions at this pioneer Off-Off-Broadway café-theatre and six at the Café La Mama, he moved to Off-Broadway in 1965 with the presentation of *Home Free!* at the Cherry Lane Theatre. In 1966, Mr. Wilson again was represented Off-Broadway, this time with a double bill, *The Madness of Lady Bright* and *Ludlow Fair,* at the uptown Theatre East. *This Is the Rill Speaking,* another of his short plays, was seen during that same season at the Martinique Theatre in a series of six works originally done at the Café La Mama.

In 1967, Mr. Wilson won a Drama Desk–Vernon Rice Award for his play, *The Rimers of Eldritch,* a haunting dramatic study of life in a small town in the Middle West. This was followed by another full-length play, *The Gingham Dog,* which opened in 1968 at the Washington Theatre Club, Washington, D.C. In the following year, it was presented on Broadway with Diana Sands and George Grizzard as stars and Alan Schneider as director. The author returned to Broadway in 1970 with *Lemon Sky,* a work that drew the following comment from Clive Barnes: "Mr. Wilson can write; his characters spring alive on stage; he holds our attention, he engages our heart."

In 1972, Mr. Wilson added another rung to his growing status when he received considerable praise for his libretto for the operatic version of Tennessee Williams' *Summer and Smoke*. The opera, with music by Lee Hoiby, was performed by the New York City Opera at Lincoln Center.

Unquestionably, his greatest success to date is *The Hot L Baltimore*. The play, written under a Guggenheim Fellowship, originally was presented by the Circle Repertory Company in January, 1973, then was transferred in March to Off-Broadway's Circle in the Square Downtown for a commercial engagement. The play ran for 1,166 performances and was festooned with honors: it won the New York Drama Critics' Circle Award for Best American Play of the 1972–73 season; the Outer Critics' Circle Award; and an Obie award for Best Play.

Among the author's other works for the theatre are *Balm in Gilead; Wandering; So Long at the Fair; No Trespassing; Serenading Louie; The Mound Builders; The Great Nebula in Orion*, introduced in *The Best Short Plays 1972; The Sand Castle*, published in *The Best Short Plays 1975;* and *The 5th of July*, a major Off-Broadway success in 1978.

Mr. Wilson has been the recipient of Rockefeller, Yale, and Guggenheim Fellowships, as well as an award from The American Academy of Arts and Letters for "the body of his work as a playwright."

Brontosaurus was first presented as the opening production of *The Late Show* at the Circle Repertory Company in New York City on October 19, 1977. The cast was as follows:

THE ANTIQUES DEALER	Tanya Berezin
THE ASSISTANT	Sharon Madden
THE NEPHEW	Jeff Daniels

Director: Daniel Irvine

Characters:

THE ANTIQUES DEALER, *a woman, well dressed and attractive, possibly forty-five*
THE ASSISTANT, *a woman about the same age or younger*
THE NEPHEW, *a young man, perhaps seventeen or eighteen; he should be presentable and not unattractive. There should not be any sign of sexual attraction between the Antiques Dealer and the Nephew*

The Scene:

The Present. New York City.
The stage is carpeted in one neutral color. The only furniture is a pair of simple antique side chairs, elegant and light.
There is no suggestion of walls or of the antique shop. The chairs are isolated by light, surrounded by dark.
The scenes alternate between the shop of the Antiques Dealer and her apartment.

The Assistant sits, her back to the audience, polishing a silver candlestick. The Dealer stands, her hand resting lightly on the other chair, looking out.

DEALER: He's not coming. He's lost in the city. She said he's a sweetheart. I should have been warned then. A real little pussycat. Half pussy, half cat, more than likely. Pussy. Cat. A bell should have tolled. I'm an innocent. I have a virgin streak in me—somewhere. I still believe. No, I don't—what I do have is a desperate need to believe. I saw a movie with a talking plant from outer space that repeated over and—
ASSISTANT: A talking plant?
DEALER: A sci-fi movie with a talking plant that said "Feed me!" And there I am. I'm an outer space plant-form demanding (*Tasting the word*) nourishment. Feed me, sustain me, make me believe. (*Pause*) Oh, he can move in. From his mother's description he's grown into more of a puppydog than a pus-

sycat. What do I care? I've got to talk to someone. I'll more than likely turn the poor child into a faggot within a week. Everyone in this business is a faggot, including me. I'm a bigger faggot than any of them, come to—dear, God, it's all about survival. What you see is what you get. Say I who am myopic. And there you have it. No, it isn't a need to believe. It's just an enormous, welling hope. An unwashed hope that's so general and vast and unspecific that it engulfs details. Fogs up edges. God, I'm hopelessly infantile. I read somewhere— I'm always reading somewhere, still blithely skipping the words I don't know; not skipping, assuming. On the fly. I must be some kind of speed-freak, I think. Everything at a rush. Catch-as-catch-can. (*Pause*)

ASSISTANT: What? You read somewhere . . . ?

DEALER: Something about maturity. Made me realize I was condemned to adolescence. Moral adolescence. Consigned.

ASSISTANT: Good.

DEALER: Umm . . . with its unbased assurance and vicious competitiveness, unconstructive criticism, unearned ennui. A welter of personal habits; all compulsive, all sloppy. And no behavior at all.

ASSISTANT: Should it be? Earned?

DEALER: (*Coming out of an abstraction*) Should what be earned, love?

ASSISTANT: Ennui. Or criticism necessarily constructive?

DEALER: (*With decision*) He isn't coming. He's four hours late. If she had told me which plane he was taking . . . Wandering in this city for four hours, he's probably a drug freak by now. I can't wait around, I'm supposed to be seven places. (*Referring to the candlestick*) That's coming out wonderfully. It'll tarnish in a day in this humidity. When my hair kinks I know I'll come into the shop and all the silver will look like nickel, the brass will be black and the copper will have begun to turn that nice aqua color. Lock up, love, pull the shade down if you stay late, and turn out the lights. (*As the Assistant stands and walks off, the Dealer turns the left chair to face right, the lights change, shift to reveal the Nephew standing, head down, beside the right chair. The Dealer continues, but with a change in her voice, more friendly)* Don't hang your head (*The Nephew raises his head*), and do try not to look so forlorn. (*The Nephew mumbles*) And please don't mumble. And don't let me frighten you. I'm all protective coloration. Under the peafowl feathers is only a peafowl. Are you tired? (*Pause*) You aren't going to be drab and lackluster and uninterested, are you?

NEPHEW: Probably.

DEALER: Yes, well, you would know, having lived with yourself for . . . what would you say if I asked you to fix me a Manhattan? (*She takes her jacket off and hangs it on the left chair*) It's been all rather long today and all rather exhausting.

NEPHEW: I don't know what a Manhattan is. I know what it is, but I don't know how to make one.

DEALER: Um. That would do. I would say fix it to what, or fix it yourself, or better still: absolutely nobody drinks Manhattans. What you probably want is a vodka stinger. Don't let me walk on you, because with the best of intentions, I nevertheless will. Which only means more than likely what I'd like—immaterial—what I would really like, actually the only thing I drink, is white wine. Wouldn't you?

NEPHEW: Where is it?

DEALER: Not "Where is it?" "You want it, what's stopping you, get it." Not where is it. (*Pause*)

NEPHEW: I don't know where it is.

DEALER: What would you like? Have one with me.

NEPHEW: No.

(*Pause. Or dead stop. The Nephew speaks in a simple, deliberate, almost uninflected tone. His rhythm, pace and lack of irony are in contrast to her, but we should feel a power and a danger in him*)

DEALER: I'm uneasy with strangers. Relative strangers. Strangers who are relatives. I hope to God sis warned you about me.

NEPHEW: She said you knew everyone and lived in a beautiful apartment.

DEALER: Um . . . "apartment." She would. Yes, I pour through catalogues looking for plants that are city hardy. Everything I touch dies of an innate sense of my ignorance of their needs. Or more likely my feigned interest in their behavior. I've never deeply accepted that "The force that through the green fuse," etcetera. They don't die, but they would if I didn't have a cleaning lady with a concern. She talks to them. And I have a feeling that the moment I leave the room they whisper back to her. About me. I don't know everyone. I don't know anyone. I used to know everyone. You're in time to see your only aunt come unglued in the humidity. (*She leaves the lighted area. The following lines are spoken from the dark*) White wine in the refrigerator for future reference, where it gets too cold; red on the shelf above, where it stays too warm. (*She reappears holding a glass of wine*) Room temperature in France is about fifty-eight degrees. There's a simple way to calculate that in centigrade, but I only remember complicated things. (*She passes between chairs and sits on the left chair*) Should you notice a crack forming, I hope you won't be self-conscious about telling me. No, the Everybodys who were Anybodys that I knew I've watched the last few years slowly realize that they had wasted their talent creating a "fashion" which, by its nature, changed and left them helplessly *derrière garde*, and clumsy about adjusting to the current whims without it being heartbreakingly obvious. If one cared. You're to be in school. Where? I mean I knew, but I've forgotten.

NEPHEW: Here.

DEALER: I know here, love. Where here?

NEPHEW: New York University.

DEALER: Umm. Do you know what you'll be studying? What's your major? If one still majors.

NEPHEW: Theology. (*Pause*)

DEALER: Did Margy show you your room?

NEPHEW: Yes.

DEALER: I can remove some of the furniture if it's too . . .

NEPHEW: No, it's fine. (*Beat*)

DEALER: "Fine." It's been described as one of the ten most beautiful rooms in the city.

NEPHEW: I like the view of the park.

DEALER: (*A little annoyed*) Yes, the window was there, I thought why cover it. The park is nice to look at but I wouldn't go into it without six strong sober adults, and I don't know any. Or at least not six. Theology as theory or philosophy or what?

NEPHEW: I'll probably be a minister eventually.

DEALER: Oh, dear . . . God. (*She sets wine glass down*) Oh, why not? Dear, yes, why not? What denomination are we—or are you—your father, I suppose, our family wasn't much on—uh, vaguely Protestant, I think. Not Presbyterian or Anglican I—

NEPHEW: Dad is a Methodist.

DEALER: Of course. I knew that. Do they drink? I mean do they approve of drinking?

NEPHEW: They say they don't.

DEALER: (*Wonders, but doesn't comment*) I read somewhere that every ounce of alcohol you drink kills four thousand brain cells which are not regenerated. Contrary to what I read somewhere else. (*She picks up wine glass*) I understand that rather than being a steady, every-night tippler, it's healthier, or less destructive, really, to go on a monthly all-out binge. Which is worth considering if one is interested in being less destructive. Which maybe I am; despite appearances. (*More expansively*) Nephew of mine, my house is yours. (*Gets up from chair and moves about the room*) Please make friends. Bring them here. I like young people. I like people, though I don't seem to sometimes. "People," you understand, no specific person. Bring them here. The "apartment" is yours. It's been photographed for every classy publication from *Abitare* to the *Sunday Times Magazine*, and in not one picture has there been a living soul. Large, flat colorless rooms in perfect order. Flowers on every table and lovely, longing, sad-looking rooms. I've never liked a single photograph. If you hate it here I'll help you find an apartment, but I hope you won't. And next spring maybe you can help me look for a house—in the country. It's past time. I don't want to live in the city. I've not found myself in the catalogues. In the winter I tell myself I have to be here for the shop, but I need a summer place where I can get away. Only I'm chicken. I want land but I see myself buying a lush seven acres and with my care watching it turn to burning desert around me. Within weeks. (*Pause*) A young theologian.

Or possibly a young minister. Well, why not? God, yes, why not? (*Pause*) I like that. You don't apologize. All my friends are apologists. Laugh at their interests and they lose interest. Pretend indifference.

NEPHEW: I didn't realize you were laughing at me.

DEALER: You're squinting. Do you need glasses?

NEPHEW: No.

DEALER: Then why on earth do—well, no matter. Your complexion can be left to a good diet. Do you eat well?

NEPHEW: I don't know.

DEALER: Do you have breakfast?

NEPHEW: No.

DEALER: Then you will. So will I. We'll all start the day as we're advised to.

NEPHEW: No. (*Pause*)

DEALER: Well, it isn't something we have to discuss now.

NEPHEW: I don't have any interest in food. I don't care what I eat.

DEALER: Well, if you don't care then there's no problem.

NEPHEW: There aren't many things I like to eat.

DEALER: Well, I'll serve what I like and you can learn.

NEPHEW: No.

DEALER: Oh, surely you can.

NEPHEW: I don't like to eat much.

DEALER: To eat much or you don't much like to eat?

NEPHEW: I don't like to eat much.

DEALER: Is this ethical or physiological? I would think with God's bountiful gifts one would be ethically bound (*As the Nephew turns and leaves, the lights change to denote a shift from home to shop, and the Assistant returns carrying a small wine table or candlestand which she places between and just downstage of the two chairs*) to enjoy the mysteries of *supreme de Volaille a la creme*, or *coquilles St. Jacques normande*—I wonder should I take that as moral indignation, physical revulsion, or tactical retreat?

ASSISTANT: He sounds shy. (*She sits on the right chair*)

DEALER: I have trouble distinguishing between shy and dull. Oh, young people! They baffle me. (*She sits on the left chair*)

ASSISTANT: I thought you had them pegged.

DEALER: Oh, I have them pegged. I know all the crap they're pulling through uninterest and disinterest and ignorance and indifference. I think they're quite right and completely wrong. I am just inadequate to dealing with it. I admire fiber. I don't understand flaccid people. Shy, retiring, flaccid—

ASSISTANT: —Fiberless—

DEALER: He's a mess, of course. His complexion, his posture. He is either an aquaphobic, or he's hypersensitive to phosphates or he has an extreme gland disorder or he just does not ever bathe.

ASSISTANT: They forget.

DEALER: They do not forget, they enjoy their own smell. They get off on reeking. I might find it ascetically bracing if they thought it was the way God intended they should smell, but no. They get off on it.

ASSISTANT: Don't you?

DEALER: (*Abstracted*) Yes, well, at that price . . . oh, it all means nothing. More than anything he gives me the feeling of being one of Tinguely's antique-looking, non-product-producing machines. Something useless and archaic and mildly amusing and above all something that makes a great deal of noise as it clanks around in its useless revolution. I learned once, some theory, that one can exhaust oneself pushing a great mass or object but if that mass doesn't move, then the effort does not constitute work. It's just exhaustion. Work equals mass times the distance moved or whatever. And I am—not lately working. (*She stands and gazes out the shop window*)

ASSISTANT: Have you gotten him to eat?

DEALER: Yes, and exactly what he damn well wants. Very stubborn streak. But I couldn't call it religious preference. No religion except perhaps his own dictates a diet of hamburgers, cokes, and French fries.

ASSISTANT: And only that?

DEALER: An occasional *Snickers* bar. An odd *Orange Julius*. Our conversations (forced on my part, nonexistent on his) are completely circular. He's been in school over a month, I ask him what he's learning (not just because I feel I should keep abreast of how my money is being spent) and he tells me yes, he is learning a great deal and I say what are you learning and he says, "Not what they're teaching." Which I suspect is true, in any case. So what are you learning that they aren't teaching? And he says, "How not to teach." How not to teach. (*She sets the empty wine glass on the table, passes between the chairs, turns, and looks at table and wine glass*) Ah, well. That looks sweet. Calculated, but sweet. A little "Bloomys," but they do all right. It's just that he never seems to be out and he never seems to be in. He's always there and he's never home. I wonder what it was I expected of him? What did I need? Or was I just madly plugging all possible gaps?

ASSISTANT: That doesn't bear too close inspection.

DEALER: (*Riding on, not picking up the inference*)—I find myself being annoyed because I suspect he's out but don't know. I find myself listening outside his room, trying to catch a light under his door. I hear him cough and think, my God, am I never to have any privacy? Probably the only reason I never married is because I am congenitally incapable of living with another human being fouling my nest.

ASSISTANT: It was your idea.

DEALER: Oh, but someone to bring life into my—laughter, joy. Someone who would listen, not someone who would only wait till I had finished. But then who knows. Who knows anything? (*Pause, she lifts the wine glass, looking at it critically. Taps her ring against the bowl and listens to ring*) "How not to teach." (*Ring, listens*) "How not to teach." (*Ring. The Nephew enters silently*) "How not to teach." (*The lights change to denote a shift back to the apartment. The Dealer turns to face the Nephew*) Could you possibly state that as a positive?

NEPHEW: How to teach.

DEALER: Ah . . . that's quite a thing to learn. (*She sets the glass on the table*) How would you teach? How would you teach me? I know nothing about theology, but I've always been a willing pupil of just about everything. Teach me.

NEPHEW: I'm going to find a place of my own. (*Pause*)

DEALER: Of course you are. I said you might. Though I

hoped you wouldn't. But I don't suppose you'll really want my assistance in finding a place. We'd be at cross-purposes, wouldn't we? I'd be looking for some place clean and convenient and light . . .

ASSISTANT: Anything else?

DEALER: No thanks, you'd better go. It's late. (*The Assistant goes. As she passes the Nephew, he crosses to stand by the left chair. The Dealer faces the Nephew from behind the right chair*) Nephew of mine, you are a puzzle. Ah, well, maybe ministers are best a puzzle. When did you decide, by the bye? If that's something you decide?

NEPHEW: I said I wouldn't stay long.

DEALER: You did not. But not to stay and not to go. To be a minister.

NEPHEW: It's something I've known.

DEALER: From birth.

NEPHEW: Since I was twelve.

DEALER: It came upon you suddenly.

NEPHEW: Yes.

DEALER: In a blinding flash.

NEPHEW: Not blinding.

DEALER: A figure of speech.

NEPHEW: A realization.

DEALER: That you were to be a minister. I wonder that other professions don't have these "callings." Imagine a bricklayer or a fireman coming to his family, his eyes glassed-over, saying: "Parents! I've *seen!*" Or "I've been called." I know that sounds cynical and pejorative, but that's only my voice. Over the years, quite independent of conscious design my voice has developed a cynicism I don't always feel. Or don't intend to convey. I am physically incapable of talking about anything involving, say, religion without it sounding as though I would like to take a bottle of lemon oil and a steel wool pad and rub it out. But I believe you understand that I do not necessarily like the sound or the impression I make.

NEPHEW: I know.

DEALER: I was sure.

NEPHEW: (*Straightforward*) I was standing at the side of the house. I don't remember what I had been doing. I don't remember anything before, immediately before, or immediately after. I stood for a while and then I went inside. I was standing at the side of the house. I had come from around behind in the shade and was standing in the sun; not doing anything, not going anywhere, just standing at the side of the house in the sun. And the hand of God reached out and touched me. That doesn't mean anything. It's abstract, isn't it? But it's the easiest way of explaining the feeling. (*Dealer sits*) I was standing there, not thinking anything that I would remember. There was a bush on my left and the corner of the house on my right. Instead of just stopping for a while and then moving on, while I was stopped I became aware that my body was changing, or something was happening, physically happening, inside my body. As if all my cells were changing at the same time. Some vibrating sensation through my body that raised me or made me feel like I was physically growing, like a—perhaps a chemical change was occurring. And I started to get scared, but instead of that happening it was gradually like I wasn't standing there anymore. For a moment it was like I had changed into a gas. I felt I was spreading, thinning out, being led over the world or shown the world. Thinning out to take it all in, to absorb it. Or I was shown what I was. I heard people speaking in languages that I understood but had never heard before, I heard bells—no, I didn't actually *hear* anything, but I seemed to *know* about bells in church towns, in the farm country around small towns where they make wine, in France; and people getting up where it was just beginning to be light, to go to work; people walking on streets, shopping, and small things growing in the wet and shade in rain forests. I didn't see them, I wasn't shown them, I just knew them. Because thinning out, or whatever it was, I *became* them. An old lady who thought in a language different from the one she spoke, dying in terrible pain in the geriatric ward of a very efficient hospital; twins just being born in the Orient; a boy my age, in India, whose job was to carry the censer with incense, swinging it, in a Catholic church: I didn't know them, I *was* them. I was *they*. They were me. We were all the same stuff, the same regenerating impulse. I just thinned out to mix with it all or to realize what I was, what I had come from, and gradually came back to my own design, my own body. But, of course, I thought about it differently, because it wasn't mine. I wasn't me. I was them. I was they. Which is grammatically correct?

DEALER: (*Pause*) "I was they" is correct, but it sounds all wrong, doesn't it?

NEPHEW: I've not tried to explain the experience before, but you asked—

DEALER: —and it's so easy and such fun to talk about oneself.

NEPHEW: Something I should try to explain. It shouldn't be all that difficult. It happened. For all I know it's the experience someone has when they say God has touched them, or when the Indians experience Satori.

DEALER: The Indians in India.

NEPHEW: The Buddhists, yes.

DEALER: I wanted to be sure we weren't into the Hopi or the Navajo.

NEPHEW: After that I decided to study theology.

DEALER: It might as easily have been biochemistry.

NEPHEW: I don't think so.

DEALER: Of course not. And you decided to come here. Where I could help you.

NEPHEW: I think we all need help.

DEALER: That's encouraging. (*She stands*) Would you like a glass of wine? (*A very long silence*)

NEPHEW: No.

DEALER: I think I would. Dear me. (*She exits with empty wine glass, and says the following lines from the dark*) It's so difficult not to be wildly cynical and experienced and cutting. I wonder why that is? The devil in us, I think. But I'll try to contain all that. (*She reappears with the wine glass filled*)

NEPHEW: It's all right.

DEALER: No, I have all my negative impulses under control. I won't make fools of us this minute anyway.

NEPHEW: I mean I'm unshakable. You can't touch that. It's there. I couldn't touch that.

DEALER: I, of course, am shakable to the core. But what religious feeling I have, although I'm not sure your experience wasn't more humanitarian than religious—

NEPHEW: Nor am I, but they're the same.

DEALER: Of course. What religious feelings I have have been sublimated into beautiful line. Into furniture and painting and those people who create them. The Protestant Ethic with taste. Maybe it should be the Protestant Aesthetic. And are you having your philosophy or whatever, your understanding, your experience confirmed? By your studies?

NEPHEW: Indirectly, yes.

DEALER: In the rain forest, I'm sorry, I may have misunderstood, that thing growing in the dark and damp. That was a plant?

NEPHEW: A fern of some kind.

DEALER: As specific as that. Then you were one with the plants as well as the—mankind or personkind. But then, "the force that through the green fuse," of course. Touché. Where exactly do you wish to move?

NEPHEW: I never intended to stay.

DEALER: You have a number of idiosyncracies for one so young, but the one that I find particularly annoying is that you do not listen to the question. I did not ask if you arrived intending to leave, I asked where you intended to go.

NEPHEW: I want to be with friends of mine.

DEALER: Now, see? One can be to the point and still enigmatic if one only tries.

NEPHEW: I never intended to stay.

DEALER: You intended only that I should pay your expenses.

NEPHEW: You said you would.

DEALER: My dear young nephew, I am liable to say anything.

NEPHEW: It would be easier for me if you did.

DEALER: I damn well bet it would.

NEPHEW: It doesn't matter.

DEALER: Of course, nothing matters. (*She places glass on table*)

NEPHEW: I want to be with my friends.

DEALER: I told you before you came. I told you as you were standing in the middle of my living room that first night—with your feet splayed and your arms hanging akimbo: bring your friends here. The house is yours. Find a delicate girl with long fingers who will set up a loom in the middle of the parlor and clack away all morning in the sunshine. Bring in an incipient and completely untalented rock group who will rehearse in the dining room, leaving beer cans on the Duncan Phyfe table. Lean back laughing and break the legs off the Federal chairs. Bring them here. These friends. All of your friends. Take a girl, or boy for all I care, into your room, and rip the bed apart. Get come stains and shit marks all over the sheets. Seat them cross-legged on the terrace and preach to them the miracle of Yoga. Use my house. (*She steps toward the Nephew*) If you have friends why haven't they been here? (*Beat*)

NEPHEW: They wouldn't like it. (*Pause*)

DEALER: Yes. (*She turns away*) As plants as people, of course. They wouldn't be happy here. Things don't thrive in order and beauty, they thrive in hardship and decay. These friends wouldn't be fertile, fecund, they wouldn't be happy here. It's too— (*A wave of the hand finishes the sentence*) Yes, I think you have made it clear that that at least is your firm if misguided . . . and you of course do not yet know of the actual efficacy of happiness. Your philosophy makes everything appear so easy. But you would say it isn't easy, it's only true, perhaps, but then what isn't? Truth is very broad and very deep and rather subjective, isn't it? You have a simplicity that's impossible for us who are competitive and . . . all those vulgar things. I must be sounding wildly condescending, but as I said that's only sound. I'm always skeptical of anyone who has it all so worked out. (*Pause*)

NEPHEW: I listen to you but I don't know how to help you.

DEALER: Maybe it's just that condescension runs in the family. But if there's something you don't know, school won't be a complete waste. (*Beat*) When I was a child, even younger than you if such a thing can be imagined, I thought I would go to heaven, and my dollies would go to heaven, and my doggies would go to heaven, but even I did not suppose that the ferns would go to heaven. But why not? If they've lived a good life. And make the journey without so much as a frost-tipped frond. Who would want heaven, after all, without the ferns?

NEPHEW: "Heaven" is here. "Heaven" is the future.

DEALER: Heaven is . . . ah. Heaven on earth? One day? (*No answer*) With the aid of science? Or without science altogether? (*No answer*) I think without. Heaven is eating roots and berries and having a knowledge of the wonder of it all— or, the sameness of it all—all life, which is a kind of promiscuous protoplasmic soup. Everyone sitting around in the altogether with a mongoloid grin: that is undoubtedly the answer. What matters? Nothing matters. Enjoy it. Or the regenerating *stuff* matters. Something like that? (*No answer*) I think that's marvelous for thirty-five people for six weeks in a warm climate. (*The Nephew crosses to behind the right chair, as the Dealer approaches the left chair*) You see, we have what would be called in personnel training a personality conflict. We see things quite differently. Paradise for you occurred once in say, Tahiti. Where there was no disease and no hardship. And you see a vision of that continuing, if the white man had not fouled paradise. While I see—without the assistance of Magellan or Cooke—one day drifts to the sandy shores of Tahiti a . . . very . . . bad . . . co-co-nut. (*Pause*) I can't get it out of my mind, purely my negative bent, that in the last few hundred years we have recognized that that life, that *stuff* we are all made from comes in some rather disturbing forms. Like the yellow fever bacilli and athletes' foot fungus. And I at least, am not going to be really content in a world without *Desenex*.

NEPHEW: Why do you think paradise would be a tropical island? It could be a desert.

DEALER: Will your desert heaven have politicians? Teachers, I suppose, you damn well bet, but—say, a form of government? (*Pause. He stares at her waiting. Finally—*)

NEPHEW: No.

DEALER: Would it have science?

NEPHEW: No.

DEALER: All those little boys who wear glasses and work in their basements on rockets and model trains at last liberated from an obligation to make a name for themselves. Would it have art?

NEPHEW: No.

DEALER: That, at least, is absolutely for the best, I'm sure. Though you may at last have discovered a model to prove art's inevitability. And no furniture or architecture or engineering. All that is . . . what? In religious terms? Vanity, isn't it? (*Pause*) And there will be no death, but people will grow old and die.

NEPHEW: Not very old, I wouldn't think.

DEALER: Nor would I. But what does it matter as long as life continues. And no one will be unkind or egocentric or ego-anything because they will know what life is. How simple. But then all great ideas are all so simple. Einstein's theory of time is like that, a continuum, but you're right not to clutter up your— I wonder why it is that I can't make myself grasp the image of deifying the hydrogen atom . . . but I'm always wrong; forever envying those who are right. That's just vanity, again, of course. I came close to the light myself once. The experience of·feeling as though I was only (or, forgive me, *supremely*) gas. When I was having a tooth extracted, as I went under, counting backwards from ten to one—I think I got as far as six—I thought for a moment that I was becoming a gas myself. But then I woke up with a mouth full of blood and a cup of tea in my hand, having missed the revelation—by one or two numbers. Had I hung on till four or three . . . but I'm a natural resister. Change, no; that's vanity too, of course. But I liken change to someone coming into my house when I'm away and moving all the furniture about. I can't seem to slough it off, all this vanity, all this world, and give myself over to it. To Christ or to someone or to some cause or to anything. Slough it all and be bathed in the blood of the lamb. How wonderful that would be. How free one would feel. How right. Damn. Go free! As with your experience, thin out and go free! God, yes. Free of it all! All this vanity! How grand and liberating. "How like a god." It must be what the sky divers feel. Or those who have determined on suicide. Or mental defectives who blubber in their bibs and smile . . . smile, my God that smile. The serenity on their faces makes them look forever young, which is what they are, of course. But I grew up. Vanity. And was guided into or decided not to slough it off quite yet, but fool that I am, to *contend* with it all for a bit. Never mind that I make nothing out of it. I am hopelessly *involved* with the world; vanity again. I do not feel, deep in my marrow, that I am one with my neighbor and the goldfish bowl, but it is to be hoped that that will come. Having never experienced Satori or received the call I must muddle around in the darkness as best I can, worrying about those mundane things like grease spots and liver spots and bills of lading and the price of psychiatry, vanity again. Without the light, I sometimes am hurtful of others and especially myself, and I find myself overcompensating for the sake of social grace and tending to make a spectacle of myself. I do at least recognize that those around me are aware that I am hanging over that goodnight by a thread, as are they, and the only comfort we have is knowing that each sees the other's pain and fear, god-damn, vanity again; but that comfort is what we live for. They know that I have not deceived, at least, anyone into becoming my friend; and have at least tried to influence no one. Living in my time, in our time, not yours, but mine and my genera-tion's time—that last generation, we honorable brontosaurs who are the last to die: that generation that plugged away those last few weeks before everlasting life was discovered; those last mad hours before everyone drank a potion and lived forever like a giant redwood or Frodo in the Grey Havens—we are the nervous dumb brontosaurs who knew only that at the very least their lives would have a form: a shape, a beginning and a middle, and for those who cared for it a progeny, and finally and blissfully, or regrettably, an end. You can have engraved on our tombs, vanity again, that we bumbled glassy-eyed, those cute little dim brontosaurus eyes, through life's humiliating, predictable metamorphoses (I pray) with a semblance of grace and compassion at times— and in a rather difficult age for intelligent beings, as we were the first and the last to make the migration purely for the sake of the journey, being fully aware of the absurdity, the biological accident, or if you would, the biological miracle of it all. And we made the migration to its no doubt ignoble end for the sake of experiencing the accident. Or for the sake of experiencing the miracle (*She picks up the glass of wine*) and with a good handful of Valium but without an excess of ameliorating philosophical palliatives. (*Beat*) You would say, of course, it doesn't end. That life does not have a form or its form has no form. That it doesn't change. That it doesn't "evolute." You would have been one hell of a wet blanket on the Beagle. (*Long pause*)

NEPHEW: May I go?

DEALER: As you say, you never intended to stay. Fly to your secrets and giggle with your compatriots about the brontosaur, with its fat ass and little brain and dim eyes. Spread the Light. God knows they need it. No point in hanging around here and being silted-in just yet. (*Pause*) Yes, go. You may go, by all means. You can't help me, you said so yourself. Don't let one failure trouble your future. You are more than likely not dangerous. Please, yes, go. (*He does not move. He is trying to find a way to help her*) Yes, go. Leave. Damnit, leave my house! (*Pause. He leaves. She places the wine glass on the table and turns the left chair so that its back is to the audience as in the opening scene. This action is accompanied by a shift in the lights to the setting of the shop. The Assistant enters, carrying the candlestick and a buff cloth. She sits in the left chair, her back to the audience*) I didn't even know the . . . he had friends. Oh, the smug, simpering, sentimental, asinine, sophomoric— Baptist! Methodist! Someone should steal his copy of *The Prophet* from his knapsack. Knapsack, I want you to realize. He arrived with an imitation leather two-suiter and left with an army surplus canvas bag. It takes no time at all to pick up the style. Though I don't believe he has friends with his "I am a rock, I am an island" phi . . . (*Beat*)

ASSISTANT: Can one be both?

DEALER: Huh? Oh, sure. Rock Island. That's the caliber mind we're dealing with. There's no talking with someone who has seen the light. Unless one has also seen the light. Is there a Dylan Thomas in the shop? Oh, never mind, I have one at home. And what good anyway, I mean the man was a bigger drunk than I. Though I'm beginning to wonder if I really understood why. Perhaps I was only humiliated at asking him to stay. Free them all. We earned it for them, didn't we? But what do they care? And what do I care? Who knows? Who knows anything? God, I wonder seriously if all reformers had aunts: did Luther have an aunt, do you suppose? Or Thoreau? But even Thoreau didn't say, "I am Walden Pond." Oh, he has no defenses. He can't sip a glass of wine and look knowing and telling and modestly arousing and throw up some smart-ass facade behind which he can quickly regroup and regain his composure. As can we. On a good day. (*Takes a sip of wine. Pause, looks at the Assistant*) Oh, leave off, darling. That's as good as that is going to get. (*The Assistant rises. The Dealer takes the candlestick in exchange for her wine glass and the Assistant exits with the glass and buff cloth. The Dealer places the candlestick on the table and puts on her jacket. The Assistant returns with a candle which she carefully places in the candlestick. As she prepares to light the candle—*) You go on. I'll lock up. I'll pull down the shade if I stay late. (*The Dealer takes the matches from the Assistant, and the Assistant leaves. As she begins to speak, the Dealer lights the candle*) So I go home to a quiet house and I bathe and sleep peacefully. So in the summer I find a house in the country and have workmen repair the roof and put in a new heating system, and I clear the weeds from the garden. I paint the rooms white and come into town for shades for the windows. So I walk out of Bloomingdales with the shades ordered and a new silk blouse in a sack under my arm: a cream silk shirt that goes with anything. So I come out of the airconditioned and carpeted, quietly bustling store into the street. The sun is very bright on the taxis and the sidewalk, and the air is very hot and not moving much. (*Pause*) So I stand for a minute, trying to decide if I want to go uptown to the apartment or if I'll walk to the shop or go directly back to the country. I stop there for a second in the heat. The curb of 60th Street is on my left as I face Third Avenue and a traffic light is on my right. I stop a minute and stand; not thinking of anything I would remember afterward, not aware of thinking of anything. Going nowhere. I stop for a minute and stand for a minute in the sun. And whatever is happening to me, I'm not afraid. (*A pause. She blows out the candle, turns to leave, turns back and watches smoke rise from candle. Lights fade to blackout*)

Steve Wilmer

SCENES FROM
SOWETO

Steve Wilmer

Published here for the first time, Steve Wilmer's *Scenes from Soweto* had its American premiere at the Manhattan Theatre Club in 1978. The play originally was seen in London at the Round House Theatre and subsequently toured Britain, Holland, Sweden, and Germany. John Simon declared in *New York Magazine* that *Scenes from Soweto* "delivers what it proposes to do with flawlessly harrowing efficacy. The work of an American writer living in England, it concerns Nelson Malubane, a black man (avowedly based on a real person) who comes back to his native Johannesburg with an Oxford degree in mathematics. He gets a good job with an Anglo-American development company and hopes to help both his family and his fellow blacks to improve their respective lots by peaceable evolution. The situation becomes unbearable as the Soweto student riots and the general strike erupt. The good but apolitical Nelson becomes politicized and, against his will, a hero and a martyr."

John Beaufort, writing in the *Christian Science Monitor,* described it as "a powerful drama" that "presents a personal case history as its protest against the suppression of individual rights. Its tone is humanitarian rather than ideological and it is admirably maintained as it movingly conveys the particular dilemma of the exceptional black intellectual at a turbulent and troubled period in South African history."

Although a resident of London, Steve Wilmer was born in Washington, D.C. and grew up in Tennessee and Connecticut. He was educated at Yale and Oxford universities and has written widely on Southern African affairs. His other produced plays include *Kachobi* (performed at the Oxford Playhouse and at the Edinburgh Festival); *The Jolly Green Soldier; Mzilikazi: Trail of Blood;* and *Say Goodbye to Britain.*

Characters:

NELSON, *a black South African in his late twenties*
COLIN, *an English student in his twenties*
IMMIGRATION OFFICIAL
SPECIAL BRANCH OFFICER
JIM, *an American executive in his thirties*
AFRICAN REPORTER
AFRICAN STUDENT
COLONEL SWANEPOEL
NEWSCASTER (*Voice*)
POLICEMAN (*Voice*)
INTERROGATOR

Author's Note

This play was written to be acted by two male actors, one black and one white. The black actor plays Nelson, the African Reporter, and the African Student. The white actor plays Colin, the Immigration Official, the Special Branch Officer, Jim, Colonel Swanepoel, and the Interrogator.

The set consists of a table and two chairs. A screen is also onstage, onto which captions and slides are projected.

Scene One

Nelson, an African student at Oxford University, sits at a table, playing chess with himself. He moves rapidly, turning the board around after every move. A John Coltrane record plays in the background. Colin, an English student, enters. A caption is projected onto the screen: November 24, 1975. Oxford University.

COLIN: Nelson?
NELSON: (*Looks up quickly*) Oh hi, Colin. (*Returns to finishing game*) Come in.

COLIN: . . . or should I say Karpov.

NELSON: Spassky!

COLIN: Ah . . . Who's winning?

NELSON: I am. Checkmate in five . . . six . . . seven moves.

COLIN: (*Sitting down*) That was a dreadful meal tonight, wasn't it.

NELSON: It was all right. Coffee?

COLIN: No, thanks.

NELSON: How is the Africa Society? (*Continues to play*)

COLIN: Wait! Don't move. Is Spassky white?

NELSON: Yes.

COLIN: (*Moves a black piece*) There!

NELSON: (*Studies the board quickly*) Oh, you made it easy. Checkmate in one move.

COLIN: Jesus! Hey look, Nelson, do you have a lot of work at the moment?

NELSON: Average. Do you want a game?

COLIN: No. You'd kill me. Look . . .

NELSON: (*Setting up board*) Come on. I'll play without my queen.

COLIN: No, I'm in a bit of a hurry actually.

NELSON: It won't take long.

COLIN: Thanks. You don't have to rub it in. Uh . . .

NELSON: Have you decided when the Africa Society dance is going to be yet?

COLIN: No . . . uh . . . you know this demonstration we're having.

NELSON: Yeah?

COLIN: Well, I've been trying to find someone from Angola to speak, but everyone has gone home for the independence celebrations.

NELSON: What about Pedro?

COLIN: No, he supports UNITA. It would have to be someone from the MPLA. Charlie Thompson is coming down from London, but we really need an African as well.

NELSON: Oh.

COLIN: I was thinking that it wouldn't have to be someone from Angola.

NELSON: Oh . . . what about Okoth? He'll speak about anything.

COLIN: Yes, except, you know, he's Kenyan. It would be better if it were someone from Southern Africa.

NELSON: Don't look at me.

COLIN: Why not?

NELSON: You're not serious?

COLIN: Yes, why not. You'd be great. You could relate the events in Angola to South Africa.

NELSON: Me? What do I know about politics?

COLIN: Don't give me that.

NELSON: No, really. If you asked me to give a disquisition on pure mathematics, I'd jump to it. But on politics, no, man. As you'd say, I'd be up shit creek without a paddle. (*Puts on jacket*)

COLIN: Come on, Nelson, you can speak from personal experience.

NELSON: I could. Fancy a pint in the Kings Arms?

COLIN: Thanks, but I've got a lot of work. But . . . I'll give you a quick game if you'll agree to say a few words.

NELSON: A few words. (*Sits*) Now, I'll play without my queen. You can be white.

COLIN: You'll speak at the demonstration?

NELSON: No, man, you asked me to say a few words. So I said "a few words." Go ahead. Your move.

COLIN: Come on, Nelson, quit clowning. This is important. We desperately need someone.

NELSON: You have Charlie Thompson, and you, why don't you speak?

COLIN: No, we need an African, a South African and you're the only one we've got in the college. What about if I just introduce you and you get up and say "Angola is free today. South Africa tomorrow."

NELSON: That's facile.

COLIN: Well, think of something else. This is important.

We have to show people that what is happening in Angola relates to the whole of Southern Africa. Mozambique became independent in June. Angola tomorrow. After that Zimbabwe, Namibia, and South Africa.

NELSON: Perfect. I told you, you didn't need me.

COLIN: But we do. We must show international solidarity. You could serve as a symbol. At least allow me to introduce you.

NELSON: No, man, I'm no good at being a symbol.

COLIN: Yes, you are, you're a beautiful symbol, beautiful.

NELSON: Thank you, but really . . . I'm an individual, I prefer not to be used. If you are so keen to have a South African, call up Anti-Apartheid.

COLIN: No, there's no time. And anyway it would mean so much more if you spoke, because people know you, and respect you.

NELSON: Colin, I'm planning to go back.

COLIN: What?

NELSON: I haven't seen my family for three years . . .

COLIN: You're going back to South Africa?

NELSON: I know it means nothing to you, but I am the eldest son. My father is an invalid. My mother needs me to help raise my nine sisters and brothers. Even now I send part of my grant home to help them out.

COLIN: (*Shaking his head*) You actually want to go back to South Africa?

NELSON: Man, you don't understand. I've got to support them.

COLIN: Get a job here. With your brains you can have your pick and then you can bring them over.

NELSON: You don't understand. South Africa is my home.

COLIN: Are you crazy?

NELSON: Things are changing, slowly.

COLIN: Changing? Yeah, they are getting worse. This bantustan homelands policy is a complete charade to make the Africans even more dependent upon the whites. It's a smokescreen. It's a con, like this business of allowing a few multi-racial games to improve their image in the western world. Do you think that because some of the firms are starting to employ a few more Africans, it's going to make any fundamental difference to the doctrine of apartheid? If you want change, you'll have to fight for it. Armed struggle is the only answer.

NELSON: Armed struggle!

COLIN: Yes, armed struggle. It has worked in Mozambique and Angola.

NELSON: But they were colonies. South Africa has four million whites.

COLIN: And twenty million blacks!

NELSON: Man, you are so naive. It's easy for you sitting in England, white, middle class.

COLIN: Oh, shit!

NELSON: South Africa has British Leyland tanks, Mirage jets, soon the atom bomb. Armed struggle! No man, things are going to change from the inside, from the pressures on the system. Where I live in Soweto, which is a suburb of Johannesburg, there are over a million people crammed into sardine cans for houses, children dying of malnutrition, smoking glue to stave off the hunger pains. One of these days things are going to explode and when they do, things will change.

COLIN: So, in the meantime, you are going to sit around waiting, kowtowing to the Afrikaners, cleaning their boots.

NELSON: Look, man, I went to jail when I was fifteen because I didn't have my pass on me, and it took my family three weeks to find me and bail me out. And during those three weeks in jail I had to defend myself from the most depraved animals you can imagine. You have no idea what it is like to be a black man in South Africa. When I was in jail, I resolved that I was going to be nobody's pawn. I have fought to get where I am, and I am not going to blow it by standing up in some silly student demonstration.

COLIN: You think it is silly? You think it is silly to try to politicize people about what is happening in the rest of the world. Do you think we should sit around in blissful ignorance of the fact that the apartheid philosophy is every bit as evil as Nazism?

NELSON: All right, maybe it's not silly for you. But it would be pretty bloody stupid of me to risk getting my picture in the paper just to say a few words. Do you know what will happen when I step off the plane in Johannesburg? (*Claps his hands*) Directly to jail.

COLIN: (*Laughs*) Do you think the South African police is going to scour the *Oxford Mail* for your mug?

NELSON: You'd be surprised.

(*Blackout*)

Scene Two

Sounds of Jan Smuts Airport. A light comes up on a white Immigration Official checking passports. Nelson enters wearing a suit and tie and carrying hand luggage. Caption: March 15, 1976. Jan Smuts Airport.

OFFICIAL: Passport! (*Nelson quickly presents his passport. The Official reads*) Nelson Malubane . . . How long have you been away?

NELSON: Since 1971.

OFFICIAL: Have you finished your studies or are you returning to England?

NELSON: I've finished. I have a job in Johannesburg.

OFFICIAL: Doing what?

NELSON: (*Proudly*) Industrial designer with the Anglo-American Corporation.

OFFICIAL: Hm. Do you have it in writing?

NELSON: Yes. Here. (*Hands over letter*)

OFFICIAL: Hm. (*Looks at letter and checks name in official book*) Hm. Yes. Can you have a seat, Mr. Malubane.

(Blackout. Lights come up on Special Branch Officer sitting behind a desk, studying Nelson's passport, letter, and a large file. Nelson sits opposite him)

SPECIAL BRANCH OFFICER: Mr. Malubane . . . Yes, we've been expecting you. The bantu designer educated at Oxford University. You were a friend of Edgar Moyo?

NELSON: Yes.

OFFICER: Are you aware of his politics?

NELSON: He was just another student.

OFFICER: Just another student! He is a member of the Zimbabwe African People's Union.

NELSON: Perhaps.

OFFICER: What do you mean perhaps? You know he is. Are you a sympathizer of the Zimbabwe African People's Union?

NELSON: No, of course not. I'm not interested in politics. My primary interest is in pure mathematics.

OFFICER: *(Looking through dossier)* Not interested in politics. This document in front of me says that you attended the Oxford University African Society. Was that not political?

NELSON: It was a social club.

OFFICER: A social club!

NELSON: Some people were political, but mainly it was a way to get together and have a good time.

OFFICER: Is that why it organized a Zimbabwe Action Day in November 1975? Is that why it invited Bishop Muzorewa to speak, as well as Wole Soyinka, Sean Gervasi, Lewis Nkosi, and other well-known communists? Not political!

NELSON: Well, as I say, some people were political, but I was just interested in seeing friends—other Africans.

OFFICER: Why?

NELSON: Sorry?

OFFICER: Why should you want to see other Africans?

NELSON: We had things in common.

OFFICER: What? Politics?

NELSON: No, we organized social evenings, dances, music.

I was interested in dancing and drinking. I'm a mathematician. I'm not interested in politics.

OFFICER: Look, you cheeky kaffir, don't try to play silly buggers with me. Not interested in politics. (*Looking at dossier*) What is your relationship with Charlie Thompson?

NELSON: Who?

OFFICER: And what were you doing last November 25th?

NELSON: November 25th?

OFFICER: Wasn't there a demonstration through Oxford that day? About Angola?

NELSON: I don't remember. Students often. . . .

OFFICER: (*Shows him a photograph*) Isn't that you?

NELSON: (*Studies photo*) It might look like me.

OFFICER: Isn't it?

NELSON: Maybe I was walking by at the time.

OFFICER: Walking by. Jere Jong! Then who is that standing next to you?

NELSON: I don't know. I don't recognize him.

OFFICER: It's Charlie Thompson, man.

NELSON: Who is Charlie Thompson?

OFFICER: Don't give me that. Don't tell me you have never heard of Charlie Thompson, one of the most notorious South African communists.

NELSON: No, I've never heard of him. I told you. I was just walking by and stopped to look at what was going on. You see I'm carrying my books. I was walking between classes and I saw a large crowd of people and so I stopped to watch what was happening. I only stayed a few minutes. Really, politics bores me. What really interests me is mathematics.

OFFICER: Don't think you can fool us, boy. We know what you have been up to. This file is just one of many on you. The special branch will want to talk to you tomorrow as well. We will be coming to your home at 125 Orlando West. Ja?

NELSON: Yes.

OFFICER: Yes, what?

NELSON: Yes.

OFFICER: Baas!

NELSON: Yes, baas.

OFFICER: Don't think you're European, just because you have been overseas. You are a bantu and don't you forget it. Now, you must report immediately to the Non-European Affairs Labour Office in the city as well as the Bantu Administration Office in Soweto to have your dompass renewed.

NELSON: Yes . . . baas.

OFFICER: Well, we're glad to have you back.

NELSON: Thank you.

OFFICER: But pasop! You better stick to mathematics or you'll be in big trouble.

(*Blackout*)

Scene Three

Slide of Nelson's family projected. Nelson in spotlight.

NELSON: You see this picture? It is my family. This is me here on the right. I'm trying to get the little one to look at the camera. That's my mother holding her. Ah. She was glad to see me when I came home from England. She had saved for months to buy me a secondhand bed. And you see this old man—this is my stepfather here with the beard, holding another little sister. He's too old to work now and he has a kind of asthma from his years in the mines. Over here on the left is my oldest sister. Yes. She's looking very proud because she has just qualified to be a teacher. I used to send her money from Oxford to help pay for her course. And the one next to her, that's another sister. She's very shy, but a hell of a good cook. In the middle here, with the striped pullover, this is my brother, Robert. He looks up to me as if I were a god or something. But he's got a big problem. The government has introduced this new law that 50 percent of the courses must be taught in Afrikaans and 50 percent in English. But my brother can hardly speak Afrikaans. The kids at his school are all very upset at having to study in a language that they don't understand. In another school the students have organized a strike. The education system in Soweto is dreadful. In my brother's class, there are about seventy students and only half of them can afford books. My brother has to share his books with the others. I'm very happy to be working at Anglo-American. Soon I'll be able to pay for him to get away from Soweto and study at a boarding school.

(*Nelson looks at picture again and walks off as lights fade*)

Scene Four

Nelson sits at his office desk, working. He picks up the telephone and dials. Caption: May 20, 1976. Anglo-American Corporation.

NELSON: (*Politely*) Hello. Is that the Cape Town depot? . . . I shipped a trunk from London to Johannesburg two months ago and it hasn't arrived. I wonder if you could check to see if it has been held up in your office . . . Yes. My name is Nelson Malubane . . . Hello? Hello? Hello? (*Hangs up the phone and starts to redial*)

(*Jim, an American colleague, enters carrying a design*)

JIM: Nelson?

NELSON: Jim?

JIM: I have to get your approval on this before making a prototype. (*Unfolds plan and spreads it on Nelson's desk*) It's a hand-operated drill for facework in the gold mines. Have you seen one of these before?

NELSON: Of course. Do you mind if I study it?

JIM: Not at all. I'll go and get myself a cup of coffee in the canteen. Can I get you one?

NELSON: Yes . . .

JIM: Milk and sugar?

NELSON: Jim . . . you understand that they have separate facilities . . .

JIM: (*Winks*) I'll hide the coffee in my attache case. (*Exits*)

(*Nelson laughs and turns to study the design. Telephone rings*)

NELSON: Malubane . . . Hello, Ma. Kulungili . . . Yebo
. . . Shopping? I OK Bazaars? (*Takes out a pad and jots things
down*) Yebo . . . Yebo . . . What sort of nyama? Beef? . . .
Yebo . . . Four pounds of rice. Kuzadula. . . . Shall I get
some flour so that Sissy can bake a cake? . . . Yebo . . . Yebo
. . . Yebo. (*Impatient*) Is that all, Ma? I'm a bit busy. (*Whispers
into phone*) I have to tell some M'lungu what is wrong with his
design. (*Laughs*) Banga ma mpala lapa! (*Laughs*) I can't help
but make an impression. I am the only black man behind a
desk . . . Yes. Anyway I have to go. (*Jim enters with coffee*) No,
Ma, I slept fine. (*Exasperated*) No, I only left early because I
had some work to do here . . . Yes, I am having some ukofi
now. Yes. Anyway I have to go. I promise I'll stay home for
breakfast tomorrow. Hamba kahle. (*Hangs up*)

JIM: She sounds like my mother.

NELSON: She wants me to do some shopping on the way
home.

JIM: Where do you live?

NELSON: Orlando. It's part of Soweto.

JIM: Is that O.K.?

NELSON: Not too bad. We're a bit cramped. Eleven of us in
four rooms.

JIM: You're kidding!

NELSON: I was thinking of renting a larger house. But the
rents are so steep and the bantu administration is about to
raise them again.

JIM: But you must be one of the best-paid people in Soweto. Why don't you get a mortgage and buy a house?

NELSON: It's not possible.

JIM: Sure it is. Why not?

NELSON: It's against the law.

JIM: Against the law to buy a house?

NELSON: It's to prevent us from settling in the townships.
They want to send us back to our so-called tribal homelands,
so they can create a white South Africa.

JIM: Jesus! It's a wonder you wanted to come back from
England. I hear the crime rate in Soweto is worse than New
York.

NELSON: It's people in beer halls, government beer halls.

They get drunk, no place to go, get into fights, and end up stabbing someone. You must come and visit.

JIM: Yeah, I could drive you home one day.

NELSON: Are you joking?

JIM: Yeah, why not?

NELSON: You would have to apply for a special permit to get into the township.

JIM: Oh, right. Well, what about next week sometime?

NELSON: Fine.

JIM: Great. Well . . . Is that O.K. or should I leave it with you?

NELSON: No, I've looked at it. It's excellent, really. You know the thing that worries me about this drill is the level of vibration. It seems to be a bit high if someone is going to operate it by hand.

JIM: No, that's standard.

NELSON: Yes, I'm sure it is. But . . . I doubt if it would be permitted in England. I don't know about the States.

JIM: But think how expensive it would be to cushion the vibration.

NELSON: Yes, but think what it must do to the nervous system of the poor chap down in the mine who has to operate it. I'm sorry, but if you need my approval I can't give it.

JIM: Hm.

NELSON: I'm sorry.

JIM: No, you're right . . . you're right. I'll see what I can do. See you.

NELSON: See you. Jim, thanks for the coffee.

JIM: Sure. Anytime.

(*Blackout*)

Scene Five

Spotlight on Jim, sitting on the edge of the desk, addressing the audience.

JIM: Hi! My name is Jim Franklin. You know, the thing that gets me about this country is the way they differentiate between the races. It's not just black and white. That's easy. Like where I come from, anyone with the smallest drop of Negro blood is black. But here they measure you. If you're half and half they call you colored. But if you are three-quarters white and one-quarter bantu, that's more difficult. They have to stick a pencil in your hair to see if it will fall out, and they examine your skin for Mongolian blue spots, whatever they are. Now with Nelson, there's no problem. You can see from a mile away that he's bantu. But I went to visit his home yesterday. Imagine having to get a special permit to see a friend. Anyway, next door there's a family who have been split up because the government decided that they didn't belong to the same race. Two of the children just happened to have such light skin that they were forced to move into a colored neighborhood. And you know foreigners are also examined. Japanese are called white, while Chinese are colored. I think there's something political in that. Cambodians are colored but people from Thailand are white . . . or is it colored? Diplomats and distinguished visitors are of course honorary whites. But if you are thinking of visiting here and you happen to have brown hair and brown eyes, let me warn you. Don't get too much of a suntan or you might find yourself riding third class.

(*Blackout*)

Scene Six

Nelson sits at his desk, telephoning. Caption: June 7, 1976. Anglo-American Corporation.

NELSON: (*Affecting an upper class English accent*) Hello. Cape Town depot? I shipped a trunk from London to Johannesburg three months ago and it hasn't yet arrived. Could you possibly check to see if it has been held up in your depot? . . . Yes. It was shipped in the name of Nelson Malubane. Hello? Hello? Hello?

(*Jim enters*)

JIM: Hey, what's the matter?

NELSON: Oh, nothing.

JIM: Something personal?

NELSON: It's just some Afrikaner at the Cape Town baggage depot. Every time I call to find out why my trunk hasn't arrived, he hangs up.

JIM: Do you want me to try?

NELSON: Yes. Would you?

JIM: Sure, give me the number. (*Dials*) You sent it from London?

NELSON: Yes. Over three months ago.

JIM: Hello. This is Jim Franklin of Anglo-American Corporation in Jo'burg. I want to enquire about the luggage of one of our employees here which was shipped from London a few months ago. (*Covers the phone*) It was a trunk?

NELSON: Yes.

JIM: It was a trunk shipped in the name of Nelson Malubane. Yes. M-a-l-u-b-a-n-e . . . Thanks. (*Covers the phone*) He's checking.

NELSON: You've got further with him in a minute than I have in a month.

JIM: Did you mention Anglo-American? (*On the phone*) Hello . . . Yes. That's right . . . I see . . . (*Laughs*) Yes, of course, I understand. Yes, well could you send it immediately.

He's been wearing the same clothes for the last three months and he smells something terrible. (*Laughs*) Yes. Thanks very much. Goodbye. (*Hangs up*) You should get it before the end of the week.

NELSON: Great, thanks a lot!

JIM: It was nothing. . . . Hey, I really enjoyed meeting your family yesterday. That was a great meal your sister cooked. What was it?

NELSON: Polisha.

JIM: Pol . . .

NELSON: Polisha.

JIM: Yeah, and I liked your brother Robert especially. He's a great chess player. Do you think he might go to college? He seems very smart.

NELSON: I just hope he finishes high school.

JIM: I'm sure he . . . oh, you mean because of this Afrikaans thing?

NELSON: If he isn't careful, he could end up in jail.

JIM: No, but he's right. Why the hell should he have to study mathematics in another language all of a sudden? It's ludicrous.

NELSON: You don't understand. They think they can boycott classes and get away with it. They are so bloody naive. It reminds me when I was a student at Fort Hare in 1968. We tried to force through a few changes and we all got expelled, over two hundred of us. And my girl friend. We were having a meeting and suddenly the police came in to break it up and they shot her in the throat. We rushed her to the hospital but she didn't make it.

JIM: Jesus!

NELSON: And now my brother and his friends are talking about a strike by the students or a demonstration. I mean, it's mad.

JIM: Yeah, maybe you're right. (*Pause*) Nelson, do you play tennis?

NELSON: A little.

JIM: Would you like to play sometime?

NELSON: Where?

JIM: My club allows mixed games on Monday evenings.

NELSON: I'd love to, Jim, but Mondays aren't very good for me. That's the night I usually teach Maths.

JIM: Oh, you didn't tell me that you're a teacher.

NELSON: Well, it's not really formal. It's just a few of the local kids who want some help. I only do it because they are so keen. They like me because I can explain things to them in Zulu or Sotho.

JIM: Hey, did you ever consider getting a Ph.D.? I'm sure you could if you wanted to. Then you could teach in a university.

NELSON: No, I'm happy here at the moment.

JIM: Dr. Nelson Malubane. Yeah. That would certainly strike a blow against the doctrine of apartheid. Anyway, think about it. (*Starts to go*) Oh, and by the way, you must come to my place some time and meet my wife.

NELSON: I'd love to.

(*Blackout*)

Scene Seven

An African Reporter sits among the audience. Slides are flashed on the screen as he speaks.

AFRICAN REPORTER: My name is Nat Temba, I was one of about twenty journalists in Soweto on June 16, 1976. It was a quiet Wednesday morning marred only by a soft cold wind. Students in Soweto schools had decided together to stage a peaceful demonstration in sympathy with seven other schools striking against the use of the Afrikaans language as a medium of instruction in their schools. By 7 A.M. several thousand school children from various primary and secondary schools in Soweto had collected and began to move towards Orlando Stadium. The pupils aged between twelve and twenty carried posters made from exercise books. "To Hell with Afrikaans," "Blacks are not dustbins," etc. They stood on both sides of the road with their fists raised and shouting "power" at the tops of their voices. They were in an extremely jovial mood. The whole atmosphere was quite a happy one. I followed the crowd through Jabavu, Mofolo, Dube and until they reached Orlando West. It was at Orlando West near the Orlando West High School where the law in its own fashion gave a hearing to their grievances. The crowd was standing at the main gate of the schoolyard and others were inside the yard when four big police vans and two smaller ones arrived on the scene. A few of the children hesitated then scattered. Some ran into the schoolyard and others along streets that joined the main tarred road, but a larger group of unshaken boys and girls remained where they were. When realizing that others had courage and were not prepared to move, those who had dashed off came back and stood their ground, although they still showed doubt. There were about four white policemen and a group of about ten to fifteen black cops. Two of the whites advanced towards the crowd. A student, Jonas Mdluli, recalls.

(African Reporter gets up and impersonates student)

AFRICAN STUDENT: The police arrived in vanloads armed with rifles, submachine guns, tear gas, and batons and formed a line in front of us. We thought they were going to disperse us with loud hailers or a loudspeaker, or maybe talk to us. But they just stood there and talked to themselves. The students were waving placards and singing "God save our nation" in Sotho and shouting "We don't want police here." Then a white policeman threw a canister, and we saw this smoking thing coming and we thought it was some kind of bomb, so we ran back, but afterwards we saw it was only smoke so we came back again. The children began picking up stones and threw back. Other policemen threw canisters and then one policeman pulled out a revolver and aimed it at the pupils standing just in front of him. A friend of mine said "Look at him he's going to shoot the kid." The policeman fired and then all hell broke loose.

AFRICAN REPORTER: In a bid to get cover as they threw stones, some of the children ran to the back of a nearby row of houses. The whole situation was now becoming a fierce struggle, stone-throwing students against bullets from police guns. Ducking and jumping from side to side, the children were advancing towards the police through the rain of bullets. What frightened me more than anything was the attitude of the children. Many seemed to be oblivious of the danger. Two boys who had been in front were shot in the legs. Four more were shot, five, six, and seven. A student came limping to our car and asked for a lift. We rushed him to the Phefeni clinic. As we drove back I saw a sight that sent a chill down my spine. (*Slides projected of Hector Peterson*) A youth dressed in an overall came running and it seemed his feet could not carry him fast enough. He carried a young boy whom I thought could be anything between the age of seven and ten years old. He seemed to be seriously hurt and was bleeding profusely from his mouth. I jumped out of our car as fast as I could and ordered the youth to jump in with the injured boy. A girl, who I took to be the little boy's sister, kept calling his name while she wept bitterly. I could not hold back my tears. I wept with her while I prayed to God for a miracle that the boy should not be dead. At the clinic we carried the boy out of the car. Then we found about three doctors, who tried the best they could for the little boy, and then they broke the worst news to us. The boy had died. Police reinforcements arrived. The vans passed through the trouble-torn spot and proceeded to the other end. The policemen who had been engaged in the fight with children rushed into their vans and also moved off, following the other vans. They were still firing. I dashed after them and I realized when I reached the corner that another battle had been going on in the other street. More students had been injured at the corner, and an old man, said to have been caught by a stray bullet, was lying dead on the pavement. The children began singing power songs along Pela Road. They were angry, uncontrollable, and hungry for revenge. They were stoning any car driven by a white man, and that is how two whites died in the area. The whole scene, which took more than an hour, was just the beginning, and what followed was as bloody. By midday the whole township was out of control. Students attacked government buildings, beer halls. Nearly all the offices of the bantu administration were burned or smashed up. Slogans were painted on the walls "we want more schools and less beer halls." Police reinforcements were brought in, including the new paramilitary anti-urban terrorism unit led by Colonel Theunis Swanepoel.

(*Colonel Swanepoel enters and addresses audience*)

COLONEL SWANEPOEL: It was the most waansinnig scene I have come across in my life. I realized that we would have to use high-velocity rifles to break up the crowd. Tear gas would have had no effect and a baton charge would have been suicide. I picked out the leader of the crowd from the movement he made with his hands. I fired a single shot at him but he disappeared into the crowd. I then fired eight additional shots at the lieutenants of the leader on either side of him and the crowd dispersed.

(*He turns and walks off as lights fade*)

Scene Eight

Nelson working at his desk. Jim rushes in. Caption: June 16, 1976. Anglo-American Corporation.

JIM: Did you hear the news?

NELSON: What?

JIM: Apparently there was a very large demonstration by school kids. I thought you probably knew . . .

NELSON: Was there any trouble?

JIM: Yeah, the radio said the police opened fire.

NELSON: Oh, no!

JIM: . . . and injured a couple of kids. No one seriously though.

NELSON: Did it mention any names?

JIM: Why? Was your brother . . .

NELSON: Yes, and maybe one of my sisters.

JIM: Should you call home?

NELSON: We don't have a phone.

JIM: But your mother . . .

NELSON: No, she phones from a call box.

JIM: What about phoning the police?

NELSON: You're joking.

JIM: What about one of the newspapers.

NELSON: Yes, the *World*. I'll call Nat. (*He looks up number in diary and dials*)

JIM: I don't think there's anything to worry about. But there's no harm in checking. You know it's this pig-headed Treunicht who's to blame, the one Vorster brought into the cabinet in December. He's the one who has been insisting on Afrikaans being taught . . .

NELSON: (*Hanging up*) Engaged!

JIM: Look, you keep trying and I'll go to my office and telephone the police. (*Exits*)

NELSON: (*Dials and slams down the phone*) How do these bloody people expect to get any news if they're always blasted engaged! (*Dials again*) Hello. Can I speak to Nat on the news desk . . . Hello, Nat. It's Nelson. Look, Nat, can you tell me the names of the students who were injured in the Soweto demonstration this morning? What? Fifty? (*Puts the receiver down slowly*) *Fifty killed* . . . (*He sits stunned and then jumps up and puts on his jacket*)

(*Jim rushes in*)

JIM: Nelson, I talked to the police. Apparently there's a big fucking riot!

NELSON: I've got to go home.

JIM: (*Stopping him*) No, Nelson, it's too dangerous.

NELSON: They've killed more than fifty people.

JIM: Look, Nelson. Wait till it cools down. It'll all be over in a few hours.

NELSON: No, man, my family needs me. I've got to go.

JIM: Nelson, how are you going to get there? They're stoning all the cars and buses. For all you know the trains aren't running. How are you going to get there?

NELSON: I'll run.

JIM: It's ten miles.

NELSON: They're murdering our children! (*He goes hurriedly out*)

JIM: Nelson . . .

(*Blackout*)

Scene Nine

Nelson enters, drunk, with beer in his hand. Caption: June 19, 1976. Soweto.

NELSON: Is this my home? Soweto? This chaos? This anarchy? Beer halls ablaze, banks and administrative offices destroyed, buses and cars burned out ruins, kids barricading streets and storming any police daring to come near. Is this my old school—Orlando High? Riddled with bullet holes, windows smashed, fences caved in, the playing field caked with the blood of children, dragged off to clinics or mortuaries. (*Stumbles around*) This is my house. Outside it looks the same. But inside I no longer recognize it. My brother Robert, always so soft spoken, now shouts and screams as he tells my parents what happened. My mother sits mortified clutching my sister who narrowly missed being shot to death. But my father, usually so tired and short of breath from his years in the mine, leans forward anxiously to hear my brother describe how the students fought back, how he helped stone the police who were shooting them; and how they managed to surround an Alsatian police dog and crush it with rocks. I try to bring my brother to his senses, to see that soon the police will counterattack in force. But all he talks about is resistance and revenge. He leads me out to the outside loo and whispers into my ear, "How do you make a petrol bomb?" As if I've had years of practice! I try to explain that "I am with you in spirit, but your tactics are wrong." He looks at me as if I'm some kind of worm. My brother, who always looked up to me.

(*Blackout*)

Scene Ten

Nelson sits brooding at his desk as Jim sits next to him, reading a newspaper. Caption: June 21, 1976. Anglo-American Corporation.

JIM: I had no idea it was this bad.

NELSON: It was worse.

JIM: It says here that several hundred kids have been detained—the ring leaders. I guess that'll be the end of it. But you know, it's incredible the way the riots have spread right across the country—Pretoria, Jo'burg, Port Elisabeth, Cape Town. . . . It's almost as if it were planned. Do you think the ANC is behind it?

NELSON: It was spontaneous.

JIM: Maybe. These students seem pretty well organized to me. It's the same story all over the country . . .

NELSON: If it were properly organized, there wouldn't be so many dead students.

JIM: But somebody must be behind it. What about this African who jumped from the fourth floor of the police station?

NELSON: Jumped?

JIM: Yeah, it says that the police were questioning him, and suddenly he broke free and jumped to his death. He must have had a lot to hide.

NELSON: Do you really think he jumped?

JIM: (*Shows him paper*) Yeah, look, that's what it says.

NELSON: Man, haven't you learned anything since you've been here? The police have been throwing Africans out of windows for years.

JIM: Come on.

NELSON: Oh God, man, you've never heard about that? They hold you out of the window and tell you that if you don't talk, they'll let go. And every so often they keep their word. The other way is to suffocate you. It doesn't leave any marks and afterwards they hang you by a rope and claim that you hanged yourself.

JIM: Do you really believe that the police. . . .

NELSON: Yes, man, it's happening again and again. The police keep claiming that their prisoners have hung themselves in prison or jumped out of windows. If the police wanted to keep them alive, don't you think they would devise a way to prevent them from committing suicide?

JIM: Do you honestly believe that the police could get away with that?

NELSON: Yes, man. I've been there. I've seen what they're like. If you give them the slightest excuse they slam the life out of you.

JIM: Nelson, calm down! I know you are going through hell at the moment. But Nelson, please try to keep your perspective.

(*Blackout*)

Scene Eleven

Nelson enters holding a leaflet which he has just been handed. Caption: September 15, 1976. General Strike.

NELSON: (*Examines leaflet*) General strike? (*Turns back*) You're joking! (*Reads*) "The racist regime has abandoned their demand that Afrikaans be taught in the schools, and Vorster is now talking of home-ownership for blacks in Soweto. . . . *Now* for greater victories—the scrapping of Bantu Education, the release of prisoners detained during the demos, and the overthrowal of oppression. We the students call on our parents to stay at home and not go to work from Monday." (*Turns back*) Till when? What is this, an indefinite strike? (*To himself*) These students are so naive. They don't realize that the South African government thought about strikes before they were even born. That's why they built these townships as totally isolated entities. All the government has to do is to cut off the food and water supplies, and within a week the strike will collapse. (*Reads*) "If you strike, you'll hit the system where it hurts." (*Crumples leaflet*) What rubbish! (*Turns back*) If you were serious about that, you would start using real explosives and not just petrol bombs and blow up the infrastructure of the country. (*Walks off*) You'd hit the banks, the police stations, the railroads, the harbors, the power stations, the electrical pylons. . . .

(*Lights fade to blackout as he exits, talking*)

Scene Twelve

Nelson working. Jim walks by and stops.

JIM: Hey, Nelson, what a surprise. I didn't expect to see you here today.

NELSON: (*Coldly*) I have a family to support.

JIM: I know, but still, you must be about the only black face in the building. None of the cleaners or the cooks have shown up. It's funny because as I was driving to work this morning and listening to the reports about the strike on the radio, I was thinking that at least here at Anglo it would be a complete failure. I figured that the only person likely to observe the strike would be you. And then I get here and you're the only one brave enough to come to work.

NELSON: (*Impatient*) Look, Jim, I've got a lot of work to do.

JIM: Sure, I'm sorry. But I just wanted to tell you how much I admire your courage in coming here. The radio said that the pickets were threatening people with knives and stones.

NELSON: Rubbish!

JIM: Well, even if they didn't bother you, it still must have taken a lot of guts. I understand that several factories have had to close down today because the staff didn't turn up. But here you are helping to keep the wheels of Anglo-American rolling.

NELSON: Jim, will you please shut up, and get out!

JIM: Nelson . . .

NELSON: I've got work to do.

JIM: Now wait a minute.

NELSON: I've got work to do!

JIM: (*Sits*) Nelson, if something's bothering you . . .

NELSON: Thanks, Jim, but it's nothing.

JIM: Nelson, you're looking tired. Look, Nelson, if you would like to come and stay at my home for a few days, you're welcome to. It's quiet where I live—big garden, lots of trees, a swimming pool, and we have two guest rooms. Any time you like you're welcome.

NELSON: Thanks, but I wouldn't want to cause you any trouble.

JIM: No, it's no trouble. The servants do all the work.

NELSON: And what would your neighbors say if they saw me swimming in your pool?

JIM: Well . . .

NELSON: Hm? What would they say?

JIM: Well, maybe swimming wouldn't be a good idea.

NELSON: Yes, it would be better to keep me inside and close all the curtains.

JIM: Cut it out, Nelson. I was just trying to . . .

NELSON: Sure. I know. Eat in plush surroundings while my people are starving because the government is preventing the food getting to the strikers.

JIM: Hey, don't blame me. Don't forget that you are helping to defeat the strike.

NELSON: No, man, I agree with the strike. But I know it can't win. If it could, I wouldn't be here.

JIM: That's the most convoluted logic I've ever heard.

NELSON: I don't believe in taking action that is doomed to failure, that's all.

JIM: Don't give me that crap! You're shit scared you'll be fired. And then where will you be? Back in the compound with the rest of them.

NELSON: You think so?

JIM: Yeah, otherwise you would be out there throwing petrol bombs.

NELSON: Petrol bombs! Where does that get you?

JIM: Nelson, all I'm trying to say is that you are really one of us. Let's face it, you really don't have much in common with your own people any more.

NELSON: Jim, do you know what really hurts? Seeing your people trampled and crushed day after day, with you powerless to help, knowing that if you take action, you will suffer as well. But there comes a point when your own security and well-being no longer seem to matter. You no longer care what the risks are to yourself. You only know that you must do whatever you can to help your people. (*Jim exits*) For me that point came on October 24, 1976—United Nations day. It was also the day of Jacob Mashabane's funeral. Jacob Mashabane, a student who died in detention. There were over a thousand mourners in the cemetery, and just as the hymn singing began, suddenly and somehow predictably, the South African police arrived in force. I'll never understand exactly what happened. I just stood there stunned, unable to move as the police opened fire. There were people screaming and running in all directions, scaling the fences and being cut down by rifle fire. But I just stood there, unable to believe what was happening. Suddenly a policeman came up to me and forced me at gunpoint to pick up a boy of about fifteen and load him into a police van. He was badly wounded and I asked him his name and address so that I could inform his parents. All he said was that he was thirsty. "Manzi. Gifuna manzi." He was thirsty; that's all he said and then he died. I lifted him into the van and walked back. I could not lift the next one. It was an old man, already dead, baba, the lines in his face hardening into a silent cry for help. I just looked at him and slowly became gripped by a compulsion to scream. The police laughed, thought I was mad or had seen a ghost. But I felt quite relieved. In that moment I had made up my mind. I knew that, no matter what the risk, I had to act.

(*Blackout*)

Scene Thirteen

Sound of an explosion, followed by the sound of a South African Newscaster reading the news.

NEWSCASTER: The price of gold continues to rise, and share prices reached their highest point since June. Minister of Justice, Jimmy Kruger, today warned the country to prepare for the possibility of urban terrorism in South Africa. His remarks followed yesterday's explosion in the Carlton Towers restaurant in Johannesburg's city centre. The bantu who lost his hand in yesterday's explosion has been identified as Isaac Seko. He and three others are being detained under the terrorism act. Two mineworkers have also been detained after forty sticks of dynamite, twenty delayed-action fuses, and two detonators were found near a mine shaft on the city outskirts.

(Spotlight on Nelson, stripped to his underwear, manacled and disoriented, standing in a cell. The voice of a policeman comes from the audience. Caption: December 10, 1976. John Vorster Square Police Station)

POLICEMAN: Nelson? Nelson? Nelson Malubane? Is that your name, Nelson? Nelson Malubane. Oxford scholar. Special bantu. We do have the right one, don't we? You are Nelson Malubane, aren't you? Nelson? What did they teach you over there at Oxford? How to make explosives? Huh? Nelson? We know all about you, Nelson. We caught your friend red-handed. Isaac. Isaac Seko. He's been talking to us. He's told us all about you. He's told us how you procured explosives and taught him how to use them. Isaac talked, Nelson. He talked because he didn't want to see his family hurt. And you'll talk, too, Nelson. You don't want to see your family hurt, do you, Nelson? Proud mother you have, Nelson. Very proud. I'd hate to see some accident happen to her. Yes, Nelson, and your little sister, very pretty with the little bows in her hair. It would be terrible if she was run over by a car. And your brother, Nelson, your brother Robert, very fit boy, very fit. Runs so fast, runs so fast on two legs, Nelson. Runs so fast on two legs. I'd hate to see him running on one leg, Nelson, hate to see him running on one leg . . .

NELSON: (*Screaming*) Run, Robert, run, run!

(*Blackout. Light comes up on Nelson, as an Interrogator enters carrying a box with wires running from it*)

INTERROGATOR: Oh, man, you look terrible. You better talk or they'll kill you. You know what happened to the others . . . dropped out of windows, beaten or suffocated to death, strangled. . . .

NELSON: I don't know anything.

INTERROGATOR: We caught your friend red-handed. He's admitted getting advice from you.

NELSON: It's not true!

(*Interrogator attaches electrodes to Nelson's genitals*)

INTERROGATOR: Look, all we need is a statement. Then we can let you go. Your friend at work, Jim, he has also told us that you were up to something.

NELSON: It's not true!

(*Interrogator turns on the current and Nelson screams*)

INTERROGATOR: We've caught another one of your conspirators who has confessed. Come on, Nelson, make it easy on yourself.

NELSON: If you have all this information, why do you need anything from me?

INTERROGATOR: We just need a statement. You showed them how to use explosives. And you showed other people as well, didn't you? You had your own little cell.

NELSON: No!

INTERROGATOR: Look, Nelson, we know that you were involved in the bombing of the police station and Carlton Towers. We know that you intended to blow up the railroads and the power station. But if you tell us about the other people, we might be able to make things easy for you. If you tell us everything, we could perhaps arrange an exit permit for you. You could continue your studies in Britain. We know how much you want to get your doctorate.

NELSON: But I don't know anything.

(*Interrogator removes electrodes and reattaches them to Nelson's ears. He walks back slowly, picks up the box and turns on the current. Nelson screams*)

INTERROGATOR: Look, Nelson. I'm not supposed to tell you this. But they've arrested your younger brother. If you don't talk, they'll beat it out of him. And if he doesn't talk they'll arrest your mother.

NELSON: Oh, God, please . . . a lawyer? . . . a phone call. . . .

INTERROGATOR: You're joking . . . Smoke? (*Puts cigarette in his mouth*) Puff! (*Nelson coughs on the smoke*) Look, Nelson, I'm trying to help you. Those people out there would kill you as soon as look at you. There are only two ways out of this room, either you give us a statement or . . . I've lost count of the number of people who have died in here.

(*Nelson mumbles something inaudibly*)

INTERROGATOR: (*Taking cigarette out of his mouth*) What did you say?

NELSON: And I won't be the last.

INTERROGATOR: Look, Malubane, I'm losing my patience. (*Removes electrodes*)

NELSON: Go ahead.

INTERROGATOR: Look, you bloody kaffir, you better talk! (*Interrogator takes wet towel and wraps it around Nelson's face and neck*)

NELSON: If I die, hundreds more will rise up.

INTERROGATOR: This is how Mohapi died. He hanged himself. See? (*Interrogator pulls the towel tight as Nelson struggles. He then releases the towel*) Now you talk, you bloody kaffir! Talk!

NELSON: (*Struggling to speak*) Hundreds, thousands will rise up! Do you hear? They are coming!!

(*Interrogator tightens towel around Nelson's face and neck again*)

INTERROGATOR: You're really asking for it. (*He releases the towel and Nelson collapses on the floor struggling for air*) Now talk, damn you!

(Interrogator gets up and lights a cigarette. He looks at him for a moment and then walks off)

Blackout followed by a slide projected on the screen. Caption: Wellington Tshazibane, on whom this play is based, died in detention on December 10, 1976. The police claim that he hanged himself.

Curtain

Frank Marcus

BLIND DATE

Frank Marcus

When *Blind Date* was first performed in 1977 at the King's Head Theatre Club, Islington, it was greeted with warmth and enthusiasm by the London press. Herbert Kretzmer of the *Daily Express* wrote: "This enchanting playlet pictures the sad, funny meeting of two unremarkable strangers on a railway platform bench. . . . Dramatist Marcus controls his forty-five minutes of story-telling time with thrift and originality, releasing his plot surprises like an experienced poker player squeezing out a straight flush." Fellow aisle-sitter John Barber of the *Daily Telegraph* was in accord: "This funny-sad comedy is a drily sardonic study of those tentative and desperate smoke-signals we send up in the hope of finding a kindred spirit. It is also, as often with this author, a confrontation of lustful dream-images with the bread-and-butter reality of everywhere around us."

Described by the author as "an anecdote," *Blind Date* appears in print for the first time in the United States in *The Best Short Plays 1979*.

Frank Marcus was born on June 30, 1928, in Breslau, Germany, and emigrated to England just before the outbreak of World War II. After completing his education and a tenure at St. Martin's School of Art, he organized the International Theatre Group, an experimental company that performed in little theatres in the area of Notting Hill Gate. Mr. Marcus contributed to the group as actor, director, and designer.

His first West End play, *The Formation Dancers,* was presented at the Arts Theatre Club, then at the Globe in 1964. Selected and published as one of the *Plays of the Year, 1964–65,* it also brought him to the attention of producer Michael Codron. The latter invited the promising young dramatist to write a play for his production auspices with a "powerful part" for a "star" actress. The resultant *The Killing of Sister George,* written in eight weeks, won him a packet of "Best Play of the Year" awards, notably the prestigious seasonal citation from the London theatre critics. Opening on June 17, 1965, it ran for 620 performances, later was brought to New York, and subsequently was filmed with Beryl Reid recreating her portrayal of the formidable title figure.

Mr. Marcus' other dramatic works include *Studies of the Nude,* produced at the Hampstead Theatre Club in 1967; *Mrs. Mouse, Are You Within?,* staged in 1968 at the Theatre Royal, Bristol, and later transferred to the Duke of York's, London;

The Window, introduced in this editor's collection, *Best Short Plays of the World Theatre: 1958–1967; Notes on a Love Affair,* presented in the West End in 1972 with Irene Worth, Nigel Davenport, and Julia Foster as the principals; and *Blank Pages,* which appeared in *The Best Short Plays 1974.*

Additionally, Mr. Marcus has made new translations of plays by Arthur Schnitzler, Frank Wedekind, and Ferenc Molnar. His version of Molnar's comedy, *The Guardsman,* was presented by Britain's National Theatre in 1978 with Diana Rigg and Richard Johnson in the leads. He also has written several original plays for television and provided the basic theme and concept of the mimedrama *Le Trois Perruques* for his close friend Marcel Marceau, the celebrated French pantomimist.

During his "moonlighting" hours, the prize-winning playwright is a regular contributor to the *London Magazine* and other publications, and since 1968, he has officiated as drama critic for the *Sunday Telegraph.*

In its coverage of one of his recent works, *Plays and Players* declared: "One of the more fascinating aspects of all his plays is that they are centered around women. In a contemporary theatre that seems to concentrate more and more on male performances, Frank Marcus probably writes better *star* parts for his ladies than any other leading playwright in the British theatre."

Characters:

ANGIE
BRIAN

Scene:

London.

The entrance hall of Charing Cross Station. Upstage right: the arched exit to the street. A clock, registering 1:12 P.M. Below it, a bench. Part of a shuttered bookstall. Timetables, signs, and the usual station paraphernalia. Angie sits on the bench in an attitude of listless resignation. She is twenty-three, fair-haired, wearing a blue denim skirt and matching waistcoat, a black-checked cheesecloth blouse with two buttons provocatively open, accentuated by a necklace, and high black boots, which look new. She looks at her watch, checks the time with the station clock, and sighs.

ANGIE: (*Singing softly*) Why am I waiting, why am I waiting . . . ? You might well ask. It's this punctuality of mine. It's incurable. They say that punctuality is the mother of something or other—all I can say it's a bloody nuisance. Nobody appreciates it. People look at you as if you were hours early and you find yourself apologizing. The one thing everyone's agreed on is that you should never be early on a first date. It looks as if you're over-eager. Date? I must be out of my tiny mind . . . It's all Nicola's fault. That girl! The things she gets up to! And I just let myself be . . . steamrollered by her. We got friendly at secretarial college and she acts as if she were my pimp. I ask you: look at me! Have you ever seen a more pathetic object? Here I am, Saturday lunchtime, waiting to meet a total stranger—who happens to be Nicola's temporary boss. A middle-aged man, married, with children. And all because she showed me a snap of him and I said he looked nice—just that, "nice"—and then he asked to see a snap of me, and then we had this weird conversation on the phone . . .

(*She giggles*) Funny how you feel sort of . . . uninhibited when you speak on the phone to a total stranger. God knows what he must think I am! Nicola told him I'm game for anything. Yes, old Nick's been up to her tricks. Do you know, I feel sorry for that man. Really sorry. Here's this office stud, expecting to find the Whore of Babylon and instead he finds—me. Angie from Bromley. (*Rising, and strolling up and down*) Except that he obviously thought the whole thing a joke and never bothered to turn up. I'll give him—(*She looks at the clock*)—exactly five more minutes, and Nick can refund my fare.

(*Brian comes rushing in from the street, nervous and out of breath. He is a slightly built man of forty, with greying hair and rather sharp features. He wears a sober, dark brown suit, with—somewhat incongruously—his cream-coloured shirt open at the neck and outside his jacket collar. He darts about hither and thither, several times passing Angie, who looks at him with circumspection*)

BRIAN: Bloody hell! It would have to happen today! Where can I have lost it? I looked in the washroom, I searched the desk minutely; Nicola looked on the floor . . . How can a contact lens just pop out? It must have gone down the sink. Good thing I've got a replacement at home. And of course I always carry a pair of glasses in case . . . She must have gone home by now—she wouldn't have waited this long. (*Giving Angie a perfunctory glance*) This child's obviously waiting for her boyfriend. I suppose I could ask her if she's seen . . .

ANGIE: Here's a right maniac—

BRIAN: No, I'll wait a few minutes, just in case. I don't want it to look as if I'm accosting a strange young girl. I'll just stand here—(*He peers at the clock*)—I suppose that *is* a clock. It's a round shape: it might be an advertisement. I don't want to put on my glasses, in case she comes. I mean, she might get a shock. They make me look so much older, and my hair's turned quite grey since that picture was taken on the beach . . .

ANGIE: He's like a ferret. That's it, a ferret. Thank heaven I thought of the right animal. It sort of nags you, it becomes almost an obsession, if you can't think of the correct animal. Most people remind me of animals. I saw a giant tortoise yesterday, and a woman in the supermarket was definitely a kangaroo—she had that funny kind of spring in her step. There's been a marked increase in pigs recently—or maybe it's me, getting more and more disillusioned.

BRIAN: Damn! Damn and blast! I ought to have got here five minutes early, not quarter of an hour late. It was Nicola's fault. Deciding at the last moment that I must take off my tie and wear my shirt collar outside. That's why I went to the washroom, and that's how I lost my contact lens. Blast!

ANGIE: (*Sitting down on the bench again*) I'll amuse myself for a few minutes longer classifying people as animals. Anyway, he might have been held up by some last-minute business call. Nicola will be with Roger by now, helping him redecorate his room. That girl's so energetic, it makes you sick. She says they'll paint it in battleship grey.

BRIAN: Nicola should have come with me and introduced me to her friend. (*He sits on the bench, next to Angie*) But that would have been conventional, and the whole idea of this . . . experiment is that it's a genuinely blind date . . . In view of the loss of my contact lenses—(*He laughs out loud*)

ANGIE: (*Moving away from him slightly*) He's a nutter, this one. I don't know—there are more of them outside than inside. Still, he looks harmless.

BRIAN: (*Pretending to convert the laugh into a cough*) Pardon me. (*He dabs his mouth with his handkerchief*) They'll have me put away, if I carry on like this. (*Pause*) Maybe I *am* marginally insane. My plan for today was, well, offbeat, to say the least. Here I am, with a devoted wife who I love—love dearly—and two delightful children, and I coldly and deliberately jeopardize their security for the sake of an adventure with a—well, with a stranger. (*He gets up again and paces up and down nervously*)

ANGIE: A lot of the things I do can be explained by the fact that I live in Bromley. Only someone living in a place like Bromley can really understand what drives us . . . The Sunday papers are full of people from places like that, indulging in satanism, cannibalism, wife-swapping—you name it, we do it. We are . . . driven to it—in desperation.

BRIAN: It all came about so naturally. Nicola showed me her weekend snaps, and suddenly I felt so jealous—no, not jealous, left behind—as though I'd missed out on something. All these young faces: grinning boys, pulling grimaces, doing vaguely obscene things with their motorcycle crash helmets. And those laughing girls, those gorgeous laughing girls. And then she showed me this picture. A girl in a swimsuit, squinting into the sun, holding back her hair which was blowing in the wind. It wasn't even a good photograph, clearly defined. Her face looked rather blurry. But I fell in love with this picture. I know it sounds daft: the sort of thing you expect in an opera or in a sentimental novel or a woman's magazine—

ANGIE: Nicola was tickled pink. "You'll never guess," she yelled at me, "my boss has fallen in love with your photo!" So I asked her what he was like, and a few days later she showed me this holiday snap, taken in Spain or somewhere, of a man on a beach. There was a palm tree, and lots of kiddies with buckets and spades. His face wasn't any too clear, but he was wearing shorts and I said I thought he had nice legs. So Nick gets busy-busy, plays Cupid, and before I know where I am I get a telephone call at the office and a complete stranger says he must see me and we must arrange to meet at lunchtime on Saturday.

BRIAN: I don't know what it was. But when I looked at that picture, I felt I had to possess the girl. Nicola said there was no problem because her friend wasn't particular—which, now I come to think of it, was a bit of an insult . . .

ANGIE: I don't know what he must think of me. I bet Nicola told him a lot of stories, all about our wild weekend parties and so on. I'm not at all clear what he expects from me—or, come to that, what I expect from him. Lunch, I think. I'm feeling a bit peckish. Obviously, it wasn't to be.

BRIAN: The sordid mechanics of adultery proved to be ludicrously easy. Jeffrey, who's in charge of sales, has gone to Scotland for a few days. He gave me the keys of his flat almost before I asked for them. I had to endure his winks and his vulgar innuendo—"Welcome to the Club" and so on—but that was a small price to pay. This will certainly change my image at the firm. Hitherto I've been a symbol of fidelity and rectitude. Jeff used to sneer: "You'll come round to it. Just you wait. And when you fall, you'll fall harder than the rest of us." How demeaning, how degrading for me to confess to him that nothing happened, that the great adventure, the great initiation rite, came to nothing on account of a contact lens.

ANGIE: We did say one o'clock, didn't we? I'm beginning to have doubts. Maybe we said half-past one? I feel all confused now. No, I'm sure it was one. Still, now that I'm here, I might as well give it a few more minutes. That fellow next to me seems to be in a bit of a tizzy. I've never come across anyone so restless. Fancy having to live with such a man—it would drive you round the bend. He's practically tying himself in knots. Maybe I should offer him a tranquilizer?

BRIAN: How long shall I give her? Is there any point—?

ANGIE: I've forgotten his name! That man, Nick's boss, my supposed date. It was quite an ordinary name. Stephen, Graham, Terry? No . . . It was one of those names that sound young. Oh, well, never mind. It doesn't look as if I'll ever meet him, anyway. (*Glancing sideways*) The ferret's behaving as if his last hour had come.

BRIAN: Once I'd got used to the idea, I developed the most extraordinary, extravagant fantasies. At first I wanted her to come straight to Jeff's. I had it all worked out. I'd undress and put on Jeff's yellow bathrobe. She'd ring the bell. I'd open. Possibly give her a drink—the drink was optional—and lead her into the bedroom. Then I'd slowly and deliberately take her clothes off. Now the point would have been that all this time neither of us would utter a word. Imagine the tension that would build up. Having stripped her, I'd lay her on the bed, stand at the foot of the bed, take off my robe, and have her. Without having spoken a word. Without first kissing her. Without any preliminaries. Sheer lust. I was going to suggest it to her on the phone—our conversation had become so reckless that anything was possible—but when it came to the point, I mumbled something about having lunch first. With a heavy emphasis on the "first." And she cottoned on to it right away, saying something about not liking to work on an empty stomach. Come to think of it, examined as it were in the cold light of day, that remark betrays a certain indelicacy, not to say vulgarity. On the other hand, there was nothing crude in her speech and certainly not in her appearance, if the photo was anything to go by.

ANGIE: I shall get myself a bar of nut crunchies in a minute. The only thing is that he might just turn up when I'm away, and if he's been held up at work he'll assume I've been and gone. He definitely didn't sound the sort of chap who'd leave me standing. He was too keen for that. Nick's only working there as a temp, but she said he was a changed man after the telephone call, Brian was. Brian! That's it—Brian. That's his name. Oh, I'm so relieved. I hate it when I can't think of a name. Well, now I know who he is, all he has to do is turn up.

VOICE: (*Over the loudspeaker*) Will . . . Swami Mahandra Gupta please call at the stationmaster's office.

(*Brian gets up suddenly and leaves by the exit*)

ANGIE: Well, you could knock me down with a feather. I'd never have thought in a million years that he was an Indian. Maybe that's why he was so nervous. Being in a strange country and all. I don't suppose they have railway stations—not like ours, anyway. Ah, well, you live and learn.

(*Brian returns, having bought a paper. He resumes his seat. Angie splutters and giggles, turning away from Brian, and extracts a handkerchief from her bag to stifle her laughter*)

BRIAN: What's got into her? (*He looks at his hands*) I haven't smudged my face or come out in a rash? My flies aren't undone. Peculiar girl.

ANGIE: Fancy my taking him for an Indian. The strain's beginning to tell.

BRIAN: (*Opening the paper*) Oh, God, I can't read it without my glasses, unless I hold it close to my face. What the hell, I'll put my glasses on. But suppose she comes just as I . . . A middle-aged man with grey hair and glasses, reading a paper. She'd beat a retreat. Never even make herself known. All a terrible mistake. Can't risk it. (*He folds the paper again*) Mind you, the same problem would arise later on in the restaurant. I'd have to look at the menu and order . . . and later on examine the bill and pay. But by then I'd have her safely with me; she'd find it difficult to get away, even if she wanted to. Besides, Nicola says she goes for older men. Even so, the first impression is all-important. Better not risk the glasses. (*He pretends to read the paper*)

ANGIE: I'm almost sure the date was for half past. I must have got it wrong. They work till one o'clock, and although it's quite near, you've got to allow a few minutes. Besides, if he'd been held up or not been able to make it, Nicola would have come to find me and tell me. So, with a bit of luck, all may yet turn out for the best. Touch wood. (*She knocks on her head*)

BRIAN: What a funny girl. Perhaps she was trying to kill some sort of insect in her hair. People do very strange things when you observe them.

ANGIE: (*Going to the exit*) I'll go and keep a lookout. Mind you, I don't really know who to look for. I'll just stand there for a bit, with a friendly expression on my face. Not too friendly, though, or I'll be had up for soliciting. His name's Brian: I must remember that. And he's got rather curly hair and nice legs. Fool, Angie! I shan't even see his legs, unless he carries me off to some illicit place of ill fame. Anyway, he's got to make the first approach. I'll pretend I've just arrived. I'm not going to let him know that I got the time wrong and have been kicking my heels for half an hour. I'll stand sort of half inside and half outside. (*She places herself in the exit*) Bloody draughty. (*She shudders, and moves inside the station again*) Come on, Brian. It's feeding-time. I haven't got all day.

BRIAN: I bet I could have picked up this girl. London's full of them. She looked at me invitingly a couple of times—at least, I think she did—it was a bit difficult to make out her expression without the aid of my contact lenses. It might be an interesting experiment one day . . . No, I mustn't let this sort of thing get habitual. After all, I am a respectable married man with a family, whose wife happens at this moment to be under the impression that I am entertaining some Middle Eastern potentate on behalf of the firm. Well, I might have . . . It's only a bit of harmless fun, when all's said and done. That rhymes! I'm beginning to speak in rhymed couplets. It must be the tension of the situation. Wouldn't it be terrible if nervousness took the form of making one speak compulsively in rhymed couplets? I believe there is such a condition.

ANGIE: (*Looking at invisible commuters*) Sheep, pigs, cattle. Occasionally chickens . . .

BRIAN: Oh, what the hell! I'm going to read this paper. Hold it up in front of my face. If or when she comes, she can look behind it or knock on it or something. Her face would then be close enough for me to recognize her. In that way . . . Ingenious idea. (*He unfolds the paper and holds it close to his eyes, obliterating his face completely*)

ANGIE: (*Leaning against the wall*) What a silly situation to be in. It's all Tim's fault. This is the kind of desperate, crazy thing you do when you've been three years unofficially engaged. Am I ever going to marry him? I wonder. And yet it seemed so exciting to start with. Our first meeting—at a fireworks party. I can see him now, outlined against a background of rockets, Roman candles, and Catherine wheels. He was organizing it all, telling people what to do, running around . . . I thought he must be masterful: a man with natural authority. He was so different in the ordinary light of day. He hardly said or did anything. I had to make all the running. Not that that's anything unusual these days. No more shy maidens with downcast eyes, blushing when they're spoken to. As for ardent wooing—"will you?" or "won't you?" is about as much as one can expect. With Tim there wasn't even that. He looked at me with an imbecile grin and said nothing. Oh, these awful, endless pauses. "What do you do for a living?" I asked him in desperation. "Electrical contractor." That was it. What can one possibly say in reply to that? Pretend to be interested in light bulbs or heating appliances? It's a real conversation stopper, that. What with the fireworks party and him being an electrician, one gets an impression of sparks flying, of things exploding, of electric shocks. Poor Tim. He's very protective about me, I'll say that for him; he makes me feel all tied up in insulation tape. That's why every now and again I feel I must escape. It's a shame, really. He's a decent lad. He trusts me. The way he looks at me with his spaniel eyes. And going to bed with him is like getting physiotherapy. Most girls complain about their boy friends being inconsiderate. Tim is so . . . anxious to please, he practically makes one fill in a form after every session. "Are you sure it was all right?" "Are you quite sure?" "Did you really come, or was I too quick again?" I keep reassuring him. "It was fine . . . lovely . . . honestly: cross my heart." The trouble is, knowing about his anxiety, I have to pretend all the time that I'm carried away by ecstasy. What with him worrying about me, and me worrying about him, it's more like mutual aid. No wonder I go off the rails from time to time. It's the only way I can keep sane. And where does that get me? Waiting at a railway station for a complete stranger who I don't even particularly want to meet. That's what a decent and considerate boy friend does to you. I must have a rotten character. I know what I ought to do: get on the next train back to Bromley and call it a day. It wouldn't be my first defeat. I see the ferret who wasn't an Indian is still waiting, buried behind a paper. I must set myself a time limit. (*She sits on the bench again*)

BRIAN: (*Startled by someone sitting next to him, lowers the paper, looks quickly at Angie*) Oh. (*He takes up the paper again*)

ANGIE: Very polite, I'm sure. (*She gets up and walks away*)

BRIAN: Now I've scared her away. Poor kid: she probably thinks I'm a psychopath. I hoped for a moment that it might be the girl—my date. Actually, if I'd been clever, I'd have cut my losses and picked up the little tart who was hanging around here when I came. I wonder if she's waiting for someone in particular or just hoping to be propositioned by a stranger. After all, I shouldn't have liked to get my face slapped. Well, it's idle to conjecture now—I've scared her away. Pity. She appeared to be quite attractive and sort of . . . provocative. I noticed that her blouse was unbuttoned on top, revealing what the papers call "cleavage." Yes, she might have helped me pass the afternoon. Wouldn't it have been ironical if . . . Ah, well, it wasn't to be. Once again, I delayed action until it was too late. The story of my life. (*Angie returns carrying a bar of chocolate*) Christ, she's coming back! It's now or never.

Courage. (*He smiles at her as she sits down, and attempts to fold his paper, crumpling it into a mess*)

ANGIE: He's trying to be friendly. At least I think that's what he's trying to convey. (*She smiles back at him*) There's a kind of fellowship that springs up between people who're kept waiting. The fellowship of the rejected or abandoned. It's foul to be stood up. I expect I deserved it, but I'll have something to say to Nicola about it. (*She unwraps the chocolate bar, breaks off a piece, and eats it*) That's better. I was starving.

BRIAN: How on earth does one start a conversation? I'm completely out of practice. The weather's a dead end, and anything more positive sounds forward—an obvious ploy for a pick-up. It would be awful to be humiliated as well as everything else.

ANGIE: Poor old Tim. I remember our first date. We'd arranged to go to the pictures. Now, when a boy asks a girl out to the pictures for the first time, and he fancies her, he usually drags her to one of those sex films. They're everywhere. And when it gets hot on the screen, you can bet his hot little paw will casually, just by chance, rest on your knee. And kindly but firmly you remove it and put it back where it belongs—that's if you're a nice girl. Then, a few minutes later, his arm will move round your shoulder and then sink down inch by inch, get under your armpit and stretch across towards your breast. Now, if you sit well away, his fingertips can only reach the outer fringe, as it were, and that usually gets them really mad. That's when they start kissing your neck and blowing in your ear. But all that's by the way. The point I was trying to make was that Tim was different from all the others. He took me to see *One Hundred and One Dalmations,* never touched me, and cried! I knew then that if anything was to happen, it would be up to me. Just like me to pick a dud.

VOICE: (*From the loudspeaker*) Will Dr. Albert Untermayer please come to the stationmaster's office. (*Pause*) Will Dr. Albert Untermayer please come to the stationmaster's office.

BRIAN: (*Scans the station with alert interest, laughs, turns to Angie, and says to her in a rather forced, jovial manner*) Surely, all

these men—there must be at least thirty—can't all be called—
er—

ANGIE: Dr. Albert . . .

BRIAN: Untermayer.

ANGIE: Sounds German, doesn't it?

BRIAN: Could be Swiss. Or Austrian. I think I'd plump for
Austrian.

ANGIE: I see.

(*Pause*)

BRIAN: It's still . . . highly unlikely . . . that all these men,
going in this direction—

ANGIE: Is that where the stationmaster's office is?

BRIAN: Apparently. According to the sign-posting.

ANGIE: Maybe it's a party.

BRIAN: A party under the supervision of . . .

ANGIE: Dr. Albert—

BRIAN: Untermayer.

(*Pause*)

ANGIE: One would expect them to be in leather shorts,
with those funny hats.

BRIAN: (*Laughing a little too loudly*) Yes. Yes, quite.

(*Pause*)

ANGIE: They called for an Indian over the loudspeaker
before.

BRIAN: Did they?

ANGIE: Yes. And I thought it must be you, because you got
up and left just as they called the name.

BRIAN: (*Muddled*) Did I? When?

ANGIE: Just now. A few minutes ago. You went out. I expect it was to buy the paper.

BRIAN: Oh, that! Yes, I see. They were calling . . . ?

ANGIE: An Indian name. At least it sounded Indian.

BRIAN: But why should you think that I—?

ANGIE: That's just it. You left straight after the an-
nouncement. I thought it must be you. I couldn't figure it out.

BRIAN: I have no Indian blood—at least as far as I know.

ANGIE: I can see that.

BRIAN: I'm not even very sun-tanned.

ANGIE: Well, the weather hasn't been any too marvellous.

BRIAN: Low pressure fronts from Greenland, I expect.

ANGIE: Pardon?

BRIAN: The cold spell, the recent cold . . .

ANGIE: Is that what it was?

BRIAN: I'm only surmising, venturing a guess. I'm no meteorologist. (*Pause*) That's two things I'm not. I'm not a meteorologist and I'm not an Indian.

ANGIE: And you're not Dr. Albert . . .

BRIAN: Untermayer. That's three.

ANGIE: I wonder what they wanted him for. I wonder why people are called—

BRIAN: Funny you should say that. I've always wondered about that myself. One can imagine at an airport—some urgent message. But at Charing Cross—

ANGIE: He was a doctor something or other, wasn't he? Maybe he was wanted by a patient? Emergency case or something.

BRIAN: You're probably right. Yes, I'm sure you're right. That makes good sense.

ANGIE: Would you like a piece of chocolate? It's a nut crunchie.

BRIAN: No, thank you. Or, perhaps . . . just a small piece. It's very kind of you. (*He accepts a piece*) Can I offer you a cigarette? (*He gropes in his pocket*)

ANGIE: (*Shaking her head*) Don't smoke. That's why I eat chocolates.

BRIAN: Very wise.

ANGIE: Bad for the figure.

BRIAN: I wouldn't say that! Nothing wrong with *your* figure! (*To audience*) That was too forward. Almost insolent. Should I apologize?

ANGIE: Thank you, kind sir.

BRIAN: Not at all. You're welcome. (*To audience*) Welcome? The wrong word. Doesn't make sense.

ANGIE: (*Unwrapping the chocolate bar*) Fancy another piece?

BRIAN: (*Startled*) What? Oh, no. I assure you—

ANGIE: I mean chocolate. (*To audience*) I've landed myself with a right dim one here.

BRIAN: Oh, chocolate. I'm ever so sorry. I mistook your—

Yes, please, if you can spare it. (*She breaks off another piece and hands it to Brian*) Oh, no, that's much too big. You're giving me half your bar.

ANGIE: No, honest. I've had enough, anyway. It's just that I was beginning to feel peckish.

BRIAN: You haven't had lunch yet?

ANGIE: No.

BRIAN: Ah, that explains it. You're waiting for someone with whom to have lunch—correct guess?

ANGIE: Yes, that's about it.

BRIAN: And the "someone"—your friend—hasn't turned up?

ANGIE: Correct, Sherlock.

BRIAN: What? Oh, Sherlock. Sherlock Holmes. (*To audience*) I thought she said "Shylock": that she took me to be Jewish, wanting my pound of flesh.

ANGIE: What about you?

BRIAN: What about me?

ANGIE: You waiting for someone to turn up?

BRIAN: Yes. No. Not actually . . . waiting . . . (*To audience*) I'd better be careful. I mean, suppose my date turns up. What do I do? It would serve her right, mind you, to find me in conversation with an attractive young girl. Teach her to be punctual.

ANGIE: I hate unpunctuality. You can waste half your life waiting for people.

BRIAN: They say patience is a virtue.

ANGIE: I can't be very virtuous then.

BRIAN: (*To audience*) Now what did she mean by that? Downright challenge I'd say. Maybe she's on the game? Can't be too careful. I could catch something from her.

ANGIE: Another one who's got to be pushed and prodded. Just my luck. I seem to attract them like a magnet. Nicola says it's because I have something protective in my ways, sort of motherly. I could do without it, whatever it is.

BRIAN: Virtue is a relative term.

ANGIE: (*Uncomprehending*) Oh, yes?

BRIAN: I mean: what's virtuous to some people is . . . vicious to others.

ANGIE: Oh, yes, that's very true. (*To audience*) Help! He's boring the pants off me. I'll have to escape.

BRIAN: (*In his stride*) Take Spain, for example.

ANGIE: Why Spain?

BRIAN: I spent my holidays there— a few years ago. Now a Spaniard's attitude to women is quite different from an Englishman's.

ANGIE: They pinch bottoms, do they?

BRIAN: (*With a forced laugh*) No, no, that's Italians. The Spaniard guards his woman's honour with fierce pride. They have a very rigid code of conduct. If you're seen walking about with a man on three successive occasions, it means you're engaged. At least that's how it used to be. Things change, of course.

ANGIE: That wouldn't suit me at all, I'm afraid. I'm free and easy.

BRIAN: (*To audience*) "Easy." I don't like her use of the word easy. It's practically an invitation, short of actually soliciting.

ANGIE: I'll have to strike Spain off my holiday list then.

BRIAN: No, don't do that. It has its compensations. Hot weather, beaches, palm trees.

ANGIE: (*Alarmed*) Palm trees!

BRIAN: Yes. Why, are you allergic to them?

ANGIE: (*To audience*) The man on the picture. The beach and the palm tree. Jesus, it's him! (*To Brian*) No, it's not that. Just an . . . a sort of connection of ideas. No, I like palm trees.

BRIAN: So do I.

ANGIE: (*To audience*) I'm out of my tiny mind. It's him. It was him all the time. I imagined him differently, somehow. I don't know: less nervous. He was so outspoken on the telephone. I can see the resemblance with the photo now. It's the way he came rushing into the station. It never occurred to me. He behaved like a lunatic. I thought he'd be a man of purpose, striding in like John Wayne or whoever it was in *High Noon.* Sort of entering and surveying the scene and making a beeline—

BRIAN: Mind you, there's a lot to be said for staying in

England. The weather's a bit unreliable, of course, but given a
nice, hot summer . . . There are so many different parts to be
explored: the Scottish Highlands, the Lake District, the Nor-
folk Broads . . .

ANGIE: (*Nervously*) Right, right. (*To audience*) Hell, what do
I *do*? I can't suddenly say who I am, and that we've been
walking past each other for the last half hour. It's too stupid.
The whole thing's been a washout. It's beyond rescuing.

BRIAN: Might I ask where you come from? Are you a
Londoner?

ANGIE: (*Absent-mindedly*) Almost. I was born and bred in
Bromley.

BRIAN: (*Startled*) Bromley!

ANGIE: (*To audience*) Why did I say that? It just slipped out.
Now I've given the game away. Suppose he tumbles who I
am? What do I DO? (*To Brian, with pretended calm*) Yes. Do you
know anyone who lives in Bromley?

BRIAN: Yes. Sometime ago. A business connection. It's in
Kent, isn't it?

ANGIE: Yes, strictly speaking, it's not in London. Although
it's usually classified as a dormitory suburb.

BRIAN: Really? That's interesting. (*To audience*) I must
know for certain. I must ask her name. And then what? Do I
make myself known?

ANGIE: (*To audience*) It's no good. It's got beyond the point
of no return. To confess the mistake now would make me look
so . . . stupid. Also it would be insulting to him, because I
wouldn't have recognized him from the photo—and, of
course, he wouldn't have recognized me from mine, which is
even worse, because it was quite a good likeness. Have I really
aged so much in those few weeks, or was it my hair blowing in
my face?

BRIAN: Well, we both appear to be in the same predica-
ment.

ANGIE: What do you mean?

BRIAN: Waiting.

ANGIE: Oh, that! Yes, you could say . . .

BRIAN: (*Suddenly*) What's your name?

ANGIE: (*Promptly*) Nicola.

BRIAN: Nicola?!

ANGIE: Yes. It's not that unusual, is it? (*To audience*) Stupid oaf, thought he'd catch me out.

BRIAN: No . . . no. It's a very nice name. Funnily enough, I know a girl . . . She's my secretary. My temp.

ANGIE: What's yours?

BRIAN: Pardon?

ANGIE: Your name?

BRIAN: Oh, it's . . . Albert—

ANGIE: (*Giggling*) *Doctor* Albert?

BRIAN: (*Confused*) No, I'm not a doctor. Why?

ANGIE: Just wondered whether you should have gone to the stationmaster's office.

BRIAN: Oh, that. No, I'm afraid I'm not Austrian. Neither Indian, nor Austrian. Just plain . . . good . . . English.

ANGIE: (*To audience*) Oh, God, that's one of Tim's stock remarks. And the awful thing is it's true. He's plain and good. Especially good.

BRIAN: (*Secure behind the mask of "Albert," is fast assuming a new, suave identity*) Nicola, eh? Do they call you Nicky for short?

ANGIE: Some do. And what do they call you? Bert?

BRIAN: No, never. It's always Albert.

ANGIE: Always Albert . . . (*She smiles to herself*)

BRIAN: What's in a name?

(*It is clear that both are aware that they know each other's true identity*)

ANGIE: What indeed?

BRIAN: Well, Nicola, we're in identical situations.

ANGIE: Waiting.

BRIAN: I wonder if we could turn . . . this coincidence . . . to some constructive use?

ANGIE: I'm not sure I know what you mean, Always Albert.

BRIAN: Come, come, there's no need to play the little innocent.

ANGIE: (*Flaring up*) I don't know what you mean!

BRIAN: Well, for example, I was wondering whether we could have a bite to eat together? And if you're not in a hurry, we could . . . go on . . . from there.

ANGIE: (*Looking at him coldly*) But I told you I was waiting.

BRIAN: For a boyfriend? Looks as if he's got delayed. Or stood you up.

ANGIE: It so happens that he's my fiancé, and he most certainly would not stand me up. He's an electrical contractor, and his jobs sometime keep him longer than he expects.

BRIAN: (*Chastened*) I'm sorry.

ANGIE: And what about you, then? Waiting for a girl friend?

BRIAN: Certainly not. I'm waiting for a train. I have a lovely, devoted wife at home, and two children. They'll be waiting for me to join them for lunch.

ANGIE: The perfect husband and father. Always Albert.

BRIAN: I wish you wouldn't call me that!

ANGIE: (*Provocatively*) Thinking of changing your name?

BRIAN: Certainly not. I am who I am. (*He rises*) No point in staying on, is there? (*They look at each other, tacitly aware of the true situation*) I'm sorry . . . things didn't work out. It would have been nice.

ANGIE: (*Shrugging her shoulders*) Who knows?

BRIAN: We'll never know now. Pity. Still, maybe it's all for the best.

ANGIE: (*Smiling*) That's one of Tim's favourite sayings. My fiancé.

BRIAN: The best laid plans of mice and men gang oft awry—

ANGIE: That's another one he always quotes. You're really very alike in many ways.

BRIAN: (*To audience*) Best *laid* is somewhat ironical in the circumstances. (*To Angie*) Well, it's been a pleasure meeting you.

ANGIE: Likewise.

BRIAN: Perhaps next time it'll turn out all right.

ANGIE: Who knows—never say die.

BRIAN: That's one of my wife's favourite sayings. Well, so long then—Nicola. The best of British luck.

ANGIE: Hey, before you go, can I have one of your cigarettes?

BRIAN: I thought you'd given up—?

ANGIE: (*Helping herself to one of the proffered cigarettes*) *I thought* I had, but there are always special occasions.

BRIAN: (*Lighting her cigarette*) I'm glad you think of our meeting as a special occasion.

ANGIE: Things never turn out the way you expect. It would be boring if they did. (*Brian stands hovering, still undecided*) Well, good-bye then.

BRIAN: Good-bye—and good luck. (*He walks away quickly*)

ANGIE: (*Draws on her cigarette a couple of times, sits back on the bench, crosses her legs and pulls up her skirt. She tilts back her head a little, and looks at the passing people. Her cigarette droops from her slightly parted lips. She undoes another button of her blouse*) Come on, *somebody*, and give me a light . . .

(*She leans forward as someone approaches. Train noises*)

Curtain

Michael Weller

SPLIT

Michael Weller

Michael Weller was born in New York City in 1942. He was educated at Stockbridge School, Windham College, and Brandeis University, where he received his B.A. in music in 1965. During his senior year at Brandeis he began writing plays and sketches for his college musical society, and after graduating he went to England to study drama at Manchester University.

His plays soon became popular with British audiences, but it wasn't until 1972 that he sprang to prominence in American theatre circles with the New York opening of *Moonchildren.* It was an occasion that evoked considerable praise for both play and author. Clive Barnes, then with the *New York Times,* called it "the best new American play of the past three or four seasons . . . a phenomenal, virtuoso display of wit and verbal imagination," while Henry Hewes reported in the *Saturday Review* that it "established Weller as a discerning and talented playwright."

Set in a student commune, *Moonchildren* began its circuitous route to Broadway in 1970 when it opened (under the title *Cancer*) at the Royal Court Theatre in London. In 1971, the play underwent a change of title and as *Moonchildren* was performed at the Arena Stage, Washington, D.C. Prompted by its reception there, the presentation was brought to New York, and although it stirred controversy as well as praise its engagement was brief. Nonetheless, *Moonchildren* was chosen as one of the ten best plays of the year, and Mr. Weller won a Drama Desk citation as one of the season's most promising playwrights. There was more to come. In 1973, the play was revived Off-Broadway where it ran for 394 performances, then toured nationally.

Among the author's other plays are *Fishing* (presented at the New York Shakespeare Festival's Public Theatre); *The Greatest Little Show on Earth* (commissioned by the Royal Court Theatre, London); *The Bodybuilders; Grant's Movie; Dwarfman;* the musical *More Than You Deserve;* and *Tira Tells Everything There Is to Know About Herself,* which was included in *The Best Short Plays 1973.*

Mr. Weller's newest work for the theatre, *Loose Ends,* is scheduled to have its premiere at the Arena Stage, Washington, D.C. in 1979, and during the same year, he will be represented on the screen as the scenarist of the motion picture version of *Hair.*

Split was first performed in the United States on April 13, 1978, at the Ensemble Studio Theatre, New York, with the following cast:

PAUL	Mandy Patinkin
MARGE	Mary Elaine Monti
WAITER	Daniel Stern
JEAN	Kathryn Grody
CAROL	Elaine Bromka
BOB	Chip Zein
JAY	Tom Noonan

Director: Carole Rothman

The play is dedicated to Alan Schneider.

Characters:

MARGE
PAUL
WAITER
JEAN
CAROL
JAY
BOB

One

Table—a cafe. Paul and Marge with coffee. Cafe noises.

MARGE: O.K. Stevie Wonder's blind. He's black and he's blind. That's a lot of things to have going against you, right, but instead of letting it mess him up he turns into this genius-level songwriter-arranger-performer who's very fulfilled spiritually according to his songs anyway plus he's famous and rich and cool and he's able to write all these incredibly happy upbeat numbers . . . and here I am this white middle-class girl with two good eyes and a college education. That's what I was trying to explain to my shrink. Stevie Wonder makes me deeply deeply depressed. The fact that he exists is really depressing to me. And of course he said I was being adolescent, which he always says. I mean I don't need him to tell me I'm adolescent. I need him to tell me it's all right that I'm adolescent. (*Pause*) Do you want to stop talking and we'll just sit for a while?

PAUL: No, that's O.K. Talk. It's O.K.

MARGE: Why don't you tell me about what happened?

PAUL: There's nothing to tell.

MARGE: Well, for instance, was it more of a thing where you left her, or did she leave you or what?

PAUL: I don't want to keep boring my friends talking about it. People split up all the time.

MARGE: A lot of them haven't been married for six years.

PAUL: A lot of them have.

MARGE: A lot of them aren't my best friends.

PAUL: It's just over, that's all. It's over. There's nothing to say.

MARGE: You know what I think, Paul? I think it's temporary. You guys just belong together. (*Pause*) Look, you want me to move in with you?

PAUL: Move in? You?

MARGE: Just for a few days. While you're getting used to Carol not being there. I'd invite you to stay with me and Bob but Bob's learning how to play Go . . . it's this Japanese game and you'd probably end up having to let him teach you how to play, which might not be kind of what you want to be doing for the next few days.

PAUL: No, it's not what I had in mind. Thanks anyway.

MARGE: I'm just trying to help. It's really lonely at the beginning. I remember when I left this guy once. He said he was a genuine Oglala Sioux Indian and I believed him for two years. Blond hair and blue eyes the guy had. He looked like Sven the Swede. Boy, was he full of shit! And I was really naive. Anyway, I really missed him at the beginning, even though I didn't like him. You don't look too good.

PAUL: There have been times in my life when I felt better, I must admit. It's crazy; last night I . . . I didn't feel like calling anyone. I didn't feel like doing anything. I was just sitting at home watching TV and getting a little drunk and I found I was thinking an awful lot about suicide.

MARGE: Well, it's something you should think a lot about before you take it up.

PAUL: I'm glad you called, Margie. And I have to start teaching again tomorrow.

MARGE: You want me to talk to Carol?

PAUL: What's the point? It's just over.

MARGE: I'll talk to her. First chance I get I'm going to talk to her. I like you guys. I hate to see this happening to you. Other people, I'm glad. You I'm not glad. (*Pause*) Oh, that's the other thing I meant to tell you about Stevie Wonder. He has this manager, I forgot what the guy's name is, but he goes around killing people. Really. This guy I'm working with, the video guy I told you about before . . . oh, I didn't tell you what he does, he takes movies, well, actually they're videotapes, he takes these tapes of himself dancing to all the hit tunes . . . all alone in his studio. That's one of the things he does, and the other thing . . . oh, and he doesn't wear any clothes. Well, he told me his sister works at a place where there's this guy who used to work for Stevie Wonder's manager and he saw the guy kill someone. He actually saw it. Isn't that amazing. Oh, and anyway, this video guy shows his tapes at parties. And all his friends dance to them, but they turn the sound off so they're only dancing to the way the guy moves and he's a terrible dancer. Don't tell him I said that if you meet him. I'll tell you next time he has a party. (*Pause*) Don't worry, Paul. I'll talk to her. It'll be all right.

(*Enter Waiter with small tray*)

WAITER: Coffee and English?

MARGE: Me.

WAITER: And ice coffee?

PAUL: And some milk with that, please.

WAITER: Did you hear something about an assassination?

MARGE: What assassination?

WAITER: That's what I was wondering. I guess you didn't hear anything, huh? A guy just said. I think that's what he said. Maybe it was "examination." Gotta get my ears checked. Milk, right?

PAUL: Yes.

(*The Waiter exits*)

MARGE: I know just what I'm going to say, too. Don't worry, Paul, really.

Two

Carol alone. A street.

JEAN: (*Off*) Carol! Carol!
(*Carol looks around. Jean enters*)
CAROL: Jeannie . . . Hi . . .
JEAN: How's it going . . . ?
CAROL: Oh, pretty good . . .
JEAN: I thought you'd be at yoga on Tuesday but you weren't there.
CAROL: Oh, you know, stuff's been happening. Hey, you look great.
JEAN: Thanks. You look . . . you shouldn't skip yoga, you know.
CAROL: Which way are you walking?
JEAN: I'm waiting for someone. Oh, Carol, this guy is so funny you gotta meet him, he's a genuine totally crazy person. You doing anything? I mean, right now?
CAROL: Yeah. Well. Why?
JEAN: Jay's taking me to this friend of his' place, he's got a loft or something. We're gonna sit around, get stoned, eat organic peanut butter, pretend it's 1968, you know. Why don't you come with us?
CAROL: Well. I don't know. I'm supposed to meet someone.
JEAN: O.K., some other time. I almost forgot. I meant to call you and everything. I found a place.
CAROL: Great. Where is it?
JEAN: No, not for me, for you guys. For next year. I got these friends in Vermont, they're renting their farm and, Carol, I want to tell you this place . . . it's like you won't believe it . . . trees all over the place and totally isolated . . . it's on the side of a hill looking over a valley with a lake . . . and . . . and and and . . . it's facing west. Well, you guys are into sunsets, right?

CAROL: Right, right. Sounds real nice.

JEAN: Real nice? Carol, this place is total nature city. And listen, all that money you guy's've been saving . . . you won't have to spend half of it. These friends of mine aren't into heavy profit. I told them about Paul writing a book and you doing a baby thing and they got so into having that kind of year happen on their farm they'll probably let you have it for free. I got their number . . . (*She checks in handbag*) Well, it's somewhere in the garbage bag here . . . look, I'll never find it now. I'll call you. (*She has pulled out cigarettes and takes one out*)

CAROL: Can I have one?

JEAN: I never knew you smoked.

CAROL: I'm just learning. Jeannie, have you been out of town or something?

JEAN: No, but I would love to get out. Maybe we could take a trip up to the farm together. Are you free next weekend?

CAROL: Very.

JEAN: O.K., I'll tell you what. I'll call you . . . tonight. When'll you be home?

CAROL: Paul ought to be back after school.

JEAN: O.K., I'll call him at five. I'll call him at school. I have the number . . . somewhere.

CAROL: Jeannie?

JEAN: What?

CAROL: I'm not meeting anyone. I told you I was meeting someone. I'm not. I don't know why I said it. I can't believe you don't know . . . I thought everybody . . . it's all anyone seems to be able to talk about and now you don't know about it and I hate that, too . . .

JEAN: What's going on? Hot news?

CAROL: Medium hot. Depends on how you look at it. Paul and I sort of parted company two days ago.

JEAN: What????!!!

CAROL: Yeah. End of marriage sort of thing.

JEAN: You and Paul?

CAROL: Me and Paul. Paul and Carol. Finito.

JEAN: I don't get it. Divorce and everything?

CAROL: Yeah. I guess so.

JEAN: This I don't believe!

CAROL: Why not? Everyone else is doing it. Don't want to be behind the times.

JEAN: Yeah, but you and Paul. I mean, you were married, you know . . . like *married* married.

CAROL: Yeah, well, now we're like split split.

JEAN: Jesus Christ!

CAROL: That's exactly what I said this morning. I woke up and there was this funny moment where I didn't know where I was because the other side of the bed was unoccupied. After one thousand six hundred and thirty eight mornings . . . And what I thought was Jesus Christ! So I went to church . . . first time in ten years.

JEAN: Carol . . . I don't know what to say.

CAROL: When I got there the place was cordoned off and there was this funny little bald priest running around telling everyone sorry, no one allowed in today . . . they're filming an episode of *Kojak*, sorry . . . and for some reason I found that really comforting. Bald priest. Bald Kojak. All these bald people.

JEAN: We should get together and talk, Carol.

CAROL: Yeah.

JEAN: Where you staying?

CAROL: The Gramercy Hotel.

JEAN: The Gramercy Hotel????

CAROL: I just want to be on my own for a while. I don't want people to know where I am . . . Everybody keeps inviting me out and I can't tell if it's because they really want to see me or they just feel sorry. I mean I don't need that . . .

JEAN: Oh shit, here comes Jay . . . JAY!! JAY!! He is so funny. OVER HERE!!! I'll call you Carol . . .

(*Enter Jay very laid back and unfunny*)

JAY: There's a great accident around the corner. You want to go over and watch it?

JEAN: Jay, this is my friend Carol.

JAY: Hi! You want to come over and watch an accident with us. They're just clearing up. It's very interesting.

CAROL: I've got to go.

JAY: After that we're going over to this friend of mine's loft and get stoned and pretend it's 1968. You can come if you want.

CAROL: No, thanks. (*To Jean*) He's not so funny.

JAY: What?

JEAN: (*Hiding laugh*) She has to meet a bunch of people, Jay. She wants to be on her own.

JAY: What's being said here? What did I miss?

CAROL: I'll see you at yoga.

JAY: You want to do some video, Carol?

JEAN: Not now, Jay. Let's go watch the accident. I'll call you, Carol.

JAY: With tape, you know. You show it on a TV screen. I'm ready to get into using a lot of new people and I get very strong vibes from you. That usually means good things for video. You have a very kinetic face. Have you ever thought about video?

CAROL: Well, I . . . No.

JAY: You should think about it. You'd be really beautiful on tape. Here's my card. Oh, yeah, that's the real estate office. You can reach me there during the day. I don't have a phone in the loft. You know, like why give people a chance to invade your trip twenty-four hours a day. Right?

JEAN: The accident's going to be over soon, Jay.

CAROL: O.K. Maybe I'll call.

JAY: Ciao.

JEAN: (*To Jay*) Be with you in a moment. (*Jay walks off, not looking back*) He's not so funny, is he.

CAROL: He's weird.

JEAN: Yeah, he is. Well, what do you do on Sundays, you know? Say hi to Paul when . . . Jesus!

(*Jean goes. Carol takes a drag on the cigarette. Forces herself to like it*)

Three

Rug—living room. Bob and Paul play Go on the floor.

BOB: No no no no no no no no no no. You remember what I told you that was called. That's Nichi not Tori. "Horse jumps pond, water goes away." That's what they call it in Japanese and it means I can take all your stones. You're not thinking conceptually. You can't play Go if you don't think conceptually.

PAUL: Bob. This looks like a good game, you know. It looks like a very interesting game, and some time I'd really like to learn how to play it. But not now, huh? Do you mind?

BOB: No. It's cool. You want to watch TV? There's the worst movie of the week on five.

PAUL: No.

BOB: Want to get drunk?

PAUL: No.

BOB: Leaving Carol hasn't made you a more interesting person to be with.

PAUL: I'm sorry. I wish someone would talk about something else.

BOB: Look. When something like this happens two things happen. One thing is everyone wants to help out, right, because everyone knows what it feels like to break up, and the other thing that happens is nobody knows what to do because everybody realizes that the person they want to help feels terrible and wiped out and probably like they're not worth helping or even being with which makes it impossible for people who want to help to help.

PAUL: Marge is working pretty late.

BOB: She's working for this jerk who does videotape. I hardly ever see her. I mean, there's nothing going on. I think he's gay in the first place. He takes movies of himself . . .

PAUL: Dancing naked, I know.

BOB: What a weird thing to do. I wonder if he'll still be at it when he's sixty. Can you just see it? Whole family comes over to his loft for Christmas and he shows tapes of himself as a young man dancing naked to *"Voulez Vous Coucher avec Moi Ce Soir."* What did your daddy do for a living? Oh, he took off his clothes and danced naked in front of a camera in an empty studio.

PAUL: I heard he makes a lot of money in real estate.

BOB: Yeah. Boy. Everything's really weird.

PAUL: Anyway.

BOB: Yeah.

PAUL: What's this all about?

BOB: What do you mean?

PAUL: You said you had something to talk to me about.

BOB: I did?

PAUL: What's the matter with you, Bob? You called me up and invited me over and you said you and Marge had been talking about me and Carol splitting up and you had this very important thing to tell me . . . isn't that exactly what happened?

BOB: We ought to wait for Marge to get home.

PAUL: Why? What's the big mystery?

BOB: There's no mystery.

PAUL: Then why are you acting so weird.

BOB: I'm not acting weird.

PAUL: You are too. You're acting very weird.

BOB: No, I'm not. I am not acting weird, Paul. Your head's in a weird place, that's all. Everything looks weird to you.

PAUL: This is a dumb conversation. Let's change the subject.

BOB: Very good idea. What do you want to talk about?

PAUL: What I really want to talk about is what you and Marge invited me over here tonight to talk about.

BOB: You're right. This *is* a stupid conversation.

PAUL: I'm gonna go home. It's getting late.

BOB: No. Look. Just wait'll Marge gets home, O.K.? We wanted to talk to you together.

PAUL: Why?

BOB: O.K. Whew! I don't know. I guess I better tell you.

Man, this feels strange. O.K. Well, it's kind of about . . . It's partly about me and Marge. And partly about . . . Has she told you much about what we've been into lately?

PAUL: Marge?

BOB: Yeah.

PAUL: No. I mean, maybe. I don't know. I mean what do you mean?

BOB: Well, we've been sort of exploring this area that we hadn't been aware of before. Well, we were aware of it. You know, marriage is . . . it can be very kind of very insular. You know? A man and a woman together all the time. Marriage can sort of cut you off from a lot of experience. And anyway, what me and Marge were thinking was that maybe you'd let that happen to you. You and Carol.

PAUL: That's what you thought?

BOB: Look, man, this isn't a criticism. Believe me. Believe me, I know what it can be like. Me and Marge. It happened to us. I mean, we didn't even know we'd gotten into such a closed-in trip and then when we realized it . . . well, we knew we had to do something about it soon or else everything that was good between us . . . fffft!! You know?

PAUL: What the hell are you talking about, Bob?

BOB: Swinging.

PAUL: Swinging? You mean two couples together? Is that what you mean? You've been doing that? You and Marge? And two other people?

BOB: . . . or more . . .

PAUL: Together? Having sex? Together? All of you?

BOB: It surprises you.

PAUL: Yeah, I mean . . . Yeah. You and Marge. Whew!

BOB: Paul, I know what you're probably thinking, but believe me, it's a beautiful thing. It's brought an incredible amount of openness in our marriage and it's helped us not to be afraid of our . . . well, ourselves. And each other and other people. We're each totally free to explore other people, but we're also together, so we can enjoy each other's explorations and it's just amazing how you become aware of the fact that society has crippled you by defining sexuality in such a narrow and limited way. And we're all victims, Paul. You take Persia and India and some of those ancient civilizations.

PAUL: Horseshit, Bob, just horseshit! Horseshit! I mean, O.K., so you and Marge are getting tired of each other and you don't know what to do about it. What's that got to do with me?

BOB: We saved our marriage, Paul.

PAUL: Oh, man! Look, if you mean like you thought you'd try to help me and Carol get back together by inviting us over here for a little group sex, I mean, no thank you. Is that what you had in mind? Is that what you wanted to talk about?

BOB: I guess I'm not explaining it right. I knew we should wait till Marge gets home. It's really more sort of her idea. I mean, I don't think it's a bad idea, don't get me wrong. I just sort of thought, I told her the timing's wrong. Anyway, it beats sitting at home alone.

PAUL: Anything beats sitting at home alone.

BOB: It's just we can't figure why you guys split up. You were such a great marriage.

PAUL: That's what everybody says.

BOB: No one expected it.

PAUL: Like that! (*Snaps finger*) Literally. We were joking around. We were making up after a fight, laughing and everything and Carol said, "Well, if we're going to fight all the time maybe we ought to just split up." It was a joke. I mean, we never fight. Never. We laugh, we laugh all the time. And instead of laughing suddenly we were talking very seriously about ending it and we were crying and stuff.

BOB: Jesus!

PAUL: Yeah. Just like that.

BOB: It was a mood. That's all. You've got to get together and talk.

PAUL: It was more than that. It must have been. I don't know what the hell it was.

BOB: You know what I think sometimes. Things just happen and you never know why. You figure out all these reasons to explain it, but it still doesn't make sense. Like a few days ago I started wondering why I was a carpenter. And I figured it out. I figured out a lot of reasons. I'm good at it. It pays a lot. I work my own hours. My uncle was a carpenter. All these reasons, but I still wonder why I'm a carpenter. I mean, I still wonder much more than I believe any of the reasons I came up with to explain why I'm a carpenter. (*Pause*) That was clear, wasn't it?

PAUL: So. You guys have been swinging, huh.

(*Paul laughs. Bob laughs. They both laugh hysterically*)

Four

Bare stage—video loft. Jay with video camera, running. Carol and the Waiter are being taped. Very awkward. Improvise.

WAITER: Well . . . Ah . . . What kind of stuff are we supposed to do, you know?

JAY: (*Filming*) That's fine. Anything that happens is valid.

WAITER: Oh? O.K. Well. Hmmm. Let's see. I'm Jeff. I'm a waiter.

CAROL: I'm Carol. I'm . . . I don't do anything at the moment.

WAITER: Hi, Carol.

CAROL: Hi, Jeff.

WAITER: Is that O.K.? Is that the kind of thing you want?

JAY: Great! Great! Keep going.

WAITER: What's your name again? Jay. That's it. This is a great loft, huh.

CAROL: Yeah. You're not a friend of his?

WAITER: I just met him. My favorite color is blue.

CAROL: What? Oh. My favorite color is . . . it used to be yellow but it's getting to be light green. I feel really uncomfortable in front of the camera.

JAY: It's great. It's beautiful. You two are perfect together.

WAITER: You want to play a game?

CAROL: O.K.

WAITER: What do you want to play?

CAROL: I don't care. Whatever you want to play.

WAITER: Do you know that one where I start a story and then I stop and you take it up where I left off until you stop and then I keep on.

CAROL: I don't know it. It's O.K. We'll play that. I mean, if it's all right. Can we play a game in front of the camera?

JAY: Why do you keep asking for permission? Whatever happens, let it.

CAROL: Well, I mean, it's your tape. I don't know what you want to do with it.

WAITER: Hey, I've got one.

CAROL: What?

WAITER: I've got the beginning of a story, O.K.?

CAROL: Go ahead. I don't know what I'm doing here, I really don't.

WAITER: Once upon a time there was a frog. (*Pause*) Go ahead.

CAROL: What?

WAITER: There was a frog. That's the beginning of the story.

CAROL: A frog?

WAITER: Yeah.

CAROL: What about him?

WAITER: You're supposed to say what happened to him next.

CAROL: I'm supposed to say what happened to a frog? I don't know. That's not what we're supposed to be doing, is it? You didn't want us to come up here to tell a story about a frog, did you? I need a cigarette.

JAY: You both keep thinking there's something that I want. Please stop worrying about it. I want whatever happens.

CAROL: I just don't know what I'm doing here, O.K.? I'm sorry. I'm standing in front of a camera with a guy called Jeff because some guy who's a friend of Jean's said come up and make some tapes and I don't know what you want. It's not like I do this kind of thing all the time. I thought I'd be watching to start with.

WAITER: I have a different story. Two trucks . . .

CAROL: I don't even know Jean all that well. I have other things to do. That's all I'm saying. I mean, I just find you really weird. Not you Jeff, I mean him.

WAITER: That's O.K., that's O.K.

JAY: Beautiful, keep going, keep going . . .

CAROL: Look, I'm getting upset. I don't want this to be on film.

WAITER: Well, I have to get to work pretty soon. I mean, if we're going to do a story we ought to start pretty soon.

CAROL: Please turn the camera off. I don't know what's the matter with me. (*Jay stops*) Thank you.

(*An awkward pause. Jay goes to Waiter*)

JAY: Jeff, that was beautiful. I want you to come by any time you're free and we'll do a tape.

WAITER: I don't have to go right away. Oh. O.K. Maybe tomorrow. This is really interesting. You got a great loft. You pay a lot of rent?

JAY: I own the building.

WAITER: Oh? O.K.

(*Waiter goes. Jay sits down facing Carol on the floor*)

CAROL: Don't say anything. I just want to sit for a few minutes. Do you have a cigarette?

(*Jay smiles. Offers her one*)

JAY: You're here in this loft. The loft is in a building. The building is in a city which is somewhere in the world which is somewhere in the universe and that makes you feel alone. But you're not alone. Do you know what that is?

CAROL: No.

JAY: Something I wrote. For you. So, tell me what's happening in your life?

(*Carol laughs, louder and louder. Blackout*)

Five

Table—a restaurant. Paul and Jean.

PAUL: Well?

JEAN: I don't know, Paul.

PAUL: Which way is it going, more yes or more no?

JEAN: I feel like you're pushing me.

PAUL: That's because I am. I'm out of practice. And of course it doesn't help a lot to know that you think of me and Carol as a kind of . . . unit. You want to arrange a signal? When it's the right time for me to ask you if you'd like to come home with me tonight, please indicate by grabbing my leg under the table.

JEAN: I feel like I'd like to. It's not that simple though. There's even stupid things. Being in the same bed . . . you know . . . that you and Carol . . .

PAUL: Oh, no problem there. We'll go to your place.

JEAN: No.

PAUL: I'll turn the mattress over. I'll buy a new one. Wait a minute. I just remembered. I don't have to. I bought a new mattress just this morning. Whew, that was lucky.

JEAN: I'm serious, Paul.

PAUL: I know. I know you are. I'm horny.

JEAN: And what if you and Carol get back together, like everybody thinks you will. Then I'll be someone who just came kind of in between for a while. That's not what I want.

PAUL: Why are you being so complicated all of a sudden? You want another drink?

JEAN: No.

PAUL: I mean, I thought I knew what'd be fun, call Jeannie, she's nice, she's a friend, we turn each other on I'm pretty sure, it'll be fun, go out, eat a nice friendly sexy dinner, see a nice friendly sexy film and go back to our place afterward . . . my place. And, you know. For the night. I don't understand it. Don't I turn you on?

JEAN: Of course you do, Paul. You know that.

PAUL: Are you seeing someone else?

JEAN: How come you can be so happy so soon afterwards. You were married five years.

PAUL: Because I'm smiling a lot and acting cute to get you into bed. Come on, Jeannie, you're too old to think that means anything. Please come back to my place.

JEAN: I don't think so. Not tonight.

PAUL: Why not tonight? What's wrong with tonight?

JEAN: I just don't want to. Not yet.

PAUL: When?

JEAN: I don't know. Soon. When I feel like I won't be being Carol.

PAUL: That was pretty low.

JEAN: It was just true.

PAUL: I really don't feel like being alone tonight.

JEAN: Neither do I, honey. That's the breaks. I have to work in the morning. You staying? Thanks for the dinner and the movie. And the drink. I like you, Paul. (*Jean kisses him on the head and starts to go*) I'll call.

PAUL: When?

JEAN: I'll call. I promise.

(*Jean exits. Paul signals an offstage waiter. Lifts glass, pointing*)

PAUL: (*Mouthing*) Same again. Right. Make it a double. Double.

Six

Couch—living room. Marge and Bob.

MARGE: I didn't have time to shop. All we have is a can of baby shrimp and some potato chips. I think there might be some beer.

BOB: That's O.K. I'll go out and get some chicken to go.

MARGE: I was seeing Carol.

BOB:　That's O.K. Oh. Carol. How's Carol?

MARGE:　O.K. She moved in with the video guy.

BOB:　Yeah? What? The guy that dances?

MARGE:　The guy I work for, Bob.

BOB:　Jay?

MARGE:　Yeah.

BOB:　I could get a pizza instead of chicken. Or we could go out. You want to go out? I got paid for a job today.

MARGE:　Either way. It doesn't matter.

BOB:　You want to though? You want to go out or eat in. If we eat in I could get a pizza or a chicken or something. Or we could just have the shrimp with some potato chips. That'd be O.K. with me.

MARGE:　Well, what do *you* want to do?

BOB:　Either way's fine with me. There's a pretty good movie on nine.

MARGE:　Are we a good couple?

BOB:　What?

MARGE:　Are we a good couple? Should we stay together?

BOB:　I don't understand. What did I say? Did I say something?

MARGE:　Maybe we're just not a good couple. I don't think we're as good a couple as Paul and Carol were and they've split up. Maybe we shouldn't be together. How do you feel about that?

BOB:　I feel . . . I feel . . . Um. I don't agree. I feel that we should be together.

MARGE:　Do you think we have a strong relationship?

BOB:　I don't know. Yeah. I guess so.

MARGE:　Do you think it's strong enough to stand on its own?

BOB:　Yes. I do. Yes. Definitely. I think so. Definitely.

MARGE:　Because I really don't want to play around with other couples any more.

BOB:　That's fine with me. Fine. Wait a minute. There was some chicken left over from last night.

MARGE:　Chicken? I don't think so. Hang on, I'll look.

(*Marge goes out*)

BOB: (*Loud*) I never liked swinging that much in the first place.

MARGE: (*Off*) Whaaa?

BOB: I said I never liked swinging that much in the first place.

MARGE: (*Off*) Just a second, sweetie, I can't hear you.

BOB: Especially the men.

(*Marge re-enters*)

MARGE: We didn't have chicken last night. There's some cheddar. What were you just saying?

BOB: I said I never liked swinging all that much in the first place.

MARGE: You didn't?

BOB: No.

MARGE: Then why did you get us into it?

BOB: Me? Me? I didn't get us into it. You were the one that kept saying our relationship was limited sexually and you thought it would be an important step to expand it into new areas. That's what you said. Those are your exact words. Almost verbatim.

MARGE: Come on, Bob. It wasn't me that started sending away for all those cheesy magazines with pictures of fat married couples and stuff . . .

BOB: You asked me to send for them. You said you were embarrassed.

MARGE: I asked you? Oh, bullshit, Bob, bullshit . . .

BOB: You asked me. I'm telling you, you asked me.

MARGE: I don't believe it. And it was me who asked you to go upstate to meet that bizarre couple with the leopard skin couch?

BOB: This is just like what Paul said. One minute everything was O.K., the next minute . . . fffft!

MARGE: Do you want a separation, Bob? Is that what you're saying?

BOB: Is that what you want?

MARGE: I asked you first.

BOB: No. I do not want a separation.

MARGE: Neither do I.

BOB: I think it's ludicrous that we're yelling at each other when we both agree that we want to stop swinging.

MARGE: I just want to talk.

BOB: Well, that's what I want.

MARGE: Well then, let's talk.

BOB: O.K.

MARGE: So. You think it would be all right for us to not have sex with other couples any more?

BOB: I do. I think it'd be all right.

MARGE: You think our relationship is strong enough to survive without it?

BOB: Yes. In my opinion.

MARGE: Good. I think I'd like to go out.

BOB: In fact, if you want to know the truth. I'm very glad we won't be with other couples any more. I'm really glad.

MARGE: I'm going to have a beer before we go out. Want one?

BOB: Yeah.

(They look at each other. Smile)

Seven

Paul with box and suitcase.
Carol enters with plant.

CAROL: That's it.

PAUL: Yeah.

CAROL: Well.

PAUL: Can you stay for a while.

CAROL: I have to go to this video thing.

PAUL: Can I come? Sorry.

CAROL: Thanks for letting me have all the Stevie Wonder records.

PAUL: I never liked him much. Marge says he depresses her.

CAROL: Everything depresses Marge. That's why she's so happy.

PAUL: Do you have a number . . . in case I have to reach you for something?

CAROL: I left it on the bed.

PAUL: Would you mind if I called?

CAROL: Would you mind if *I* called?

PAUL: I asked first.

CAROL: Maybe we shouldn't. For a while.

PAUL: Yeah, I guess you're right.

CAROL: You seeing Jeannie?

PAUL: A little. How'd you know?

CAROL: Friends.

PAUL: Good old friends.

CAROL: Good old friends.

PAUL: Carol. What the hell happened?

(*Phone rings*)

CAROL: Maybe it's for me.

PAUL: I'm expecting it.

(*Carol picks up things. Paul puts plant in box*)

CAROL: You better get the phone. Bye, Paul.

(*She goes*)

End of play

Israel Horovitz

HOPSCOTCH

Israel Horovitz

Hopscotch is the fourth work to be published here from Israel Horovitz's *The Quannapowitt Quartet*, a quadruple bill of related short plays. The complementary plays are *Spared* (*The Best Short Plays 1975*), *Stage Directions* (*The Best Short Plays 1977*), and *The 75th* (*The Best Short Plays 1978*). And while *Hopscotch* is the final play of the quartet to be included in these pages, the author designed it to be the first to be performed on stage.

Under the direction of the author, *Hopscotch* initially was presented at the Manhattan Theatre Club, New York City, with Lenny Baker and Swoosie Kurtz. Subsequently it was produced in Milwaukee, Wisconsin; Denver, Colorado; at Yale University in New Haven, Connecticut; and at the American Cultural Center in Paris, France. *Hopscotch*, along with the other plays comprising *The Quannapowitt Quartet*, is now scheduled for production at the New York Shakespeare Festival's Public Theatre, under the auspices of Joseph Papp.

Mr. Horovitz won his first acclaim in 1968 with *The Indian Wants the Bronx*, a powerful and terrifying study of violence on a New York street. A striking Off-Broadway success with Al Pacino in the pivotal role, it also scored heavily in other major American cities, at the 1968 Spoleto Festival (Italy), the World Theatre Festival in England (1969), as well as in numerous other foreign countries. The play (which was published in *The Best Short Plays 1969*) won a 1968 Drama Desk–Vernon Rice Award and three Obies, as well as a commendation from *Newsweek* magazine citing the author as one of the three most original dramatists of the year.

Israel Horovitz was born on March 31, 1939, in Wakefield, Massachusetts. After completing his domestic studies, he journeyed to London to continue his education at the Royal Academy of Dramatic Art and in 1965 became the first American to be chosen as playwright-in-residence with Britain's celebrated Royal Shakespeare Company.

His first play, *The Comeback*, was written when he was seventeen; it was produced in Boston in 1960. In the decade that followed, Mr. Horovitz's plays tenanted many stages of the world. Among them: *It's Called the Sugar Plum* (paired with *The Indian Wants the Bronx* on the New York stage); *The Death of Bernard the Believer; Rats; Morning* (originally titled *Chiaroscuro*, the play was initially performed at the Spoleto Festival and later on the triple bill, *Morning, Noon and Night*, Henry Miller's

Theatre, New York, 1968); *Trees; Acrobats* (introduced in *The Best Short Plays 1970*); *Line* (included in this editor's anthology, *Best Short Plays of the World Theatre: 1968–1973*); *Leader;* and *The Honest-to-God Schnozzola* (for which he won a 1969 Off-Broadway Obie Award).

His other works for the stage include *Shooting Gallery; Dr. Hero; Turnstile; The Primary English Class* (a 1976 Off-Broadway success with Diane Keaton as star); *The Reason We Eat;* and an adaptation of Eugene Ionesco's French drama, *Man With Bags.* He also has written extensively for television; most recently, a dramatization of Herman Melville's *Bartleby, the Scrivener,* presented by the Public Broadcasting Service in 1978.

Mr. Horovitz's most ambitious project to date is his full-length trilogy, *The Wakefield Plays.* Set in Wakefield, Massachusetts, where he grew up, the three plays are *Alfred the Great, Our Father's Failing,* and *Alfred Dies,* and they are planned for a major Broadway production in the near future.

A collection of his plays, *First Season,* was published in 1968. His first novel, *Cappella,* was issued in 1973, followed by the novella *Nobody Loves Me* in 1975.

Twice the recipient of a Rockefeller Foundation Playwriting Fellowship, he also won a similar fellowship from the Creative Artists Program Service, funded by the New York State Council on the Arts. In 1972, he received an Award in Literature from the American Academy of Arts and Letters, and in 1973 he was honored with a National Endowment for the Arts Award.

The author, who divides his time between New York and Massachusetts, with frequent sojourns in France, also has written several major screenplays, notably *The Strawberry Statement,* which won the *Prix de Jury,* Cannes Film Festival, 1970.

The play is dedicated to Paul Simon.

The People of the Play:

ELSA, *calls herself Lorali, thirtyish, youthful body, blonde hair, fair.*
WILL, *calls himself Earl, thirtyish, tall, dark-haired, dark-complexioned, thin.*

The Place of the Play:

Park playground, overlooking Lake Quannapowitt, Wakefield, Massachusetts.

The Time of the Play:

September, sunny afternoon.

A Note on Music:

Paul Simon's song "Was a Sunny Day" should be used to begin and to conclude play.

Lights out in auditorium.
Music fades in.
Lights fade up.
Asphalt patch, small park playground.
Small traditional green park bench, baby carriage set at bench's outermost corner, facing upstage.
Elsa is discovered, drawing hopscotch grid on asphalt with yellow chalk. She marks the word "HOME."
She throws a pebble into the first square and hops to it, picks it up, continues hopping to end of grid, turns, returns to starting position: her game has begun.
Music plays to completion.
As Elsa plays, we sense she is bothered by something or someone offstage, beyond auditorium.
As music fades out, Elsa calls out into and above auditorium.

ELSA: You like what you're seein'? (*No response. She returns to her game. When she reaches the end of the grid, she turns, stops, calls out again*) Hey, c'mon now, will ya! If yo're gonna gawk, gawk from where I can gawk back! Fair's fair! (*No response*) I'll turn my back, I won't watch. You can either come out and show yourself . . . or go away . . . (*Pause, calls louder*) Either way's okay with me! You gotta do one or the other, *okay?* (*She turns her back to auditorium. A moment of silence passes. A young man, Will, appears in auditorium. He will stop a moment and then walk swiftly and directly on to stage, directly to Elsa. He will never alter his course, once he begins to move to her. She turns, sees him. She is obviously frightened*) I'm not frightened, you know . . . (*Will continues his move to her*) This place is crawling with people, you know that? (*Elsa is frozen in fear. Will continues to move to her*) You better just back down, huh? This place is crawling with people . . . I mean, there's no danger here, right? . . . (*Will reaches Elsa. He takes her in his arms and kisses her on the lips. She is overwhelmed by his size and acquiesces, at first, to his embrace and kiss. She then responds with noticeable strength and emotion. They hold their kiss a while. They break apart, holding a fixed stare between them*) That was a good one . . . (*She smiles*) Strong silent type, huh?

WILL: (*Looking in baby carriage*) Where's the baby?

ELSA: Playing. Why?

WILL: Yours?

ELSA: Sure. (*She throws the pebble and begins her hopscotch game again*)

WILL: Where's your husband? Working?

ELSA: It's daytime, isn't it? (*Points to sky*) That big round bright thing up there's the sun. When you can see it, you can pretty much figure it's daytime. And when it's daytime, people are working . . . (*Smiles*) *Most* people.

WILL: This what you do for a living?

ELSA: (*Smiles*) Naw. Not yet. I'm not turning pro 'til after the next Olympics . . . (*She throws pebble again and plays. Will sits and watches a moment*) You married?

WILL: Me? Naw.

ELSA: Ever close?

WILL: To being married? (*Pauses*) Naw. Not even close.

ELSA: How come?

WILL: I looked around me. All my married friends were spending their weekends playin' softball. Their wives were home spending their weekends complaining about bein' left alone . . . while their husbands were playin' softball.

ELSA: That's why?

WILL: Sure. I hate softball. All's I needed was to get married and havta start bullshit like *that!* You know what I mean? (*He smiles*)

ELSA: You've got a lot a charm and a wonderful sense of humor.

WILL: You noticed?

ELSA: MMMmmm. I never miss a trick. (*She begins to play again*)

WILL: I see you waited . . .

ELSA: For what?

WILL: Babies. (*She looks at him, suddenly. He nods to carriage*) I could tell from the age. Still in a carriage and all.

ELSA: Oh, yuh. I waited. (*She smiles*)

WILL: Boy or girl?

ELSA: Well, now. It's gotta be one or the other, right?

WILL: Nine chances outta ten, yuh.

ELSA: Girl.

WILL: Name?

ELSA: Lorali.

WILL: How's that again?

ELSA: Lorali.

WILL: That's pretty. Yours? (*He is staring into carriage, lost in a memory*)

ELSA: (*Stops; looks at him*) My name? (*He smiles*) The same: Lorali. (*She resumes play*) I'm Lorali the Second, she's Lorali the Third. My grandmother was Lorali and my mother was Lorali, Junior . . . (*Smiles*) Very common name around these parts.

WILL: No kidding. I never heard it in my life before, now I hear of four of them . . . And in a jerk town like Wakefield, too . . .

ELSA: Very well-known and very well-respected name, too . . .

WILL: Around these parts, huh? (*Stands*) Wakefield, Massachusetts, United States of America, North America, Western Hemisphere, Earth, Universe, Infinity . . . (*Smiles*) I'm very deep.

ELSA: Oh, yuh. So's the lake.

WILL: What d'ya call it?

ELSA: The lake?

WILL: Yuh. The lake.

ELSA: Janet. I call it Janet. See these shoes? (*Points to her shoes*) These are the twins. (*Nods to bench*) The bench is Nanny Mary Poppins and you are what we see of Silver as he rides off into the sunset: a horse's ass! (*Stops; controls her anger by turning away from him*) Unbelievable! (*Faces him again*) Lake Quannapowitt. Named for the local Indians . . . a tribe that vanished.

WILL: Oh, right . . . I forgot . . .

(*Silence. Ten count*)

ELSA: You wanna know about my husband?

WILL: Sure. What does he do for a living? Break backs?

ELSA: Naw. Not for a living; he just breaks backs as a weekend hobby kind of thing . . .

WILL: He sounds nice . . .

ELSA: He's a minister.

WILL: No kidding?

ELSA: No kidding.

WILL: What kind of minister?

ELSA: Protestant.

WILL: A Protestant minister. You don't say? What denomination?

ELSA: Baptist. (*Pauses*) Blonde. (*Pauses*) Blue eyes. Both of them . . . (*Pauses*) Six-five-and-a-half . . . (*Pauses*) Square jaw, thick neck . . . (*Pauses*) He's a hunk.

WILL: He is?

ELSA: Mmmm . . .

WILL: A hunk?

ELSA: Mmmmm . . .

WILL: Of what?

ELSA: Huh?

WILL: A hunk of what?

ELSA: (*Resumes her game*) You just passing through . . . or are you planning to set up a business here? (*Smiles*) Hey! Maybe pizza. Wakefieldians eat a hell of a lot of pizza. Santora hit it big with subs. Maybe you could be pizza! A pizza-place with a real gimmick could be a real hot-shit success!

WILL: Anybody ever tell you you've got a mouth like a toilet?

ELSA: Oh, yuh. Couple a' guys. They didn't get too far with me, though . . . not with an obvious line like that. (*Smiles*) You know . . . maybe a quick feel, but nowhere solid. (*Pauses*) I've never been a sucker for an obvious come-on line. I like something more subtle . . .

WILL: A gun, a knife? That sort of thing?

ELSA: No. Uh-uh. (*Smiles*) Money's more what I had in mind.

WILL: (*After pretending to fish in his pockets*) Je's . . . what a shame! (*Smiles*) I used all my spare change on the train from North Station . . .

ELSA: Hey, well, listen! You can't win 'em all! I had a guy here just the other afta'noon . . . a real blowah' . . . real bullshit ah'tist-type, ya' know . . . he tried to pay me with magic beans . . .

WILL: No kidding?

ELSA: No kidding.

WILL: Was he youngish?

ELSA: Yuh, youngish . . .

WILL: Sho't?

ELSA: Yuh. Wicked sho't. Nearly teensy . . .

WILL: Was he leading a cow on a rope?

ELSA: That's him!

WILL: Never heard of 'im!

ELSA: You do night work, huh?

WILL: Huh?

ELSA: You work anywhere?

WILL: Yuh. I work.

ELSA: What kind?

WILL: I work for a big company . . . construction.

ELSA: Oh, really? You construct things?

WILL: Me, personally? Nope. Opposite. I tear things down. I'm in the destruction end . . . wrecking.

ELSA: Gee, it, well, sounds like you've done really well with yourself . . . very successful. (*Pauses*) Wrecking, huh? (*Pause*) They pay you a lot of money to do that?

WILL: Money? Sure, well . . .

ELSA: Sounds like it took a lot of schooling . . .

WILL: Schooling? Well, I . . .

ELSA: You have a big desk? . . .

WILL: C'mon . . .

ELSA: . . . a big *position!*

WILL: You s'posed ta be *cute* now or somethin'?

ELSA: Me? Cute? Uh-uh.

WILL: (*Forces a calm pitch to his voice*) I have a middle-sized position . . . middle management, they call us. (*Smiles*) It's a middle-sized position.

ELSA: Do you like it?

WILL: (*Yells*) *My position? Do I like my middle-sized position???* (*There is an embarrassed pause*) I'm still awful tired from traveling. My nerves are all edgy . . .

ELSA: Don't sweat it. (*Hops*) I can understand that . . . (*Pauses*) I meant "the town."

WILL: Huh?

ELSA: When I asked "Do you like it?" I meant "Do you like the town?" (*Smiles*) Being here.

WILL: Oh, I getcha. You wanted to know if I liked being here. (*Smiles*) I love it.

ELSA: I figured you did. (*Stops*) Most everybody here was born here . . .

WILL: Really? . . .

ELSA: . . . And stayed! (*Pauses*) You know what I mean?

WILL: Your parents? Are they still . . . ?

ELSA: My parents, are they still? Sure. Still as they come. (*Smiles*) Two days apart. (*Pauses*) Happens.

WILL: I was gonna ask about their house and all . . . I never even guessed . . .

ELSA: *That* happens, too . . .

WILL: How long ago?

ELSA: How long ago what?

WILL: How long ago did you lose them?

ELSA: Lose them? (*Pauses*) You mean, like in Filene's Basement . . . You make it sound as though I were careless! (*Pretends to be talking to third person*) Excuse me, but I seem to have lost my parents . . . (*To Will again, timbre of voice suddenly changed*) Last month. Four weeks ago. You just missed the excitement . . . the hustle and the bustle . . .

WILL: I'm sorry . . .

ELSA: Don't be.

WILL: I am . . . I really am.

ELSA: Long time comin'. Just as well . . .

WILL: I'm really very sorry to find out . . .

ELSA: Yuh, I was, too . . . (*Looks directly at Will*) I'm not scared of you at all anymore, not at all. So, just don't get that into your head, okay? (*Resumes playing hopscotch*) I used to hate boys . . . (*Pauses; throws pebble*) I grew up . . . (*Hops; stops*) Things changed. (*Hops; stops*) Now I hate men. (*She smiles*)

WILL: His heart?

ELSA: Huh?

WILL: Your father. Was it his heart?

ELSA: What do *you* think?

WILL: And your mother? She was sick long, too?

ELSA: Take a wild guess . . .

WILL: (*Angrily*) *Aren't you getting tired of this???*

ELSA: *Where . . . have . . . you . . . been???*

WILL: I . . . dunno' . . .

ELSA: That outta state? (*Pauses*) I don't hear an answer!

WILL: Newport News.

ELSA: Where's that?

WILL: Virginia.

ELSA: What d'ya wreck there? Men? Women? Buncha kids?

WILL: Navy yard. Tore it down.

ELSA: (*After a pause; she stops the game*) He had his heart attack, finally. Waited long enough, worryin' . . . (*Pauses*) Shot outta his chair like he'd been kicked by a mule . . . watching Miss America.

WILL: Were you there?

ELSA: Sure.

WILL: That musta frightened you.

ELSA: I don't know. I s'pose . . .

WILL: Your husband?

ELSA: What about him?

WILL: Was he . . . with you? . . . then?

ELSA: Then? No. Just me.

WILL: And your mother?

ELSA: On display. Being waked. In the living room.

WILL: Oh . . . I see. (*Walks to her*) And you were . . . alone, huh?

ELSA: That's what I said, right? You've got yourself a sho't-memory problem, don'tcha? (*Throws the pebble; hops to it*) You know who won? You maybe know her. (*Pauses; no reply*) Miss Virginia. A brunette with mushy big brown eyes, a wicked dumb drawl, mouth always open real slutty-like, and a pair of tits shot, no doubt about it, full of sand . . .

WILL: C'mon . . .

ELSA: Your type . . .

WILL: Don't be vulgar!

ELSA: But I am! Born vulgar, grow up vulgar, die vulgar; it's kinda a tradition around here . . . among those who stay and miss out on the sophistication of world travel . . . (*Pauses; then quietly*) Must be nice. (*No reply*) Your life.

WILL: (*Smiles*) It's the greatest.

ELSA: You speak any languages?

WILL: Je's, I thought I'd been doin' it since I got here . . . fact is, I thought we'd both been!

ELSA: (*Flat, childish reading*) Ho. Ho ho. Ho ho ho. Some rapid fire slashing wit, ya got there! (*Pauses; throws pebble*) Foreign tongues is what I meant.

WILL: Nope. You?

ELSA: Whatta *you* care?

WILL: I don't. I really don't.

ELSA: I know. I really know.

WILL: You ever been outta here? Outta Wakefield?

ELSA: Too happy ta wanna leave! Everything I'll ever want is right here . . . right in Wakefield . . . squashed in between

Reading, Stoneham, Greenwood and Lynnfield . . . (*Smiles*)
Everything I'll ever need is right here. Always been, too . . .
(*Pauses*) Everythin' else is bullshit. That's the way I see it.

WILL: You finish college?

ELSA: (*After a long pause; quietly*) Noop . . . never started.

WILL: How come?

ELSA: I was busy!

WILL: Oh, yeah? Doin' what?

ELSA: You own anything?

WILL: You always answer questions with questions?

ELSA: I try to. Okay with you?

WILL: Fine with me. Sure.

ELSA: You own anything special?

WILL: What, exactly?

ELSA: How about weird belts? I always notice that men
who travel around, like you do, get to wearin' a lot of weird
belts . . . you know . . . hand-carved stuff . . . sometimes
with studs . . . the kind quee-ahs sometimes wear . . . (*She
smiles*) You know what I mean? (*There is a long pause. Will slowly
lifts his shirt and displays his waist to her. There is no belt around his
waist*) You've lost weight. You're skinny.

WILL: I'm not skinny. I'm thin. You get tired of airport
food. You don't eat. You get thin . . .

ELSA: I use'ta be skinny, 'til high school. I got a big
stomach in high school. (*Pauses*) Gone now, but it used to
worry me a lot. In high school. (*Pauses*) Sometimes I used to
wake up worrying, in the middle of the night. Sometimes I
used to wake up maybe two or even three times a night.
(*Pauses*) I used to have to go into the bathroom. We had a
full-length mirror on the door. I use'ta stand in front of it and
hoist up my nightgown, about to my chin, and stare at my
stomach. (*Pauses*) It really worried me a hell of a lot! It sorta
. . . well . . . it sort of ruined me, you might say. My twirling.
(*Pauses*) I used to twirl. I was very good at it. Some people
used to think I could twirl wicked . . . I still could . . . if I
had to. (*Pauses*) You're pretty weird, you know that?

WILL: Do we *have* to???

ELSA: I'm gonna be thirty soon. Next month . . .

WILL: You look younger . . .

ELSA: Yuh, that's what they tell me . . . (*Stops; looks at him*)
You ever been anywhere that you actually thought was . . .
you know . . . exciting? Worth stayin' at, maybe?

WILL: I guess . . .

ELSA: Someplace where you might send somebody like
me?

WILL: You might like cities . . .

ELSA: I've seen cities!

WILL: I think I've seen 'em all; every city. (*Pauses*) My line
of work. It's indigenous.

ELSA: What's that supposed to mean?

WILL: Indigenous? "Peculiar to."

ELSA: I'm not stupid!

WILL: I never said you were!

ELSA: You travel a lot, huh?

WILL: Sure, wherever they have a big demolition job, I
have to go there first and estimate the costs . . .

ELSA: Sounds really crappy.

WILL: It's pretty bad. (*Pauses*) Do you think I'm dull?

ELSA: Yes. I really do.

WILL: I don't talk to people much.

ELSA: It does show a little, yuh. (*She throws pebble, plays a
while; stops. She turns to him*) Here's a fact about me you probably missed: did you know that I was very nearly Miss America?

WILL: C'm'off it, will ya?

ELSA: It's true! (*Pauses*) I came really close. I did! (*Pauses*)
I twirled for my specialty.

WILL: How close?

ELSA: Very. (*Pauses*) Fourth. (*Pauses*) State runoffs . . .

WILL: You get any money? (*No reply*) What did you get?

ELSA: (*Suddenly angry again*) You've got no right to just
come around and stare at people and start up all sorts of
bullshit, ya' know!!! (*Pauses*) What the hell do you think ya get
for fourth in the goddam state runoffs!??? (*More softly now*) I
got nothing.

WILL: I bet you were cute.

ELSA: (*Carefully*) The things . . . they . . . promise . . . you.
(*Silence*)

WILL: I've personally always found twirlers to be . . . you know . . . a little *stupid,* but . . . you know . . . stimulating. (*She looks up. He smiles*) It's true! It always turned me on. Maybe it's the way you fingered the aluminum stick . . .

ELSA: Thanks a lot.

WILL: But it's true! You are! (*She looks at him, tight-lipped*) Cute. (*He smiles*) You're more than that. You're really pretty . . . beautiful.

ELSA: (*Looks at him, directly*) You got feelings like the side of a hill, you know that?

WILL: I keep hearin' that. Yuh.

ELSA: Did it ever occur to you that I might be special?

WILL: Special? (*Smiles*) Never. (*Pauses*) Not at all.

ELSA: I do a lot of special things . . . I have special talents . . .

WILL: Like what? Acrobatic dancing? Musical saw? (*Looks at hopscotch grid*) Oh, *this,* you mean . . .

ELSA: I'm good at voices. Especially on the telephone. (*Smiles*) You ever make any dirty phone calls?

WILL: A few. Maybe twenty, thirty. That's about it.

ELSA: I mean really *filthy* phone calls. The kind you don't even read about . . . The kind you just sort of muse over . . . Really *filthy* phone calls . . .

WILL: Oh, I thought you just meant *dirty* phone calls. Filthies? Oh, sure, I guess I've done several hundred filthies . . . (*Pauses; adds quickly*) This month!

ELSA: I did thirty-one straight days in a row.

WILL: I think I read about it.

ELSA: I called the butcher.

WILL: What the hell are you talkin' about anyway?

ELSA: I called the butcher. (*Pauses*) Every time I use'ta walk by his butcher shop, he use'ta call outta me . . . usual things like "Hey, blondie, you want some of my meat?" or "How about some nice loins, cutie?" That kind of thing. (*Smiles*) I called him every night from the 1st of July right through til the 31st, inclusive. Gave *him* something to think about!

WILL: You like it?

ELSA: I loved it! (*Pauses; smiles*) At first he was really made nervous, you know, by my language and all . . . but by the middle of the month . . . even earlier . . . by the 10th, or so, he'd calmed down really quite a lot. By the 20th, he'd worked it out to get his wife and family to stop picking up the phone. He worked it out most of the time to get them right outta the *room!* (*Pauses*) He started whole conversations! (*Pauses; excited*) You know what he said on July 28th?

WILL: If I knew, it's somehow slipped my mind!

ELSA: I love you.

WILL: What?

ELSA: (*After a pause*) That's what he said: "Miss, I want you to know that I really love you." That's what he told me. I asked him if he wanted to meet me, but all he wanted was my telephone number . . .

(*N.B. Following section to be played quickly*)

WILL: C'mon, will you . . .

ELSA: It's true! He kept avoiding the question. He just kept asking for my number . . .

WILL: What time of day did you call him?

ELSA: What the hell kind of weird question is that?

WILL: I just wondered . . .

ELSA: Time of *night*. Five minutes to eleven . . . just before the news.

WILL: Every night?

ELSA: Religiously.

WILL: How could he get his family out of the room, every night, five to eleven?

ELSA: (*Smugly*) *He was dedicated!*

WILL: *You're* the weird one here!

ELSA: How come you're all jittery?

WILL: Me?

ELSA: On the 31st, I walked into his shop and asked him if he liked my halter top . . . it was hot and I had a halter that was kinda loose-fitting, wicked thin . . . no bra or anything . . . and shorts that were kinda wrecked from bein' washed so much . . . you know . . . holey. (*Smiles*) Nothin' underneath them, either . . . (*Pauses*) He pretended he didn't know me. Even when I did the same sentences I did on the phone, over and over again to his face, he pretended he didn't know me. He said he'd have to call the cops if I didn't stop my dirty talk. Can you imagine? We were all alone in the shop . . . me, just talkin' the sentences over and over to his face. Him, standing there with his bloody hands and apron. *A look of honest-to-God shock on his face!*

WILL: (*Suddenly*) This is an awful thing, but it's on my mind . . . I've forgotten your name!

ELSA: What?

WILL: I know it was pretty, but I can't remember it exactly . . . (*Pauses*) I'm sorry.

ELSA: (*Furiously*) *What the hell do you want from me, anyway?*

WILL: I don't want anything from you. It was a sunny day, I was walking, I saw you, I thought it might be interesting . . .

ELSA: Bullshit! You've been following me for a week now!

WILL: I saw you over here by yourself . . . hopping around like some kind of weird kind of retarded hooker, you know . . . and I estimated that it might be interesting . . .

ELSA: (*Interrupts*) Drop dead!

WILL: (*Yells*) . . . *to pick you up!*

ELSA: *Was it???*

WILL: *Was it what???*

ELSA: *WAS . . . IT . . . INTERESTING???*

WILL: (*After a long pause; softly*) No. Not very. (*Pauses*) Not *bad*. (*Pauses*) You're not stupid. Just not very . . . (*Smiles*) . . . interesting. (*She throws pebble and misses mark*) You missed.

ELSA: I wasn't concentrating. (*She picks up pebble, throws it into square, hopping to it. Again and again, in succeeding squares. Will picks up her yellow chalk, writes "Elsa" quite visible on top slat of bench. Adds* ♥➤) It's Lorali. (*Spells the name aloud*) L-O-R-A-L-I is the way we spell it.

WILL: I don't think that's correct. (*Smiles*) Okay. I'm . . . Earl. Earl the Third. My grandfather and father were both Earls. (*Will suddenly writes "Earl" in large letters scrawled over her hopscotch grid. He suddenly grabs her and pulls her down on to the hopscotch field with him, pinning her arms behind her, holding her down to the ground with him. He yells angrily*) I'm Earl the Third! (*Pauses*) Maybe even Earl the Fourth! Who's keepin' score, huh? (*Screams*) How about *Mister* Earl??? (*He forces her to kiss him*) Is that any better?

ELSA: Let me up!

WILL: When I want to!

ELSA: *You let me up!*

WILL: When I *decide* to!

ELSA: *YOU LET ME UP!!!*

(*He kisses her again, roughly, forcing her into a somewhat docile state. Elsa is quite visibly shaken, frightened. Their difference in size is unquestionable. Will breaks the kiss*)

WILL: Is that any better?

ELSA: Yuh. (*Quietly*) Just what I've been waiting for. Must take a lot of courage to throw around somebody who's half your size.

WILL: I'm ready to hear about this frocked and collared husband of yours . . . (*Pauses*) Do you two enjoy each other? (*No reply*) I expect an answer here *please* . . .

ELSA: Yes, we do.

WILL: How? I'd really like to know how. Speak to me. Tell me . . . some of the good things you do together.

ELSA: You're hurting me!

WILL: Good . . .

ELSA: Son of a bitch!

WILL: C'mon, Lor-ah-*liar!* Let's hear what you and the Reverend do for your jollies! (*Leans even closer, bending over her*) I'm really curious. (*Lets loose of her arm now*) You're free. (*Sits back, watches, as she weeps*) You gonna tell us?

ELSA: (*Weeping*) You've got no right . . . (*Pauses*) Rides . . .

WILL: You say "rides?"

ELSA: We . . . take rides . . . together . . .

WILL: Horses?

ELSA: In our car. We take rides. That's what we do . . . (*Quietly, weeping*) That's what we do around here. We ride up one-twenty-eight to the shopping centers . . . up in Burlington . . . down in Peabody . . . usually after they're closed . . . we sit in our car and look at the outsides of the stores . . . (*Pauses*) Everybody does it. (*She sobs a moment*) We don't talk much. Hardly at all. If he died during the rides, we'd crash. If I died, nothing much would happen . . . (*She regains her composure*) You've really got no right . . . no more . . . (*Pauses; then deep-throated, carefully*) I . . . am . . . so . . . unhappy.

(*There is a long pause*)

WILL: (*Smiles*) Is he a good driver?

ELSA: Who?

WILL: Your husband. Does he like trying new roads? Branching out . . . being . . . inquisitive?

ELSA: This isn't fair . . .

WILL: What is it? I'd really like to give it a try . . .

ELSA: What are you talking about?

WILL: Your number. What is it? I'll give you a ring, huh? Here. Write it down . . .

(*He throws a piece of chalk at her. She takes it and writes her number in huge letters on the asphalt. She stands, her attitude changed, composed*)

ELSA: I should call a cop!

WILL: (*Pauses*) You invited it. (*Pauses*) You forget so soon? A week ago, Park Street, outside the Greyhound Station. (*Smiles*) I couldn't believe my goddam eyes! (*Pauses; attitude changed now*) You forget? Ahhhh, that's too bad. (*Leans in; he is quite angry*) I just got off the bus. Still carrying my suitcases. You were leaning against the building . . . with the others . . . a real pro, huh? Wicked tough!

ELSA: You're crazy!

WILL: Oh, yuh, really crazy. (*Pauses*) You smiled, I smiled.

ELSA: I never saw you outside of any bus station! What the hell are you talking about?

WILL: Who was he? (*No reply*) *Who was he?*

ELSA: Who was who?

WILL: Answer me who were you waiting for?

ELSA: You're making this all up!

WILL: (*Yells*) *Come off the shit!*

ELSA: Okay, fine. That's what you need. That's what you get! I don't know who he was! Just somebody passing through! Okay.

WILL: "Somebody passing through?" What the hell is *that* s'posed ta mean?

ELSA: It just means . . . somebody. (*Turns to him; suddenly*) *I have to have somebody!*

WILL: You could leave.

ELSA: I can't.

WILL: *I* did.

ELSA: But you're back! How come?

WILL: Just passing through, believe me. Nothing here that interests me enough to stay around this jerk town.

ELSA: I loathe you.

WILL: You're really a tramp, aren't you? I mean, when you get right down to the bottom of things, you just whore around, don't you? Isn't that right? (*No reply*) How many?

ELSA: (*Yells*) How many what?

WILL: (*Same volume*) How many men? How many men do you have to have?

ELSA: (*Spits her words*) *As many as I can get!* (*Silence*) My husband . . . he went to a Baptist clergy council meeting in Worcester to give a speech on family planning. That's his specialty: family planning. He likes to use Gray Line buses instead of driving . . . gives him time to study his notes. He likes his speeches to be perfect.

WILL: Your mother? How'd she die?

ELSA: She just did.

WILL: That's no answer . . .

ELSA: What's the goddamn difference to you, huh?

WILL: I'd like to know . . .

ELSA: She's *my* mother, not yours!

WILL: I'd like to know.

ELSA: You shoulda stuck around! You woulda known!

WILL: Elsa . . .

ELSA: Fourteen years! Nothing! Not a word! You marry me on a Tuesday, and by Friday you're gone. Not a call not even a pigeon with a note, not even a bottle floating in the lake with a message. Fourteen years and not a word. *Nothing! What do you want?*

WILL: Want?

ELSA: Here? Now? What do you want?

WILL: A look.

ELSA: A look? Okay, fine: look! (*She spins once around, faces him again*) You had your look. Now, leave!

WILL: I don't know anybody around here any more, just you . . .

ELSA: (*Screams*) Join a club!

WILL: Elsa, please . . . (*He reaches for her. She pulls away, slapping his face, sharply*)

ELSA: Don't you *for-Jesus-Christ's-sake! ever* put your hands on me again!

WILL: I was seventeen!

ELSA: I was sixteen!

WILL: I'm sorry.

ELSA: You've got no *right* to be sorry. (*Faces him*) Sixteen years old and pregnant and terrified and you just fucking leave me here to . . . to *what*? To die? To what? What did you figure I was gonna do? Run the bank? Drink the lake? I'm really curious, Wilbur. I really am!

WILL: I was seventeen. I was scared.

ELSA: How about when you were nineteen? How about when you were twenty-five? How about when you were twenty-seven? (*Pauses*) I'll tell you what's really on my mind right now, Wilbur . . . what's really right on the tip of my tongue as I stand here lookin' at you face-to-face . . . (*Clearly*) I wasted so much of my time worrying about you and you're nothing! I've had dozens more interesting boys than you right here in town. Practically *all* of them!

WILL: Shut it up, now, okay?

ELSA: Can't take it, huh?

WILL: I don't give a fat shit about you *or* your boys . . .

ELSA: I gave yours away.

WILL: What's *that* tidbit s'posed ta mean?

ELSA: I was pregnant, remember? (*Pauses*) Did you forget? I gave it away.

WILL: Boy or girl?

ELSA: Which d'ya want it ta be?

WILL: Don't be stupid!

ELSA: But I am!

WILL: Elsa!

ELSA: Boy?

WILL: Boy?

ELSA: Girl!

WILL: Which?

ELSA: Both. Twins. Triplets. A litter! I had a litter! You shoulda stuck around. It was quite a show . . .

WILL: Listen to me . . .

ELSA: Nope. Sorry . . .

WILL: Listen to me!

ELSA: Nope.

WILL: *Listen to me!* If you had a son . . .

ELSA: (*Quickly, correcting him*) Daughter!

WILL: If you had a son . . . and he were seventeen . . . and he got a local girl knocked up . . . and he could either stay here and . . . be married to her . . . or he could get the hell outta Wakefield . . . once and for all . . . *which would you want him to do????*

ELSA: (*She lunges at him. He throws her down on to the hopscotch grid*) You filthy rotten son-of-a-bitch!

WILL: Elsa, listen!

ELSA: You filthy rotten bastard!

WILL: Elsa!

ELSA: There's no son! I killed it! I killed your son! It's true. I couldn't take his crying. I couldn't take his noise. (*Pauses*) He had your face. That's what I *really* couldn't stand . . . That's what I *really* couldn't take. He was you! (*Pauses*) It's true.

WILL: I didn't make a mistake at all, did I? I did just the right thing, didn't I? (*Pauses; then suddenly*) I think you're a *monster!*

ELSA: Swell. Great. That's just great. Is that what you came back here for? To tell me that?

WILL: (*Touches baby carriage.*) Whose is this?

ELSA: It's not mine. You said that, not me. It probably belongs to somebody young. Town's full of young families. The town's crawling with young families . . .

WILL: I'm sorry about your mother and father. I really am
. . .

ELSA: Save it, okay?

WILL: I'd hoped to see them . . . to talk to them . . .

ELSA: To what? To get them to forgive you? They didn't.
They never would've, believe-you-me. (*Pauses*) That's a fact.

WILL: I would've liked to have tried to explain . . .

ELSA: Hey, listen, be my guest. Try. Explain. They're
buried right over there in Lakeside. You know the spot, don't
you? Right next to yours . . .

WILL: I never guessed you'd still be so . . . involved.

ELSA: Now what's that s'posed ta mean, hmmm?

WILL: You just seem so . . . involved . . . with me. Still so
passionate . . .

ELSA: You're really unbelievable, Will. You were an unbelievable kid and you ran away and saw the world and grew up
and now you're back here and I can see you've become just an
unbelievable middle-aged adult. It's all just unbelievable.
(*Pauses*) I'm really happy to see the way you've turned out
. . . to see what a stupid little asshole you turned out to be
. . . (*Pauses*) I can see exactly what you are. I . . . am . . . so
. . . lucky. (*Suddenly*) *I WISH YOU WERE DEAD!*

(*There is a substantial silence. Will moves to her, faces her, but
cannot touch her. She stands, facing him. He is suddenly eloquent;
precise. He is somewhat aloof*)

WILL: I'm getting married. (*Pauses*) I've met a girl. She's
very nice. I think you'll like her. (*Pauses*) I've decided to stop
. . . you know . . . moving around. (*Pauses*) I'm coming
back. (*Suddenly angry*) We're settling here . . . home. (*Pauses.
Yells*) *Aren't you going to say anything?* (*Pauses. No reply*) We'll
talk. I'll call you. (*Moves away from her, stops; turns and faces her
from new distant position*) I'm sorry it's so . . . awkward . . . so
awkward between us . . . still. (*Pauses*) I was sure you'd . . .
well . . . you'd understand. (*He moves away from her, to edge of
stage, at point from which he entered play. He stops there a moment,
silently. He then speaks, angrily*) I never played hopscotch with
you! I don't know what the hell you think you're doing!

(He exits the play. The music fades in. [N.B. Simon song used to lyric "Her name was Lorelei," through end of song.] Elsa sits on bench, alone, in front of her name and the ♥. *Graffiti written with her yellow chalk, all around, her telephone number, his name. She looks at the marks on her hopscotch grid; she is weeping. Music plays to completion. Lights fade with music)*

The play is over

Frank D. Gilroy

THE NEXT
CONTESTANT

Frank D. Gilroy

Frank D. Gilroy makes his second appearance in *The Best Short Plays* series with *The Next Contestant,* published here for the first time. A satiric look at media "game shows," the comedy originally was presented as part of "Marathon '78"—a festival of nineteen short theatre pieces—at the Ensemble Studio Theatre, New York, a creative and prolific community of playwrights, actors, and directors functioning under the artistic stewardship of Curt Dempster.

The author was born in New York City on October 13, 1925. He attended DeWitt Clinton High School in the Bronx and soon after graduating went into the U. S. Army. While in service he managed to do some writing and contributed two stories to the divisional paper. Coming out of the army with "a burning desire and determination to write," he enrolled in Dartmouth College, and although he had been writing poems and stories for some time, a playwriting course taken in his junior year made him realize that drama was his proper genre. During his tenure at Dartmouth, he wrote two full-length and six short plays that were produced at the college. He also served as editor of the college newspaper. Graduating from Dartmouth in 1950 *magna cum laude,* he won a year's postgraduate study at the Yale School of Drama.

After Yale, Mr. Gilroy held a succession of odd jobs, all the while continuing to write. Television drama was coming into its own at the time, and he decided to make "an all-out total assault" on the medium. The breakthrough came in 1952 when he sold a sketch for Kate Smith. This soon was followed by other scripts performed on almost all of the major dramatic shows during television's Golden Age. He also started to write for films, notably the screenplays for *The Fastest Gun Alive* with Glenn Ford, and *The Gallant Hours* with James Cagney.

He next invaded the theatre with *Who'll Save the Plowboy?*, presented Off-Broadway at the Phoenix Theatre in 1962. The play and author were hailed by most reviewers and it brought him his first theatre award, an Obie for the best new American play of the year.

The Subject Was Roses, his second produced play in New York, opened at the Royale Theatre on May 25, 1964, and it was greeted with critical acclaim. Richard Watts, Jr. declared in the *New York Post* that Gilroy had written "a powerful drama" and "established himself as one of the high hopes of the American theatre." The play ran for 832 performances and won drama's triple crown: the Pulitzer Prize, the New York Drama Critics' Circle Award, and the Antoinette Perry "Tony" Award.

In 1967, Mr. Gilroy was represented again on Broadway with *That Summer–That Fall,* with Jon Voight and Irene Pappas. This was followed in 1968 by *The Only Game in Town,* a three-character vehicle that costarred Tammy Grimes, Barry Nelson, and Leo Genn. It later was filmed with Elizabeth Taylor.

Mr. Gilroy also has served as author and director of several films including *Desperate Characters* starring Shirley MacLaine, *From Noon Till Three* with Charles Bronson and, most recently, *Once in Paris . . . ,* which he also produced.

The author's drama, *Present Tense,* appeared in *The Best Short Plays 1974.*

Characters:

MASTER OF CEREMONIES
WALTER CARTRIGHT, *thirty*
CATHERINE HORTON, *twenty-eight*

Scene:

Stage right is a radio studio; stage left, a girl's room.

At rise, a program is in progress. An M.C. is at the mike. The girl's room is blacked out.

M.C.: And now, on The Big Challenge, we bring up our next contestant, Mr. Walter Cartright. (*Walter appears, takes his place before the mike; there is applause from the audience*) How do you do? Nice to have you with us.

WALTER: Thank you; it's nice to be here.

M.C.: Where are you from, Walter?

WALTER: I'm from New York.

M.C.: What do you do for a living?

WALTER: I sell business machines.

M.C.: Have you any idea what we're going to ask you to do?

WALTER: No, sir.

M.C.: Well, let me tell you it's a beaut. (*Laughter from the audience. Walter smiles*) I understand you're engaged.

WALTER: Yes, sir. Being married next Saturday. My fiancée is out in the audience.

M.C.: Have a house picked out?

WALTER: Yes, sir.

M.C.: Furnished?

WALTER: Somewhat.

M.C.: Well, then you might be able to use a new Hydro-Surf Spray washer and dryer, a complete bedroom suite designed by Viking, a Royal console radio, TV and stereo?

WALTER: Yes, sir. We could sure use them all right.

M.C.:   Well, they're yours, along with other gifts too numerous to mention, provided you meet your Big Challenge . . . Are you ready?

WALTER: Yes, sir.

M.C.:   All right, here it is . . . We challenge you, Walter Cartright, to call up an ex-girl friend who knows you're engaged and get a date with her. You can say anything you want with the exception you can't tell her that you're on this program or that you've broken your engagement. (*Some audience laughter*) Do you accept your Big Challenge?

WALTER: (*Hedging*) Which old girl friend?

(*Laughter*)

M.C.:   That's up to you.

WALTER: Where would I call from?

M.C.:   Right here. From the Big Challenge Isolation Booth. (*A booth is wheeled out*) We'll be able to hear everything that's said by both of you . . . but you won't be able to hear us. Are you game?

WALTER: I don't know.

M.C.:   A Hydro-Surf Spray washer and dryer. A Viking bedroom suite. A Royal console. Plus the Big Bonus Jackpot . . . if you meet your challenge.

WALTER: Gee, I don't know.

M.C.:   Well, let's get your fiancée's opinion. (*Looks out in the audience*) Will Walter's fiancée please stand up? (*Spots her*) There she is. And very pretty. (*To Walter*) What's her name?

WALTER: Doris.

M.C.:   (*To Doris*) Doris, you've heard the challenge. Is it all right with *you* if Walter tries it? . . . She's nodding her head. She says yes. That's a game little girl. (*Applause for Doris. M.C. turns to Walter*) Well, Walter, what do *you* say?

WALTER: Okay. I'll try it.

(*Applause*)

M.C.:   What's the name of the girl you're going to call?

WALTER: (*Ponders*) Catherine Horton.

M.C.:   When was the last time you saw her?

WALTER: About a year ago.

M.C.: She knows you're engaged?

WALTER: Yes.

M.C.: Okay, let's get started. What's her number?

WALTER: Murray Hill 4-2325.

M.C.: All right, you go into the Big Challenge Isolation Booth and dial the number. Good luck.

(*Walter enters the booth*)

M.C.: (*To the audience*) Hasn't seen the girl in a year but remembered her number like that. Watch out, Doris!

(*General laughter. Walter dials. The girl's room lights up. Catherine Horton, in her slip, is ironing. She does this in a vacant, listless preoccupied way. The telephone, on a stand in her room, rings. She looks at it a moment. Decides to ignore it, continues ironing. The ringing persists. The persistence of it gains Catherine's attention. She stops ironing, regards the phone. She goes to the phone, puts her hand on it, hesitates, then raises the receiver. The ensuing scene is punctuated by audience laughter*)

CATHERINE: Hello?

WALTER: Hello?

CATHERINE: Hello?

WALTER: Hello, Cathy?

CATHERINE: Yes. Who's this?

WALTER: Walter.

CATHERINE: Who?

WALTER: Walter.

CATHERINE: Walter who?

WALTER: Walter Cartright.

CATHERINE: Walter Cartright?

WALTER: That's right.

CATHERINE: No, it isn't.

WALTER: What?

CATHERINE: This isn't Walter Cartright.

WALTER: Sure it is.

CATHERINE: No, it isn't.

WALTER: Why not?

CATHERINE: It isn't.

WALTER: Why?

CATHERINE: It isn't.

WALTER: Well, it is.

CATHERINE: No, it isn't.

WALTER: I tell you it is.

CATHERINE: It doesn't sound like Walter.

WALTER: Maybe it's the connection.

CATHERINE: Who *is* this?

WALTER: *Walter Cartright.*

CATHERINE: No.

WALTER: I tell you it is.

CATHERINE: No.

WALTER: Why not?

CATHERINE: It can't be.

WALTER: Well, it is.

CATHERINE: No.

WALTER: Look, you know Ronnie Parker?

CATHERINE: Yes.

WALTER: And Dot Finley?

CATHERINE: Yes.

WALTER: Well, if I know your friends doesn't that prove I know you?

CATHERINE: I guess so. But it can't be you.

WALTER: Well, it is.

CATHERINE: Where are you?

WALTER: In midtown . . . You convinced that it's me?

CATHERINE: No. I think I'm going to hang up now.

WALTER: Please don't.

CATHERINE: What?

WALTER: I said please don't hang up. Look, remember that time at the circus when the elephant almost knocked your hat off?

CATHERINE: Yes.

WALTER: That foggy night we went to hear Frank Sinatra. Do you remember?

CATHERINE: Yes.

WALTER: Well, how would I know these things if I wasn't Walter Cartright?

CATHERINE: I don't know.

WALTER: So that proves it.

CATHERINE: I don't know.

WALTER: Well, you test me. Go ahead, ask me things. Anything. Go on . . . About places we went and all. Go ahead, ask me anything.

CATHERINE: Lake Tindale?

WALTER: We visited Joe Bathgate there. We went on a picnic and got lost. They were just about to send out a search party when we got back.

CATHERINE: We were too late for supper.

WALTER: So we went into town to the Log Cabin.

CATHERINE: We had barbecued ribs.

WALTER: We split a third portion. Then we went to that dinky movie. *Now* do you believe it's me?

CATHERINE: It *is* you.

WALTER: That's what I've been trying to tell you.

CATHERINE: But it can't be.

WALTER: Well, it *is*. How have you been?

CATHERINE: Fine, thanks. You?

WALTER: No complaints.

CATHERINE: That's good.

WALTER: What?

CATHERINE: I said that's good.

WALTER: I bet you're wondering why I called.

CATHERINE: Yes.

WALTER: I want to see you.

CATHERINE: Oh?

WALTER: How about tomorrow night?

CATHERINE: Tomorrow night?

WALTER: Yes. All right?

CATHERINE: No. No, I can't tomorrow night.

WALTER: Why not?

CATHERINE: I have a date with this fellow. That's who I thought it was when the phone rang. He always calls about this time.

WALTER: Then let's make it the next night.

CATHERINE: I can't. I have a date with the same fellow.

WALTER: Could you break it?

CATHERINE: No.

WALTER: Well, then you pick a night. Any night.

CATHERINE: This week?

WALTER: This week or next week. I don't care. Just pick a night.

CATHERINE: Do you think it's all right? I mean you're still engaged, aren't you?

WALTER: Yes, but it's all right. Doris doesn't object if I see other girls.

CATHERINE: I'll bet!

WALTER: Honest. She's very liberal that way. What do you say? . . . She's away for a few days.

CATHERINE: I don't know.

WALTER: Don't you *want* to see me?

CATHERINE: I don't think it's right.

WALTER: I just want to talk to you.

CATHERINE: I'll bet!

WALTER: I mean it.

CATHERINE: All right, go ahead.

WALTER: Not on the phone.

CATHERINE: Why?

WALTER: It has to be in person.

CATHERINE: Why?

WALTER: Because it does.

CATHERINE: Why?

WALTER: It's important.

CATHERINE: Well, I can't imagine what it could possibly be . . . You're not in trouble, are you?

WALTER: No.

CATHERINE: Then what is it?

WALTER: I just want to see you.

CATHERINE: You *really* want to see me?

WALTER: Yes. What do you say?

CATHERINE: I don't know.

WALTER: Come on, what do you say? . . . What do you say?

CATHERINE: . . . All right.

WALTER: When?

CATHERINE: Now.

WALTER: Tonight?

CATHERINE: You can't make it tonight?

WALTER: Sure. Sure, I can.

CATHERINE: Where?

WALTER: Wherever you say.

CATHERINE: The Zebra Bar?

WALTER: All right.

CATHERINE: I'll meet you there in an hour.

WALTER: Okay.

CATHERINE: In an hour. The Zebra Bar.

WALTER: Okay. It's real swell of you to do this.

CATHERINE: It's a pleasure, Walter. Believe me, it's a pleasure. I'll see you in an hour. Bye now.

WALTER: Bye.

(*They hang up. The girl clasps her hands, clenches them tight together, brings them to her bowed head, stands rocking, eyes closed, in an attitude of fervent gratefulness and prayer. Walter steps from the phone booth. The M.C. leads him to the mike*)

M.C.:   Is this boy an operator or is he an operator? (*The audience applauds and laughs*) Well, you certainly met our challenge. Now let me tell you what you've won.

WALTER: (*Interrupts*) What about the date I made?

M.C.:   You don't have to keep it . . . unless you want to. (*The audience laughs*)

WALTER: No. But she'll be waiting there.

M.C.:   No, she won't. At this very minute, one of my assistants is calling her to explain the whole thing and for being such a good sport, she'll receive a Monarch clock radio. Now let me tell you what *you've* won.

(*Catherine suddenly becomes very animated. She rushes about laying out clothes. Holds several dresses up to herself before a mirror. The M.C. begins reciting the list of gifts. The audience "Oh's" and "Ah's"*)

M.C.:   A Hydro-Surf Spray washer and dryer. A bedroom suite by Viking. A Royal console radio, TV and stereo. And the Bonus Jackpot! A silver service for eight by Brock. Your choice of wall-to-wall carpeting for any room in the house from the huge selection available at Morrow, Inc.

(The telephone rings in Catherine's room. She picks it up)

CATHERINE: Hello? Yes, speaking.

M.C.:   . . . A marble top coffee table from Bowman and Fine.

CATHERINE: Who?

M.C.:   . . . An electric blanket by H.Z.

CATHERINE: What? I don't understand?

M.C.:   . . . A complete set of lighter-than-air luggage designed by Miss Warren.

CATHERINE: Yes? Yes? What?

M.C.:   . . . A Randolph automatic toaster.

CATHERINE: Please say it again.

M.C.:   . . . Two weeks all expenses paid at the beautiful Marlin Hotel in Miami Beach.

CATHERINE: *(After a moment)* Again . . .

M.C.:   . . . A Dekto movie camera to record your happy stay there.

CATHERINE: *(Softly)* Yes. I see. I see . . .

M.C.:   . . . And all because you met your BIG CHALLENGE!

Curtain

Corinne Jacker

THE CHINESE RESTAURANT SYNDROME

Corinne Jacker

Once again, Corinne Jacker won warm approval from the New York press when her triple bill, *Other People's Tables,* had its premiere at the Off-Off-Broadway Billy Munk Theatre. Mel Gussow of the *New York Times* wrote: "In the last two years, Corinne Jacker has emerged as an extremely versatile dramatist, with the naturalistic *Harry Outside* and the darkly comic *Bits and Pieces.* (Note: The latter play was introduced in *The Best Short Plays 1977.*)

"It is clear that she has a particular affinity for creating female characters and that she often writes with wry humor about the competitiveness within even the closest relationships. . . . The author's ear is acute and there is an urbanity to her dialogue.

"*The Chinese Restaurant Syndrome* (which was part of the tripartite program) is about a long-standing friendship and never-ending rivalry. Because of their closeness and the airlessness of their association, two women have shunned each other's company for seven years. Now, at a moment of crisis in one of their lives, they meet for lunch in a Chinese restaurant, and almost immediately after the greeting, old ire rises."

A winner of a double Obie award for *Harry Outside* and *Bits and Pieces,* the author was educated at Stanford and Northwestern universities where she took her B.S. and M.A. In 1954 she was named a Lovedale Scholar, and in 1955, a University Scholar.

Her other published and produced plays include: *Travellers; Night Thoughts; Seditious Acts; The Scientific Method; Breakfast, Lunch, and Dinner; Among Friends;* and *My Life,* performed by the Circle Repertory Company, New York, in 1977. Her most recent work for the stage, *After the Season,* was presented at the Academy Festival Theatre, Chicago, during the summer of 1978 with Irene Worth as star.

Additionally, she has published the following books: *The Biological Revolution; The Black Flag of Anarchy: Antistatism in the United States; A Little History of Cocoa; Window on the Unknown: A History of the Microscope;* and *Man, Memory, and Machines: An Introduction to Cybernetics.*

Miss Jacker also has written extensively for television, notably *John Adams, President,* acclaimed as one of the most dramatic episodes in the series, *The Adams Chronicles;* and was presented with an Emmy Citation for her participation in the *Benjamin Franklin* series.

The Chinese Restaurant Syndrome appears in print for the first time in *The Best Short Plays 1979.*

Characters:

SUSAN LEMMERER
MAGGIE STEWART
WAITER

Scene:

A Chinese restaurant on the Near-North side of Chicago. It's about two in the afternoon. If there was a lunch crowd, it's long gone now; the place is empty except for one customer, Susan Lemmerer. She is bored, anxious, and annoyed because the person she is waiting for has not shown up. She pours the last of a pot of cold tea, looks around for the Waiter. He is nowhere to be seen.

SUSAN: *(Calling out)* Waiter! Waiter! *(No answer. Then the Waiter comes through the door with a tray on which there are two martinis)* No! Please! I told you to wait with those until my friend came. Please. Just bring me some hot tea. *(The Waiter looks at her, then takes the teapot into the kitchen)* Some *hot* tea, please . . . *(She opens her paperback, begins to read, mutters to herself as she reads)* No hot tea. No wonton soup. Not even a Chinese waiter.

(At that moment, a drenched Maggie Stewart comes rushing in. She literally shakes herself free of the rain. As if to make her point, there is a thunderclap outside)

MAGGIE: Hi!

SUSAN: Hi, there!

MAGGIE: It's coming down dogs and cats.

SUSAN: Needles and pins.

MAGGIE: Cups and saucers? . . .

(They laugh, it's an old joke between them)

SUSAN: For God's sake, get out of that coat. You're soaking.

MAGGIE: That's why I'm late. I mean, no one expected. There I was, on the Outer Drive, and I literally had to stop my car. I mean, we all stopped, crawled to a halt . . . ground to a halt? . . .

SUSAN: Either. Will you get out of that ridiculous coat? You look like a wet collie or something.

MAGGIE: I'll keep it on for a while . . . I'm cold.

SUSAN: Of course. Because you're standing there in a wet coat. You'll start sneezing in a minute. You always catch cold. (*Calling*) Waiter! Waiter! . . . Will you come over here and take off the damn raincoat and sit down? (*After another moment of hesitation, Maggie does take the coat off. She discloses under it exactly the same chic pants suit as Susan is wearing*) Oh! That's why you wouldn't take the coat off!

MAGGIE: You look better in it.

SUSAN: No, I don't.

MAGGIE: But it's your color.

SUSAN: My best color is black.

MAGGIE: Is something wrong, Sue?

(*The Waiter returns and puts down the martinis*)

SUSAN: Thank you . . . Two Manhattans, now, please.

(*Susan drinks her martini very quickly*)

WAITER: You mean two martinis.

SUSAN: Manhattans.

WAITER: You're drinking martinis.

SUSAN: Why aren't you Chinese?

WAITER: I speak the language.

MAGGIE: Isn't that interesting.

WAITER: Why? You can't work in a Chinese restaurant without knowing Chinese. The cook doesn't know any English! (*He smiles at her*)

SUSAN: Manhattans. Please. How do you say Manhattans in Chinese?

(*He shrugs, leaves them*)

MAGGIE: (*After a moment*) These are martinis.

SUSAN: You don't remember, do you? (*Maggie looks at her*) We swore that some day we'd go right down the drinks that were our letters of the alphabet. Remember? I remember it so clearly. We were juniors then, or maybe beginning our senior year. And we were applying to college. And we said that when we got accepted, we'd celebrate. When we got accepted and when we turned eighteen. And that's what we'll do today— Maggie—M—martinis, Manhattans, Margaritas, Susan—S— screwdrivers, sidecars . . .

(*A pause. Maggie sips her drink. The Waiter comes back in, looks at them. He still doesn't have the drinks with him*)

WAITER: You ready to order? The kitchen closes in eight minutes.

SUSAN: Almost. Come back in another minute, okay?

(*The Waiter leaves for the kitchen again*)

MAGGIE: I think it's an omen or something. I mean, both of us choosing the same thing. I went into the closet this morning and without hesitation, I looked at this outfit and I thought it's exactly the sort of thing Susan would like . . . Maybe I thought that when I bought it.

SUSAN: Where'd you get it?

MAGGIE: On sale at Field's.

SUSAN: I made mine.

MAGGIE: You don't know how to sew.

SUSAN: *Didn't.* I didn't know how to sew. Now, I know how to sew. I was passing this Singer's store—and there was this terrific sale on sewing machines and there was this particularly gorgeous one—it zigzagged and embroidered and but-tonholed and threaded its own needle, and I thought—"God, I have to have that." So I went in and I took the course, and—voilà.

MAGGIE: You must save a lot of money.

SUSAN: We don't need the money. But it's a creative chal-lenge. Vogue patterns, designer fabrics, my brain and hands working together . . . How much did you pay?

MAGGIE: It was a real bargain.

SUSAN: Come on. How much? A hundred? (*Maggie shakes her head "no"*) More? (*Maggie hesitates. Before she can respond, the Waiter comes in, puts down the drinks, takes out his pad, waits to take the order*) Well, how much? I want to be able to tell Jack. I mean, this one outfit probably paid for the whole sewing ma-chine. (*She gulps down her Manhattan. Then, to the Waiter*) Two Margaritas, please. (*The Waiter does not move*) Come on, 'fess up. Some sale—what'd they do? Take ten percent off? You never could manage money, always overspending your allow-ance. Now, I'll tell you first. Then you tell me. The whole thing—fabric, thread, buttons, zipper, the pattern—which is reusable—the works cost me . . . $35. Now how much? I did it for 35—

MAGGIE: $29.95 . . . But mine's falling apart already. Look at the hem, coming down here and here. And the buttons are coming loose. And the zipper got stuck three times. And look here—there's a defect in the fabric.

(*The Waiter gives up and leaves*)

SUSAN: You never could have gotten a bargain like that ten years ago.

MAGGIE: Sure. We change. Everybody changes . . . Ted's changed. He's not the same person he was when we got married. You wouldn't recognize him. He's all—he jogs and does yoga and he eats proteins. He looks ten years younger than I do.

SUSAN: Come on, Maggie, drink up.

MAGGIE: . . . What's wrong?

SUSAN: Does something have to be wrong? I'm celebrating the fact that two very old friends have gotten together after so many years—seven years.

MAGGIE: I was so glad when you called.

SUSAN: You made the last call. Exactly seven years and one month ago. Give or take a week. You just picked up the phone and dialed my number and I said hello and you said hello, and then, flat out, cold as ice, you said—let's cool it, let's see less of each other for a while. And we talked a little more. And hung up. And now it's seven years later.

MAGGIE: Were you waiting for me to call you, all that time?

SUSAN: Well, Christmas, summer vacation, we sent you baby announcements.

MAGGIE: So did we.

SUSAN: But you didn't call back, no invitations to lunch, or a barbecue—not even bridge.

MAGGIE: That's why I was so glad you called.

SUSAN: Well—you were right. You were absolutely right. We were just becoming too much alike, same perfume, same dishes, same clothes—(*She looks at her clothes and Maggie's, smiles, they laugh together*) Come on, drink up! It's no fun if you don't play, too.

MAGGIE: You'll drink more. You always could. We always had to turn everything into a competition . . . Ever since the day we were born. I knew I was three ounces heavier than you.

SUSAN: You were three inches longer.

MAGGIE: And born first—V-E day.

SUSAN: Then I was born on V-J day.

MAGGIE: Flags on both our birthdays.

SUSAN: But I had more. V-J day ended the war. V-E day was only the end of *part* of the war.

MAGGIE: It doesn't matter. We both had significant birthdays. That's important, you know, occasions, meaningful dates. Like both of us getting married on the same day.

SUSAN: Two years apart.

MAGGIE: I was jealous—for a while, I was really jealous, but then, I thought, don't worry about it, so she sold out, so you'll be a lawyer.

SUSAN: What happened to all that?

MAGGIE: What? Being a lawyer?

SUSAN: That, too . . . I sent away for a catalog—continuing education—and I marked all these courses—Russian, social history, the philosophy of television—

MAGGIE: Well, we're both happy. That's what counts.

SUSAN: Fulfilled.

MAGGIE: Both parents alive, never lost a child in the war, both married.

SUSAN: Satiated.

MAGGIE: God, I just wish I had more time to read.

SUSAN: Are you scared? About the first—you know, tragedy, whatever? That something's going to go sour?

MAGGIE: (*After a moment*) Yeah . . . Well . . .

(*Neither has any words. They look at each other, pick up their glasses, clink them together and drink. The Waiter comes back from the kitchen. He has two more drinks*)

SUSAN: What's that?

WAITER: Bloody Marys . . . M—Mary. I didn't count the B.

MAGGIE: That was very clever of you.

WAITER: I'm getting my doctorate. Physics. Solid state. Cryogenics . . . The reason I wanted to know Chinese was—when the war starts, or the detente, or whatever, and they come over here to invest and to run the country and to take promising scientists to Shanghai—see, I'll be prepared. Chinese is an asset. (*A pause. The women look at one another; they have nothing to say to this*) You want to order?

SUSAN: We're still drinking.

WAITER: How about some more tea?

SUSAN: Are you sure you're not with the CIA?

WAITER: The CIA is last week's news, lady. (*He leaves*)

SUSAN: (*Calling after him*) You can start us on the S's when you're ready—sidecars . . . (*Maggie takes out a cigarette, lights it*) You still smoke?

MAGGIE: Don't you? . . . I thought you were too—you know, all that scare stuff, in the cigarettes, in the food, cancer here, cancer there, so—I like smoking. Ted tried to cajole me into stopping—he offered me a mink jacket. It's not worth it. (*She smokes, then smiles at the memory that's come to her*) Remember when we learned how to smoke? Oh, God!

SUSAN: Oh, God!

MAGGIE: Why does anyone do anything like that—it tasted like shoe soles.

SUSAN: Dirty socks.

MAGGIE: Jock straps.

SUSAN: Oh, God! That was the year. Had to get everything in before sweet sixteen . . . Listen, I never asked, did you? Get everything in?

MAGGIE: Did you?

SUSAN: Almost. All I planned on. Necking, and French kissing—I just got that in a week before. But not—

MAGGIE: Oh, no.

SUSAN: Oh, God no! . . . How we used to live in one another's pockets.

MAGGIE: Sometimes, I thought I'd die if you went away.

SUSAN: The two of us. The Bobbsey Twins.

MAGGIE: Grammar school, high school, summers. Until I went away to the convent.

SUSAN: You wrote me this incredible letter—after you were there about five weeks, about getting up at dawn, and how you were afraid they'd cut off all your hair.

MAGGIE: Well—I didn't have a vocation after all.

SUSAN: I knew that. We all knew that . . . But, the possibility of your staying was so awful!

MAGGIE: Well, you could have entered one, too. (*She contradicts this sharpness by taking Susan's hand*) I suppose we'd better order.

SUSAN: I'm on a diet. I lost five pounds.

MAGGIE: Me, too. Seven!

SUSAN: I meant five pounds this week. (*Pause*) You've been on my mind so much lately. I had to call you.

MAGGIE: I'm getting drunk.

SUSAN: Me, too . . . Does Ted snore? Jack does. Every night. I keep trying to fall asleep in time. Most of the time I'm too late, though.

MAGGIE: He grinds his teeth. I never get any sleep.

SUSAN: There we go. Trying to be best again. (*They laugh together*) Let's make a rule. No more contests. No more tests.

MAGGIE: Agreed. (*They shake hands on it*) How many kids do you have now?

SUSAN: Four.

MAGGIE: Me, too. Two of each.

SUSAN: Three boys.

MAGGIE: Two of mine are twins.

SUSAN: (*After a thoughtful sip of her drink*) My oldest has six toes on his left foot.

MAGGIE: Really? One of the twins has dyslexia.

SUSAN: My youngest is allergic to food. He can only eat soy beans.

MAGGIE: The twins are both overweight!

SUSAN: All four of mine are in therapy!

MAGGIE: The last time we saw one another was at your Timmy's birthday party. He was two. Just two. And he wanted to blow out the candles, and he cried out "Mommy, Mommy," and he turned to you, and then he turned to me. Of course he couldn't tell us apart. We walked alike. We wore the same shade of eye make-up. Cut our hair the same way. We were growing up to be Siamese twins. You were president of the Junior League. I was chairman of the United Fund. We were in this ridiculous three-legged race. And we were dragging our husbands in with us. And our children. And right then, I had this epiphany. I didn't want to be in contests any more. So I chose to withdraw. Before I lost. Or you lost. And there were no more chances to win.

SUSAN: I didn't know you felt like that.

MAGGIE: (*Taking her hand for a second, squeezing it*) I'm so glad I came today.

SUSAN: I needed to see you.

MAGGIE: I really wanted to see what you'd become.

SUSAN: Me, too. I thought maybe you'd changed. You sounded different on the phone.

MAGGIE: Oh, no. I haven't changed. The world's changed, walked right out from under me. On the way here, I was wondering how *you'd* changed.

SUSAN: And?

MAGGIE: I guess we're more alike than we were before.

SUSAN: Or more different. Who's to know?

MAGGIE: Maybe we never knew one another at all.

SUSAN: I know your favorite color, and what you like for breakfast, and how you respond to tickling. Isn't that it? Isn't that what we are?

(*The Waiter again comes to the table, takes out his order pad*)

SUSAN: Listen, it doesn't matter. You pick. Order us a lunch. *We'll* be very happy with it.

WAITER: What're you going to do? When the third world takes over? It's not far away.

MAGGIE: Laundry. We'll do their laundry.

SUSAN: I'd like to be a concubine.

WAITER: (*Pulls up a chair, sits down*) Why won't you take me seriously? Is it because I'm a waiter?

SUSAN: We're trying to talk to one another.

WAITER: You don't have to talk. You should feel. Words are a waste of time. Symbols. Energy. That's the point of calligraphy . . . How come you wore matching outfits?

SUSAN: We're twins. Identical twins.

WAITER: You don't look alike.

MAGGIE: She meant fraternal twins.

SUSAN: Did I?

MAGGIE: Two different eggs instead of the same one split in two.

SUSAN: Sure.

WAITER: We all come from the same cell. Originally. Millions and millions of years ago, the same amoeba, split in two, and split again, and again.

MAGGIE: (*To the Waiter*) Are you content? Really content?

WAITER: What does that mean? The word "content"? What sort of symbol would you draw to represent it?

MAGGIE: You're not content. You couldn't even give me a straight answer. Power. It's all about power. You want to know Chinese because it'll give you more power . . . That's what I've been telling her—Susan—I don't want to be in power struggles any more. I want to secede. To sit on the sidelines.

SUSAN: No, you don't.

MAGGIE: Yes, I do.

SUSAN: No, you don't. You're just afraid. You're afraid to be second. You'd rather be last than second.

WAITER: The cook left. He took his wok off the fire and he left. He won't be back till supper time. You want to wait until then?

SUSAN: See. You, too. We're intimidating you, so you change the subject.

WAITER: I'm trying to do my job. You won't let me do my job.

SUSAN: How much a week do you make in tips?

WAITER: Hey! Do you know how many women start talking to me every week? They come in here alone, late, for lunch, with their paperbacks or their magazines, and soon they're talking to me. Wanting to know what I'm doing in a Chinese restaurant, and then they're trying to seduce me.

MAGGIE: She wasn't trying to seduce you.

WAITER: How do you know what she was trying to do?

MAGGIE: She's my best friend.

WAITER: (*Pauses, gets up, goes back to the kitchen*) I'll cook you up something . . .

SUSAN: Was I trying to seduce him?

MAGGIE: I don't know. How can I tell?

SUSAN: I think what I object to most is that the whole face of this city's changed. Nothing's where it belongs. The loop isn't the loop. All the expressways. All the high rises. I feel I can't depend on it. The city.

MAGGIE: (*After a moment*) Do you think it's true? That we never knew one another?

SUSAN: We knew one another.

MAGGIE: If I didn't know you, I didn't know anyone.

SUSAN: Are you all right?

MAGGIE: Why not?

SUSAN: It's almost two-thirty.

MAGGIE: How do you know?

SUSAN: There's a clock over there. I've been watching it, looking at it from time to time.

MAGGIE: You have to leave?

SUSAN: No. I have to make a phone call. That's the reason. The reason we're here. I mean, I suppose you wondered. Why I turned up, like that, on the phone.

MAGGIE: No . . . Well, yes.

SUSAN: I needed you to be with me. At two-thirty. That doesn't make any sense. Unless you know . . . Last week, on Wednesday—no Tuesday. I woke up at seven-thirty, and made breakfast, and then when everyone was gone, I read the *Tribune,* and I decided to take a bubble bath, just on the spur of the moment, I decided, because I was depressed—

MAGGIE: (*Interrupting*) Are you afraid you're starting change of life?

SUSAN: (*Looks at her. Doesn't reply. Goes on*) Well, I was washing and—it was just like in the movies—I felt this lump, right here, on my left breast. (*She takes Maggie's hand*) It's very little. But I felt it . . . So I went to the doctor. And he took tests. And I'm supposed to call at two-thirty today. For the results. And I'm scared, Maggie. I'm really terrified.

MAGGIE: It could be nothing. A cyst.

SUSAN: And all week, I walked around with this secret. I couldn't tell Jack. Or my mother. Or the kids. And I'd look in the mirror in the morning, to see if I looked different. If I should wear less lipstick, or darker eye shadow, if people could see the difference. Like not being a virgin any more. And when we made love, I pretended I had only one breast, and I tried to see if he was going to be disgusted. So then, I wouldn't let him touch me. And he's angry. He's hurt, you know . . . And I desperately had to see you. And all week, every hour I've been waiting with the secret, I've changed. I look at things and they're bigger or smaller than they were, or their colors are different . . . I stopped wanting a Mercedes . . . One night I got an absolute craving for Mallomars.

MAGGIE: It's all right. I'm here.

SUSAN: I figured it out after I called you. Why I called you. That's the biggest change of all. See, it wasn't—what did you call it? Power? We weren't running against each other. We were running against ourselves. In a mirror. Reflections. Shadows. So here we are.

MAGGIE: It's two-thirty.

SUSAN: He can wait.

MAGGIE: I can't.

SUSAN: (*Fishing in her wallet*) Do you have a dime?

MAGGIE: (*Gets one out*) Here . . . Want me to come with you? Want me to hold your hand?

SUSAN: I just remembered why I stopped eating Chinese food. It's the MSG—the headache you get from it. I almost fainted once. (*Susan settles in, she will not yet face the phone*) You know, I went to take the mammogram, and—well, standing there with this strange doctor in a dark room, and he took my breast and he put it on the machine, and I got goose bumps right away, and then he pushed the top down and down, squeezing me against the plates, and he smiled and said, "That's some sandwich," and how many hundreds of women has he said that to, do you think?

MAGGIE: Will you please get the hell to the phone?

SUSAN: Maybe I won't call. Maybe I'd rather not know.

MAGGIE: You want me to call?

SUSAN: You could pretend you were me. Then, if the new,
is bad—

MAGGIE: I have to go to the toilet.

SUSAN: Not right now, please . . . (*She takes Maggie's hand*)

MAGGIE: It's just nerves.

SUSAN: If it's anything serious, he'll call me.

MAGGIE: I'm here . . . Really . . .

(*Susan waits a moment, breathes, then she goes to the phone, dials a number, waits. Maggie finishes her drink. Then she picks up Susan's drink, pours the remains into her own, and finishes that, too*)

SUSAN: (*While Maggie is drinking*) Dr. Rice, please . . . Mrs. Lemmerer . . . Dr. Rice? Hi, Susan Lemmerer . . . Oh, you do? Oh, and . . . I see. I see. Of course; thank you. Bye. Thank you. (*Susan goes back to the table, looks for her drink, which is, of course, all gone. Maggie offers her the last sip of her drink*) Thanks.

MAGGIE: Well?

SUSAN: Well . . .

MAGGIE: Come on, come on. It's okay, isn't it? I can tell. It's okay.

SUSAN: Well, he's not a hundred percent sure. But probably—"almost certainly"—it's benign. Nothing to worry about.

(*Unwittingly, almost unconsciously, Maggie has begun to feel her own breast, but very surreptitiously, turned away from Susan*)

MAGGIE: I knew it! You always did dramatize. You always could scare me out of my wits.

(*The Waiter comes, puts down some dishes, leaves*)

SUSAN: I'm starving . . . (*As soon as he goes*) Isn't that nice? I thought he was being hostile . . . What's wrong? What're you doing? Are you crying?

MAGGIE: No. I'm not crying.

SUSAN: What's gotten into you?

MAGGIE: Nothing.

SUSAN: Something.

MAGGIE: Nothing. I was just checking. I mean, seeing if I—

SUSAN: Oh, my God! That's really too offensive. That's

really too gross. You have to outdo me, even in that! You want a bigger lump than mine. I suppose you want cancer because mine was benign. Maybe we should have a race to see who dies first. Would that be winning? You want a bigger funeral than mine? What cemetery? What size tombstone? Well, don't get your hopes up, I plan to be cremated!

MAGGIE: Come on! Come on, Sue. Don't cry . . .

SUSAN: I don't understand it. I have this vague feeling of being let down. I mean, I should be so relieved, and I am, but—you know?

MAGGIE: That was cruel—accusing me of competing. At a moment like that.

SUSAN: I'm sorry.

(*Pause. Maggie picks up the cover, looks at the food, smiles at Susan*)

MAGGIE: We might as well share. (*She dishes out some food*)

SUSAN: You moved, didn't you?

MAGGIE: Uh-huh . . . To Skokie.

SUSAN: That's nice . . . for the kids.

MAGGIE: Sometimes I miss the neighborhood . . . Do you have a house now?

SUSAN: A nine-room ranch. In Kenilworth.

MAGGIE: That used to be restricted.

SUSAN: Did it?

MAGGIE: Ted put in a sauna last year . . . And a swimming pool.

SUSAN: All the appliances. You have to have a special utility room—washer-dryer, dishwasher, garbage compactor, mangle—

MAGGIE: (*Interrupting her*) I know—self-defrost walk-in freezer. Walkie-talkies in every room—

SUSAN: Well, the microwave oven doesn't take up much room. And it saves so much time.

MAGGIE: Don't they say that gives you cancer?

SUSAN: Do they? (*A pause. They eat a bit*) This is the worst Chinese food I've ever eaten.

MAGGIE: Well, I don't know anything much about science.

SUSAN: If we could—if we could just—you know.

MAGGIE: Oh, I know. Could we?

SUSAN: Do we want to?

MAGGIE: I do.

SUSAN: Oh, so do I—I'm different now. I don't need to measure myself so much . . . I missed you.

MAGGIE: I missed *you*. Somehow, the friends you make afterwards, they aren't the same. They didn't go through the pimples, and the bras, and the twist.

SUSAN: The thing I like best about you is that I don't need all those words.

MAGGIE: Oh, God, yes. All those explanations—I love you.

SUSAN: I love you, too . . . Come to dinner. You and Ted. Next week. Next Saturday.

MAGGIE: Saturday? No, we can't . . . Thursday?

SUSAN: No. Not Thursday. Friday?

MAGGIE: (*Almost simultaneously*) Friday.

Curtain

Michael Shurtleff

SAILING

Michael Shurtleff

Something of a Renaissance man of the performing arts, Michael Shurtleff has functioned in the theatre and films as a casting director, director, teacher, and playwright.

Born in Norway and raised in the Middle West, Mr. Shurtleff was educated at Lawrence University and Yale University, where he received his M.F.A. He got his start in the professional theatre by way of operating a switchboard in the office of a performer's agent. However, he soon moved upwards in the theatrical ranks by becoming a production assistant and, later, David Merrick's casting director for the musical *Gypsy, Becket, The Matchmaker*, and assorted other shows, working with such luminaries as Jerome Robbins, Peter Glenville, Bob Fosse, Gower Champion, and Joshua Logan.

His debut as a playwright came in 1961 with the Off-Broadway success, *Call Me by My Rightful Name*. The drama, with Joan Hackett, Robert Duvall, and Alvin Ailey in the leading roles, received a spate of fine notices. Henry Hewes wrote in the *Saturday Review* that "this work provides a theatrically elating evening and places Michael Shurtleff at the top of the list of new playwrights of the present season."

Other productions of Shurtleff plays followed, including *So It's All Rashomon* (with Gene Hackman and Estelle Parsons); *Life Among the Young People; Coming to Terms; When the Sun Goes Down;* and *A Fine Summer Night.*

From the stage, he moved on once again, this time to films as casting director for *The Graduate, 1776, The Sound of Music, Jesus Christ Superstar,* and as director of the movie version of his play, *Call Me by My Rightful Name,* with Don Murray and Cathy Lee Crosby.

For more than a decade, Mr. Shurtleff has taught, both in New York and Hollywood, "How to Audition" classes for performers. A result of these successful sessions was the recent publication of his book, *Audition,* which advises actors on how to prepare to handle every conceivable auditioning situation.

Sailing was the 1977 winner of the Second Annual Metropolitan New York Original Short Play Festival, and it appears in an anthology for the first time in *The Best Short Plays 1979.*

Characters:

WALTER
HARI

Scene:

Walter and his wife, Hari, are sitting on the terrace of their country weekend home. It is on a bluff overlooking a valley and a bay. The bay is blue and large and filled with sailboats and provides an endless breeze for them.

She is reading a book. He is reading the newspaper and finds the news irritating. Finally, he puts his paper aside to survey the beauty of his landscape. He breathes deeply, rises and crosses down right and performs his ceremony, which consists of intaking large gasps of the fresh air followed by beating his chest to express his great pleasure. Each time he beats his chest or makes the intake noise, she is ready to kill. She contains herself. He crosses upstage to invite her to join him in breathing. At that moment, she exhales smoke into his face accidently. He crosses down left and repeats his breathing ceremony. She extinguishes her cigarette. He then crosses back to his chair as he says:

WALTER: I shall always adore the Winstons.

HARI: I have a whole leg of lamb in the frig. I do not adore the Winstons.

WALTER: I love it when guests cancel out at the last minute.

HARI: Do you?

WALTER: It means solitude. It's like stolen ecstacy, being here alone.

HARI: Do you wish I weren't here?

WALTER: *(Sitting)* We don't want to quarrel, Hari.

HARI: *(Pursuing her question)* Do you? Wish I weren't here?

WALTER: *(Concealed behind his newspaper)* I didn't say that, dear.

HARI: Answer my question, Walter! *(She pushes his newspaper aside)*

WALTER: Of course not.

HARI: (*Teasing him*) Don't you know me well enough after all these years to tell the truth?

WALTER: (*Smiling in agreement*) Of course, one does secretly hanker for total solitude at times.

HARI: (*She knew it all along*) Ah ha.

WALTER: But only at times.

HARI: Shall I go back to town?

WALTER: You ask me to tell the truth, then you want to quarrel over it. Is it any wonder I avoid? (*Once again, conceals himself behind the newspaper*)

HARI: (*Following a pause*) Marriage is a terrible state.

WALTER: (*Peering at her*) Sometimes.

HARI: Mostly all the time. Imagine, two people sitting side by side, watching one of the prettiest views of the most beautiful harbor and the most expansive bay in the east, all those divine sailboats gliding by, and wishing they weren't together. (*She shakes her head ruefully; then he does the same*)

WALTER: I wish I had masses of steel gray hair and a craggy face.

HARI: (*Looking at him in amusement*) There's nothing wrong with your hair. (*She ruffles it lovingly*) You're lucky you've got hair.

WALTER: My kind of face is not going to age well. Juvenile type faces never do. It's going to make me feel even more absurd in the years to come. (*Surveying the bay; suddenly*) My God, that catamaran went over!

HARI: Boats are always going over in the bay, dear.

WALTER: (*Watching the capsized boat*) Not catamarans! That's the whole point of a cat—it's not supposed to go over.

HARI: Life never works out the way it's supposed to, does it, dear?

WALTER: (*This reply aggravates him. He changes the subject*) What's the Winstons not coming got to do with you've got a leg of lamb in the frig? I love leg of lamb.

HARI: (*Always the sensible one*) Do you know what it costs now?

WALTER: Oh! It's good enough for the Winstons, but I don't deserve it?

HARI: (*With finality*) It's too much for two people.

WALTER: I love it cold. We'll take it back to the city with us.

HARI: Maybe I'll freeze it for next weekend . . . for the Andersons.

WALTER: (*Looking at her distrustfully*) And what will I have this weekend?

HARI: I've got plenty of vegetables.

WALTER: (*Forcefully*) But I want meat!

HARI: (*Putting him on with a great show of shock*) Do you hear yourself? That's a crude thing to say. We should all give up killing animals.

WALTER: I don't kill animals. I eat the animals other people kill. Man has done that from time immemorial. (*Changing the subject to get back at her*) Even with the face I have, this non-craggy face, it's interesting that women still find me attractive.

HARI: (*Slyly*) It is interesting.

WALTER: (*Enjoying himself greatly*) Of course, you don't see it. You see me every day. But I'm not speaking macho talk. I'm as surprised as you are. Young girls especially. I don't know what they see in me. I don't encourage them, but there they are. You can see that look in their eyes. They all want to hang around and they want to talk.

HARI: What do they want to talk about? (*Angry at herself for being interested*) How can I read if you keep talking?

WALTER: You keep asking questions.

HARI: (*Very annoyed*) I know I do. (*She goes back to her book with a vengeance, but she's forgotten what came before*)

WALTER: (*After a slight pause*) They want to talk about themselves, of course. Young girls never cease wanting to tell about themselves. But some of them want to know about me. I rarely answer them.

HARI: What do you do?

WALTER: I imply mystery.

HARI: (*She pretends to be dumbfounded*) *You* imply mystery?

WALTER: Don't ask me, if all you are going to do is put down what I say about myself and my experiences.

HARI: Sorry. I am getting to be a terrible nag. It's the way wives get, and I hate it, and why do I do it? You irritate me so! (*She rises and crosses to center*)

WALTER: (*Quietly, curiously*) Do I?

HARI: (*Simply being very frank and honest*) Every goddamn thing you say drives me up the wall.

WALTER: (*A simple question*) Perhaps we should stop living together?

HARI: How can we?

WALTER: Other people manage.

HARI: Other people are even more foolish than we are.

WALTER: Foolish?

HARI: (*She returns to her chair*) Unrealistic. We can't afford to live separately.

WALTER: Is that really true?

HARI: Of course. We'd end up in one-room studio apartments, counting our pennies.

WALTER: Two really live cheaper than one? (*They share the humor of this*)

HARI: We're trapped, Walter. In each other's company. (*She takes his hand*)

WALTER: (*Lovingly*) I don't mind it as much as you do.

HARI: Why not?

WALTER: I've managed to screen you out, at times.

HARI: (*Withdrawing her hand*) How?

WALTER: I put my mind elsewhere.

HARI: Like?

WALTER: (*In his mind's eye*) A desert isle. A beautiful sandy beach, a sunny day, walking alone along the beach for miles and miles. Naked! No one, no one around.

HARI: (*Playing with him*) Oh? No beautiful naked girl comes along . . . and wants you, only you?

WALTER: I can add that at any time, can't I?

HARI: I see. (*Looking out to the vista*) It seems so . . . so juvenile, fantasizing like that, at our age.

WALTER: (*Rising; enjoying this memory*) When I was in the army, we used to have so damn many shots, getting ready to go overseas. I was very sensitive to them. Not afraid, sensitive. I'd keel over every time they gave me one. It was embarrassing. (*Sharing the humor of this with Hari*) So, I learned finally to put myself somewhere else, totally. (*Crossing, as he demonstrates*) I'd stand there in line and put myself on a deserted beach, all by myself, and they'd have to poke me to tell me I'd had my shot and move on. (*Turning back to Hari*) I'd made myself totally oblivious.

HARI: (*Not at all happy with the thought*) And that's what you've done with me? Made yourself totally oblivious?

WALTER: (*They look at each other for a moment*) Yes.

HARI: God! (*She shudders, hurt by this. He crosses to her, positioning himself just above her chair and comforting her by his touch*)

WALTER: People weren't meant to live together like this, day in, day out. Remarkable people, perhaps, but not people like you and me, everyday humdrum people.

HARI: We're not that.

WALTER: (*Gently, in an effort to make her understand*) We thought we weren't going to be. I've made a success out of my business, we've had money. We built this fine home, we've got a view of the bay clear across to Connecticut . . . (*An afterthought*) on a clear day. We've had children, although I think that is more of an accomplishment in your eyes than in mine. I haven't really cared that much for them. And, I've managed to make myself pretty oblivious to them, too, most of the time . . .

HARI: Leaving me to raise them.

WALTER: You wanted them.

HARI: Yes. I wanted them.

WALTER: (*Staring at her for a moment, then:*) I've learned to love being alone. You'd better learn that, Hari. (*His concern for her creates in her a concern for him. A pause. Hari applies suntan lotion to her arm*)

HARI: Has it been an embarrassment for you, having a wife named Hari?

WALTER: (*Chuckling*) At first, I spelled it for them: H-A-R-I. But then that didn't really help. So, I referred to you as Harriet.

HARI: (*Indignant*) But my name isn't Harriet!

WALTER: (*Gently*) Somewhere along the way I got this absurd notion that it's better to solve problems than rail against them. You always preferred railing. (*This reminds him*) My mother is going to drive us to the madhouse. What are we going to do with her? Way out in California, yet the vibrations of her discontent shake the very foundations of this house. I think she's really going bonkers this time, Hari.

HARI: It's just senility.

WALTER: But it's so unpleasant for everyone around her. Nothing is ever her fault. To hear her list of grievances, everyone has damaged her. I damaged her when I sold the house. She told me she couldn't take care of it anymore, couldn't get help, it needed a million repairs, she wanted the peace and quiet of a mere apartment. Now she says that I sold the house out from under her . . . and at a loss, at that. I wish she didn't exist.

HARI: That's a terrible thing to say!

WALTER: (*Weighing what he has said for a moment, then:*) I know it is. I don't mean I wish her dead, but I do mean I wish she didn't exist, always reminding me of all those unhappy experiences, going back . . . going back . . . I don't want to go back. (*Moving to his chair and sitting*) To hell with it! It's all over and done, and I'd never give the past a thought, but there she is— (*Visualizing her*) a constant, insistent, unpleasant reminder. What's the good of living to eighty, as she has? Making life hell for the rest of us. If she seemed to get some enjoyment out of being alive . . . but all she does is pile up injustices, sits there suffering, blaming, blaming . . . I don't want to get like that, Hari. I'll manage to kill myself first. I swear I will.

HARI: And leave me to cope with all this by myself?

WALTER: Did you hear what you just said? (*They laugh*) Men always die first anyhow. Prepare yourself for that.

HARI: (*Looking at him for a moment, then:*) I'm not going to spend the best years of my life doing all this preparing for eventual calamities, Walter. Shut up! (*She returns to her book, he to his paper. After a few moments, Walter reads something that displeases him greatly*)

WALTER: I hate human beings.

HARI: Walter, you don't!

WALTER: Yes. I hate all human beings . . . even my friends, well-meaning as they may be.

HARI: But why?

WALTER: (*Adjusting his chair for a more direct confrontation*) This morning, I walked down to the store. I got the things you'd put on the list and I got in line at the cash register. The man in front of me piled his stuff out of his cart onto the counter and then, just left the cart there . . . right there in front of the counter. No room for the next person, which was me. I said, (*Visualizing the experience from his memory*) "Pardon me, sir, but you've left your cart," and he turned and said, "I know I did." Defying me. I thought, "Now, Walter, don't get into one of your fits just because another injustice has been done. *Function!*" Well, I took the cart back to where it belonged so that I could put my groceries on the counter and when I got back . . . just a minute it took . . . four people had gotten in line in front of me. Well, they didn't know that I had gone to do A Good Deed, so I waited in line again. Finally, I got up to the counter, put all my groceries on it and took *my* cart to its proper resting place and when I got back, three more people were in front of me. The cashier waited on them, then another person snuck in ahead. I said, "Please! Several people have gotten ahead of me, may I have my turn now?" She said, "How do I know it's your turn? I look at the stuff on the counter, not at the people." "But, that's my stuff on the counter," I said. "How do I know what's next? I take what they put in front of me." "Yes, but my stuff *is* in front of you." "No, it's not, it's to one side. I take what's in front of me." (*He pauses, looks at Hari, smiles and then, sweetly*) Well, I thought of killing her. Right there, quietly and efficiently. Pow: dead! (*Building to a crescendo*) I thought of taking the eggs and breaking them, one at a time, over her head and then pouring the milk over her and then smashing the ice cream into her face. And you don't understand why I hate human beings?

HARI: (*Smiling at him with understanding*) Yes, Walter. I understand why you hate human beings.

WALTER: (*After a moment*) You mean we all do.

HARI: But we get over it.

WALTER: (*Turning away from her*) I don't.

HARI: (*Kindly*) You've got to, Walter. You can't live like that.

WALTER: (*Very agitated, he rises and moves away*) Every day, people do these things. It's piling-up. I can't get over it, I can't stand it. I don't want to be near human beings.

HARI: But, dear . . .

WALTER: (*Interrupting her, moving, demonstrating his problem as he describes it*) Do you know, nine times out of ten when I go down an escalator, the person in front of me gets off the escalator and JUST STANDS THERE. Stands there! Deciding if she'll go right or left. Of course, the person behind her piles into her, has nowhere to move. Doesn't she know that? Do nine out of ten people have so little consideration for their fellow human beings that they never think what's happening to the person behind them?

HARI: (*Overlapping*) I know, but—

WALTER: (*Elbowing the imaginary crowd*) Why do all those people jam into the subway before letting the others off? (*Laughing at the madness of it all, but furious*) Don't they know you can't give them the space they want until you get off and vacate it?

HARI: They're just—

WALTER: (*Moving to her*) They're just selfish. They're just stupid. They're ruining the world. There are only 9,000 cheetahs left in the entire world. Men have killed them all off. One of the most beautiful of all animals. (*Looking at the beach*) Twice this year, this beach has been covered with sludge so we can't use it. Do you realize, they pour their shit into the rivers and the bays and the oceans. They're killing us! They're killing themselves. (*Confronting her*) They go right on doing it. I can't stand it.

HARI: (*Rising to comfort him*) Darling, calm down . . .

WALTER: Calm down!?! (*He takes his newspaper to show her*) Bergman . . . that man who runs the old people's nursing homes . . . locks them up like prisoners, steals their pensions, rips off medicaid for millions . . . and he gets twenty-seven days in jail! *Twenty-seven days!* I can't sleep at night thinking about Bergman. All those poor, old people who are his victims and he's going to go right on doing it. (*Frightened at the thought*) We'll be old soon.

HARI: You make it sound like tomorrow. We're nowhere near old.

WALTER: (*Shaking his head positively*) Soon. Soon. And then Bergman will get us or the shit in the ocean will or there won't be any water fit to drink. Human beings are selfish. Inutterably selfish.

HARI: (*A pause*) And you hate me, too?

WALTER: Yes. (*Short pause*) And myself. Everyone. I hate being a human being.

HARI: But what about love?

WALTER: (*Scoffing at her*) Love?

HARI: You felt love once. (*She moves to him*) You must have.

WALTER: (*Relenting, he takes her head in his hands*) Do you want to know the reasons I never succeeded at love? I lived in constant dread the person I loved was going to change her mind and leave me. I lived in fear of being boring. I like a fight but I can't stand domestic quarrels, which are different from other fights . . . they take the heart right out of me. I should never have gotten married.

HARI: Then why did you?

WALTER: I didn't know these things then.

HARI: (*Moving away as she speaks*) *I* should never have gotten married.

WALTER: (*Surprised*) What? You, too? (*She nods affirmatively to him*) Yes, but you had to—you wanted children.

HARI: I had them. They're gone now. The marriage goes on. Look . . . another boat capsized! A lot of Sunday sailors today. (*With apprehension*) Or perhaps the wind is treacherous. (*She shivers. The wind is ominous*)

WALTER: (*Crossing to her and touching her gently*) Would you rather live alone?

HARI: (*With difficulty*) I'm worse off than you are. I would rather not be alone.

WALTER: Oh. You just don't want to be with *me* anymore?

HARI: I have to be with someone.

WALTER: (*This hurts him. He retreats, but he considers her*) You are worse off.

HARI: I look like an ordinary woman, but I didn't get married for ordinary reasons.

WALTER: Didn't you?

HARI: (*Still surveying the bay*) I wasn't romantic. I didn't have stars in my eyes or dream ours was a great love affair. I got married to get even with my mother.

WALTER: (*Surprised at this revelation*) What did she do to you?

HARI: (*Watching the boats*) Another one over! The currents must be tricky today. It doesn't look it. (*They both gaze at the new disaster but the day is so benign that it belies the disaster below*) She said I was unloveable, I'd never get a husband. I showed her; I trapped you. You loved me or you thought you did. (*Turning away from him and laughing gently at this*) The really awful thing about mothers is that in the end they always turn out to be right. Unforgiveable—mothers. (*She stands, shading her eyes, looking out toward the bay*) Walter . . . I think that boat's really in trouble. Do you suppose we ought to call the Coast Guard?

WALTER: They aren't signaling for help. I don't feel one should call the Coast Guard unless people want you to.

HARI: (*Very surprised*) Why?

WALTER: (*Strangely angry*) I think it'd be embarrassing to have the Coast Guard bearing down to rescue you if you didn't want them to. You'd have every right to resent the people who've called them. (*He crosses back to his chair and sits. Hari follows him a step or two*)

HARI: But to be helpful? Neighborly? Concerned?

WALTER: Mind your own business.

HARI: People have to learn to reach out . . . to offer help to each other.

WALTER: If people want help, they'll ask for it.

HARI: (*She looks at him oddly, then back to the bay*) Ah, another craft is coming up to them. Thank God! There's something odd about . . . Walt, you know how they say so many auto accidents are really suicides, only we never know; d'you think that's true about boats, too?

(The thought is not a new one to him, but he attempts to disguise this)

WALTER: Nonsense. A man would never lose his boat that way. He'd simply drown himself swimming.

HARI: *(She is watching the boats. She suspects them)* I suppose so . . . still . . . *(She looks oddly at him, then out to the bay again)* I try not to resent them.

WALTER: *(Incredulous)* Who? Boat owners?

HARI: Our children. I try not to feel neglected. *(Moving to her chair)* After all, I knew this was coming. I did the same thing to my mother. She deserved it. *(A revelation)* My God, I suppose ours think I do, too. They always were more fond of you than me. You indulged them. *(Taking her chair)* I had to do the disciplining; of course they like you better. Still . . .

WALTER: Still . . .

HARI: Going to all that trouble, raising them. It is a lot of trouble, Walt, only to have them resent you, detest you. Why did I do it?

WALTER: *(With a great deal of love and appreciation for her)* If you had it to do over, would you have them?

HARI: *(She weighs the question a moment)* Yes. Isn't that absurd?

WALTER: But why?

HARI: Because I wouldn't know then what I know now. You can't live your life for how it turns out. *(Walter studies the horizon. Hari has an afterthought)* And then there's the life force. Something that makes us have children even when it doesn't make sense to. These days . . . *(Pause)* Walt.

WALTER: *(Very involved with his thoughts)* Yes.

HARI: *(Pause)* I don't hate you.

WALTER: *(Looking at her)* Oh.

HARI: It's just . . . I've known you too long. *(Short pause)*

WALTER: I'd prefer it if you did. *(His saying this touches her. It also puzzles her. Why does he think this? There is a long silence. They both watch the boats in the bay. Finally, he rises)* I think I'll go for a sail.

HARI: Do you want me to come with you?

WALTER: (*Simply*) No. (*He takes several steps downstage surveying the bay and beauty of the day. Finally, as though in anticipation and enjoying the thought, he adds:*) I wish summer would not end. I don't want winter any more. I want it to be this way, always. (*As he sees it before him*) Beautiful, summery, solitary. (*He stands a moment, gazing across to the distant Connecticut. Hari watches him, puzzled. Something does not feel quite right to her . . . something he is feeling. Then, without a glance at her, he exits*)

HARI: (*A pause. She has a premonition and calls after him*) Walter, be careful . . . the wind is coming up . . . (*She rises and moves downstage a step, listening, then:*) Walter . . . (*She has the feeling that she will never see him again*)

Curtain

Samuel Shem

ROOM FOR ONE WOMAN

Samuel Shem

Published here for the first time, *Room for One Woman* also marks the debut of Samuel Shem in *The Best Short Plays* series. A touching dramatic study of the complexities facing three less-than-young English women, the play had its initial production at the Loeb Experimental Theatre at Harvard University. Additional staged readings followed, and now the play (and its companion piece, *Napoleon's Dinner*) is scheduled for a full-scale presentation at the Off-Off-Broadway Impossible Ragtime Theatre in 1979.

In response to a request for biographical information, the author supplied the following: "I was born in 1944, and grew up in upper New York State. At Harvard College I wished to write for the theatre, but my pre-med studies did not allow time, and instead, I acted in several plays. I spent summers as a toll collector on a bridge, working the midnight-to-eight shift so that I could read.

"After college, I went on a Rhodes Scholarship to Oxford, England, where I began to write. Living in a small village in the Cotswold Hills, I became friendly with the English people on whom *Room for One Woman,* and a companion play, a comedy for three English men, *Napoleon's Dinner,* are based.

"After completing a Ph.D. in Neurophysiology at Oxford, I returned to Harvard Medical School, where I completed my M.D. degree. I spent a year as a medical intern, and then did a three-year residency in psychiatry. Currently, I am in the private practice of psychiatry.

"In addition to the aforementioned short plays, I've written five full-length dramas: a verse trilogy and two plays set in New England."

The author's first novel, *The House of God,* was published in 1978.

Characters:

PEDLEY
LIL
BEESLEY

Scene:

A small furnished room in England. Late afternoon. The room, dimly lit by a single shaded bulb, is sparsely furnished: narrow bed with uncovered cushions, straight-backed chair, table. In rear wall a window, shade pulled, and a portrait of a young man dressed formally, high collar and cravat. Steep stairs lead down to room from offstage right; narrow ramp leads down from room offstage left. A single open suitcase lies on the bed, half-filled with an old woman's possessions.

Pedley, a woman of seventy-five, sits in the chair center stage, two canes hooked over the arms.

Lil, a woman of forty, is busy packing the remaining possessions into the suitcase.

LIL: (*Straightening up*) Good Christ, my poor aching back! I've got to lose some weight—I feel like my figure's getting bigger than me! It's so close in here—we need the rain to clear the air. Thundery all afternoon, and not a drop of rain. Wish it would come. Sweating makes me feel even fatter. I can't stand these uncertain seasons—they say it's the moon what does it. (*Yawns, stretches*) I'm so tired today! Didn't get to sleep 'til halfway through the night, and do you know why? (*No response from Pedley*) You won't guess what my dear husband brought home with him last night—a magician! A conjurer! Both of them drunk as fishes, pounding at the front door, screaming to be let in—he never can find his key when he's tight, and if he does find it, he's never yet been able to put it in the hole and twist it! So I open the door and there he is, and beside him this . . . this wreck, this disaster—a little tiny red-eyed hairy man wearing a bashed-in top hat and a great old coat that covered his boots and was soaking up the water from the puddle he was standing in. "Lil, Lil, my pet," says he, "this gentleman beside me is named Grigg. Simeon Grigg," says he, "Professor Simeon Grigg, formerly the Foremost Conjurer of the World Itself!" Foremost Conjurer? Foremost Gut-Stripper, or Foremost Compost Heap, he should have said, I mean you couldn't even stand in the same room with this man Grigg, for the stink off his clothes. Ugh! (*Yawns*) So then he and this Grigg make their way up the stairs—we live on the third floor, you see—but they don't stop there, oh no, not them, they keep right on. "The lads," says my husband, "wait 'til the little lads see the tricks Professor Simeon Grigg has in store." So they wriggle and flip up the next flight, falling and tripping and cursing the steps and then they go shouting into the lads' room and rouse *them* up and there they stay, drinking whisky and doing these cheap conjuring tricks 'til halfway through 'til morning. You should have seen them—little James sitting up on his bed, eyes as wide as two fried eggs, and Matthew half asleep beside him. Oh, they enjoyed it all right, but still, I mean children that age need their sleep, now don't they? I tried to get rid of them, but there's no doing anything with him when he's got tight. They were still asleep when I left this morning. I didn't have the heart to wake them for school. And this Grigg had left some of his tricks behind—a deck of cards, some silk handkerchiefs, and a rubber chicken! Looking at Grigg you wouldn't think he could stand up by himself, much less muck about with the rabbits and the hats. It's got to stop, this. I'm afraid to think where it'll end, with this drinking and bringing home these dosshouse wrecks like Grigg. Grigg! (*Pause*) Now what else is there to pack? The lampshade? Do you want to take the lampshade with you? Pedley?

PEDLEY: What?

LIL: Do you want to take the lampshade with you?

PEDLEY: What do I care about a lampshade?

LIL: I'm not asking you about caring. Is it yours? Was it here when you came?

PEDLEY: I don't remember.

LIL: Don't sulk, Pedley. There's no use you sulking.

PEDLEY: I'm not sulking. I don't remember.

LIL: Well, shall I take it for you or not?

PEDLEY: Leaving this room after fourteen years, and you ask me about a lampshade?

LIL: I'll take it anyway. There might not be a shade in your new room. There's nothing more lonely than a bulb without a shade.

PEDLEY: Nothing more lonely than that?

LIL: (*Removing shade; bright light*) I'll take it.

PEDLEY: And what about the woman coming here? She'll be sad, without the shade.

LIL: And suppose she brings her own shade with her? Think of the waste—two shades here, and a bare bulb in your new room.

PEDLEY: I wouldn't mind anymore. Things are dark enough, even so. But she might mind. She might mind. Who is she?

LIL: I don't know anything about her.

PEDLEY: Will we meet her?

LIL: I suppose we will. She's to be here before dark.

PEDLEY: Is it dark?

LIL: (*Going to window, raising shade*) Not yet, but darkening.

PEDLEY: Help me up. I want to see.

LIL: (*Helping her up*) It's so warm today, so close. Thundery all afternoon, but not a drop of rain. Wish it would come, it would clear the air.

PEDLEY: (*Hobbling to the window*) We'll have enough trouble going, without the rain. We'll get soaked, if it rains.

LIL: We could leave now, before she comes.

PEDLEY: No! I don't want to go. I'm afraid of leaving. It won't end well, this leaving. (*Pause*) I won't leave, no. I shall stay.

LIL: Don't start that again, Pedley.

PEDLEY: I shall. I shall stay.

LIL: You can't stay. You know you can't stay here—

PEDLEY: I shall stay with this new woman. She'll be a kind person, she'll let me stay here with her, as a kind person would, the two of us, together.

LIL: You can't stay. The room is for one woman, it won't take—

PEDLEY: I'll ask her, the new woman, to let me stay here

with her. She'll let me stay, you'll see. I'll say to her nicely, politely, like a lady: "Won't you let me stay on here, with you?"

LIL: You won't. Things are all settled. You'll keep quiet about staying, do you understand? You won't say a single word.

PEDLEY: I'll ask her nicely, politely, like a la—

LIL: QUIET!

PEDLEY: Don't be short with me. How could you understand? It hasn't happened to you—coming alone to a room like this, making a home of it somehow, and then having to leave and go to another room, the same but worse because you bring less life to it. You don't know what it's like—

LIL: If you don't stop I'll leave and let you move by your-self.

PEDLEY: I can't. You know I can't. I can't even walk, without these two sticks of mine.

LIL: I'm sorry. I'm just tired. Tired and sweaty. It's so close in here! (*Pause*) I won't stand for this, coming in at all hours with these human disasters dragging along behind. It started when he had the job driving the lorry—he'd pick up anyone, for company. Started bringing them home, giving them a place to sleep. I'd go into the sitting room in the morning and someone would shout out: "Wait just a second, luv!" and there'd be some great tattooed fellow in there pulling on his undies. It got so you didn't know what you'd run into about your own house! (*Pause*) Ah, but sometimes it's funny, sometimes he's such a laugh. When he had that job in the center of town he'd have to take the Tube in and out, and he'd get in all right, but when he tried to get back out in the evening there'd be no end of trouble. You see, there was a pub on the corner of the bus stop, and while he'd be waiting he'd say, "Well, I'll just nip in and have a pint," and there he'd sit, get drunk as a showman and miss the last bus and have to walk home, and living in the estate development like we did he'd lose his way and knock on the wrong door. There he'd be down the street screaming, "Lil, Lil, where the hell are you, Lil?" Once he even tried to climb into the wrong window, and a constable came up and said "Is there anything wrong, sir?"

and he said, "I'm just trying to get into my flat. My key won't work," says he. Imagine! Him and his keys! So the constable looks in his wallet and says "No wonder your wife won't answer you, sir, you're shouting outside the wrong address!" The little clown! It's comical, isn't it? (*Pause*) Ah, but they do need us, they do, I suppose. They do need us, these men. And sometimes he's so dear. I keep catching myself thinking that it'll get better, that sometime we'll have a house, and a garden, and a fishpond with white lilies and little green rubbery frogs, and that we'll take the kids to the country on the holidays and go out to shows ourselves. We used to do that, sometimes. He used to take me with him, early on, to one of his pubs, and there'd be all sorts of people there—workingmen, students, actors even—all kinds of people, and we'd sit and talk and sing—yes, we'd even sing!

PEDLEY: (*Looking out the window*) It is thundery. Those plants have died. Even with them alive it was a dismal view, down below the level of the pavement. I'll pull the shade—the new woman won't enjoy this view, her first evening here. It almost broke my heart. (*Pulls shade; turns and looks about*) It's an evil thing, this room. I came down those stairs alone, carrying my own bags, and now I can't get up them at all, not even with your help. We'll have to leave the other way, on the ramp.

LIL: We'll do all right, don't you worry.

PEDLEY: The stairs haven't changed, really. Nothing's changed, really, but me. I wasn't as sad as this when I first came here. (*Looks at the portrait*) Yes, I was. I was even more sad, then. He had just died.

LIL: He was your husband?

PEDLEY: Yes. In that portrait, then, an alderman. Alderman Pedley, youngest alderman in the country. He was so proud! Men can be so proud! Men can be **so** proud about things like that! Didn't have a penny, then, but he strutted about, seeing to his cases, while I was out working. I always used to say "Oh, he's not unemployed, he just won't work." (*Pause*) I remember the day he was appointed—he rang me up at work and I left to get home early, and I was hurrying along the Raddlesbury Road and I slipped on a loose pavingstone and nearly broke my ankle. So I said to myself, "Right, I'll have to report this," and I noticed that it was just outside of number fifty-five, and jotted that down, and that it was on the left side of the street, and jotted that down as well, and I got home and I said to him, "Alderman Pedley?" "Right," said he. "Well," said I, "this is your first case. There's a loose pavingstone outside of number fifty-five Raddlesbury Road, and a law-abiding woman named Mrs. Pedley was walking along there this afternoon and she stepped on the corner of this loose stone and the other end came up and struck her a great blow on her ankle and she's reporting it to you and demands that you do something about it right away, before someone falls and breaks their necks." So he says, "Right," says he, and rings up the Council Offices and says "Right, this is Alderman Pedley and I'd like to speak to the Superintendant of the Roads." Sure enough, next day on my way to work what do I see but a great vanload of men sitting round their coal burner in the middle of Raddlesbury Road, sipping their tea and watching some chappie bashing away at the pavingstones outside number fifty-five. And when I walked home that evening, there wasn't a loose stone in sight. (*Pause*) Books? There wasn't a book written that he wouldn't read, once he'd got his hands on it.

LIL: He was a handsome man.

PEDLEY: At that age he was. We all were, handsome . . . (*Pause*) He gave me my children, and he did put a bit of a spark into me, and into them, a little bit of a spark, he did. He did that to everyone, you know—if you met him you got a little something out of him, a little thrill, a new way of looking at things. He always said he was going to make something of his life, but he never did. I think that was the high point, somehow, right then, that first job as alderman. (*Pause*) Still, it was good. Perhaps, now, I'd even say it was grand. People always said they admired us, him and me. They said—yes— they said we were "a great success." Success? (*Pause*) He died. I came here. Strange—I found myself hating him! Oh, I hated him so much. Why? I didn't know why, then. (*Pause*) I couldn't leave his portrait behind. My first evening here, in this terrible place, I unpacked all my things, and then, last, I unwrapped his portrait, but I couldn't bring myself to hang it up, no. I turned it round to face the wall. Imagine! So hard to come down here after living high up where you could look out over the rooftops and treetops and catch snatches of the river twisting through the city on its way to the sea. But here there was nothing—not even covers on the cushions, then. The new woman won't like these bare cushions. We should leave the covers, Lil. (*Pause*) But I made a little garden out there, and I had a little cat. At first I couldn't stand the thought of looking at his portrait, and yet I couldn't throw it away. And then I stopped tending the plants, and then the cat left, and didn't come back. I got these sticks to help me get about, but even with them, I didn't get about, much. And then one day I hung up his portrait.

LIL: You don't hate him anymore?

PEDLEY: No. These walls ordered my grief, gave me solace, even forced me to understand: I didn't hate him. I hated myself.

LIL: Well, everything's packed. We'd better get out before the rain comes. Here, I'll help you.

PEDLEY: No, not yet.

LIL: It's no use dragging it out, it just makes it worse—

PEDLEY: Please. Let me stay until the new woman comes. I can't leave without asking her.

LIL: It's time we were going.

PEDLEY: Don't you tell me when it's time. Don't you dare tell me!

LIL: (*Irritated; picking up suitcase*) Come on, I've heard enough—

PEDLEY: NO!

LIL: YES! I've other people to think of besides you, Pedley. I've my own family, wondering where I am—

PEDLEY: Your family? What kind of family is it when your man comes home drunk at night, dragging another drunk with him, and spends the night doing magic tricks instead of in bed with his wife?

LIL: (*Angry*) It's more of a family than what's here. It's more of a family than what's left to you!

PEDLEY: Oh, yes, it's so easy for you to say. But you

wait—wait 'til you start losing things, those things that made you a wife, and a mother, and a woman that a man might want to watch, as you pass by—

LIL: They still watch, you can be sure of that—

BEESLEY: (*Offstage at the top of the stairs, shouting*) HELLO? HELLO? YOO-HOO, ARE YOU THERE? HELLO?

LIL: HELLO! COME DOWN THE STAIRS!

(*Pause*)

BEESLEY: *DOWN* THE STAIRS?

LIL: THAT'S RIGHT. DOWN HERE. (*To Pedley*) She's come. Now mind you, Pedley, not a word about staying.

PEDLEY: (*Pleased*) Yes, yes. The new woman. She's come.

(*Beesley enters. She is a robust, cheery woman of sixty, loaded with packages and cases*)

LIL: Good afternoon to you.

BEESLEY: Good afternoon. Good afternoon and God Bless to all who's here.

LIL: You're the woman who's come to—

BEESLEY: Yes, to take the room. My name is Beesley, Mrs. Beesley.

LIL: Well, this is Mrs. Pedley, and my name is Lil.

BEESLEY: How do you do. Yes, I'm delighted to meet you both. Yes, yes . . . I'm . . . (*Looks about the room, disappointed*) Delighted. I didn't realize it was . . . that it was a basement room. I mean, there was no mention that it was a basement room.

LIL: Mrs. Pedley is the former tenant.

BEESLEY: Oh? Ah, yes, well isn't that grand. (*Looking around*) Well, it's quite nice, isn't it, really? It's just that . . .

LIL: Yes?

BEESLEY: Oh, nothing, really. It's just that I'm used to living—how shall I say it—I'm used to living *above* the ground, do you know? A bit higher above the ground—second floor, third floor, something along those lines. I've just come from a third floor arrangement, actually. (*Pause*) But it's quite nice, really, this. It's, yes, cosy, isn't it really:

(*Awkward pause; Beesley wipes sweat from her face*)

LIL: Warm, isn't it?

BEESLEY: It is close, yes.

PEDLEY: Thundery as well.

BEESLEY: It might thunder, yes.

LIL: I wish it would come, it would clear the air.

BEESLEY: Well, this is the thing, isn't it? They say it did rain in Coombe today, and last evening I went to Chadlington and the Hanborough Road was just covered with water, just covered, it was.

LIL: It's the closeness is what it is. Just raise your little finger and you're dripping with sweat.

BEESLEY: (*Opening suitcase to find handkerchief*) And it's always the way with moving, isn't it? I mean either the sweat is running down into your eyes and you've to stop and put down your bags and wipe the stinging away, or it's ever so bitter cold and there's a wind cutting through your overcoat and your hands get numb and your nose starts to run and you just about can't walk at all, for the numbness in your toes and the shivering. Do you have far to go, dear?

PEDLEY: Not too far, no.

BEESLEY: There's always the buses, but they're so dear these days, though, aren't they? The only thing to do is walk, isn't it? But I don't go walking much, anymore, do you?

PEDLEY: I can't go walking much anymore.

BEESLEY: Oh, I'm so sorry. I completely forgot—I mean you carry yourself so well—I hardly noticed that you were . . . that you had a . . . a . . .

LIL: Disability.

BEESLEY: Yes, a disability. I mean you carry yourself so well. But health is everything, isn't it though? If you don't have your health where are you? I mean that's right, isn't it?

PEDLEY: I should say it is, yes.

BEESLEY: Of course. You could be as lovely as the Queen Herself from the waist up, but if you didn't have two strong sturdy legs under you, where would you stand then? Answer me that, where *would* you stand?

LIL: I should think you'd be sitting, if you were the Queen—sitting in the Palace on the throne itself, good legs or bad.

BEESLEY: Oh, you'd have a good sit-down on the throne, if you were Queen, there's no denying that, no. But I mean how would you feel, sitting down all day not being able to get about? Not to mention those great balls the King was always holding for you, as well.

LIL: Those great balls the King was holding? Why, Mrs. Beesley!

BEESLEY: Oooh! I didn't mean—now isn't that something then? But if you was confined to your chair, and couldn't get about, you wouldn't feel like the Queen, now would you, really?

PEDLEY: I wouldn't know. Good legs or bad, I've never felt much like the Queen, no, to be sure, I did not.

BEESLEY: (*Emphatically*) Well, this is the thing! Yes, your health is everything, isn't it, really? I mean look here, look at this. You see this thumb? See that split in it? (*Proudly*) Poor circulation of the blood! It's been driving me crazy, right round the bend, it has. I can't touch anything with it, it's so tender. I was always so proud of my nails, you see, even though I come from a large family where there was a lot of work. I was always the best in the class, when I was a girl, for my nails. They used to call me "the lady," at home, because I had the best nails of any. Now my sister is different from me in that she's not at all attractive, and she never wore any makeup, but I always wore makeup, always. I think a woman has to make the best of what she's got, don't you? But this thumb of mine—right round the bend! You see, it's the poor circulation of the blood from the 'eart to the thumb, and it's just split like that, do you see? Not to mention the pins and needles I get in my hands, both hands, from the poor circulation. I start to do some knitting and then I have to stop for the pins and needles. I mean where are you, if you can't do your knitting?

PEDLEY: Knitting can be very pleasant. I used to enjoy an evening's knitting, now and again.

BEESLEY: Of course you did and well you should. I expect Lil does, too. We all enjoy our knitting, now don't we? And look at *this!* This *other* thumb! See I had a whitlow taken off there when I was young, and it ruined the looks of that thumb, and I have to file it down but I can't file it down too much because it's right down to the skin, do you know? (*Takes Pedley's hand*) Here—feel it, do you see? And I have to run it against some cloth to make sure that it's smooth and doesn't catch. Here—you feel it, Lil. I still have to pare it down some, now, when it gets too big. Imagine! (*In amazement*) I've been paring down that whitlow all my life! But it just goes to show that you just don't know where you are, if your health starts to go, now do you?

PEDLEY: You learn to make do with what you have.

BEESLEY: Well, this is the thing, after all. You come to realize this, yes. (*To Lil*) Your friend and I are at an age to realize this, but you're lucky, young lady, you can still look ahead to a good few years of health. Ah, it's a grand age, isn't it, my pet?

PEDLEY: All the same, I shouldn't like to go through it all again.

BEESLEY: Oh, well, yes, I suppose there's something in that, yes.

PEDLEY: If your only worry right now was to be a splitting on your thumb, Mrs. Beesley, you might be thankful, I shouldn't wonder.

LIL: Well, then, it's time we were leaving you. I've a family of my own to tend to, you know—

PEDLEY: No! Not yet!

BEESLEY: What's that, Mrs. . . . . Mrs.—I'm sorry, I've forgotten your name.

PEDLEY: Pedley. Mrs. Pedley. Surely I should show you round the room, Mrs. Beesley, show you round, before I leave.

LIL: I'm sure Mrs. Beesley can find her way about. It's not like moving into Waterloo Station, now is it, Pedley?

BEESLEY: Waterloo Station! Now that *is* a confusing place! I mean, they should have more signs up, for the destinations, do you know? I mean where are you without your signs, in a great bustling place like that?

PEDLEY: (*Looking round the room*) But it is larger than it seems.

BEESLEY: Waterloo Station? Larger than it seems?

PEDLEY: No, no, the room. When I first came here it seemed small, quite small, but then as the years passed, it seemed larger. I couldn't see living in a larger place, now. Why, this room is even large enough for two. Don't you think it's large enough for two, Mrs. Beesley?

BEESLEY: Well, I don't know, really. It might be. I'm used to living in several rooms, so I don't know about living in just the one.

LIL: Pedley, we must leave Mrs. Beesley to settle herself in—

PEDLEY: Large enough for two, no question of it. But let me give you a bit of a show-round, Mrs. Beesley. After all, in fourteen years I've gotten to know a few things about this room.

BEESLEY: It's not a short period, fourteen years, now is it? I should think you would get to know a place, in that length of time, yes. Even Waterloo itself wouldn't be such a great puzzle, if you spent fourteen years looking round it—why, you'd not miss your trains after fourteen years, surely not!

PEDLEY: Yes, it is larger than it seems. In fact, I should think it would easily take two beds that size, isn't that so?

BEESLEY: Why, yes. The bed appears to be quite comfortable. And those cushions are your own?

PEDLEY: No, they come with the room.

BEESLEY: Oh, I see. And the covers for them?

PEDLEY: There were covers, yes.

LIL: They were Mrs. Pedley's covers, actually.

BEESLEY: Oh, not to bother. As a matter of fact, I've brought some covers with me. (*Rummaging in suitcase; putting covers on cushions*) Now where did they go? Here we are. Isn't that a coincidence? Just the other day I said to myself I must just make some covers for the cushions on my couch at Briarly Road—that's where I used to live—I love doing things like that, don't you? Why, you can spend twenty minutes, half an hour, wondering which way to arrange the different colors so they don't come up the same when you go round the cover face. And with the different shapes, as well. I save everything.

Everything! I've had to leave so many of my things behind, moving here. Still, I'm always doing something to keep busy. It used to be with the children when they was growing up, mending the punctures in the boys' bicycles or fixing their fishing rods—I've always wanted to learn to crochet, but I can't. I'm too old, I suppose, to remember this change and that change and how many stitches here and there— (*Endearingly*) I'm a bit thick, really. (*Covers are now on the cushions*) There—now isn't that much better, then?

LIL: They look quite nice, yes. You're quite handy, Mrs. Beesley.

BEESLEY: Well, it makes you run your brain a bit, to do things with your hands. When you get older you learn to like doing things like this, don't you? Yes, they'll brighten up the room, my cushion covers will, they'll add a little color.

PEDLEY: Yes, we didn't know whether to leave the covers or not, and Lil thought you might have brought some with you.

BEESLEY: Wasn't that clever of her, yes.

PEDLEY: Yes, and the lampshade, as well.

BEESLEY: The lampshade as well?

PEDLEY: Yes, the shade that covered that bulb. Lil thought I should take the shade, that you would have brought one with you. I thought we should leave it for you. A bare bulb can be so sad, at first.

BEESLEY: Yes, that's true enough, yes.

PEDLEY: You have brought your own lampshade then, have you?

BEESLEY: Why, yes. Well, I mean, no, I haven't, actually, no.

PEDLEY: Oh, well, then I must leave you it.

BEESLEY: Well, is it your shade or does it belong to the room?

PEDLEY: It's been so long, I just can't remember.

BEESLEY: In that case, why don't you take it. You're probably quite attached to it, and you can use it in your new arrangement.

PEDLEY: Oh, no, I'm not attached to it at all—Oh, Mrs.

Beesley—I've just had a marvelous thought!

BEESLEY: A thought?! Good for you. And what is it, Mrs. Pedley?

PEDLEY: I could leave the shade, and as you said there's easily room enough for two beds here, and this room can be so lonely with just the one, and we could solve all these problems quite easily, I should think, if—

LIL: Pedley, I'm warning you—

BEESLEY: Warning?

PEDLEY: Yes, you're such a kind woman, Mrs. Beesley, and—

BEESLEY: Why, isn't that sweet of you, Mrs. Pedley—

PEDLEY: Yes, so kind, and I was wondering, if in fact, I might stay on here with you.

BEESLEY: Stay on?

PEDLEY: ·   Yes. The two of us here, together.

BEESLEY: Stay on? Stay on together?

PEDLEY: Yes. That's it, yes.

BEESLEY: Oh. Well, I should say that's a fine thought, Mrs. Pedley, yes. Interesting that you should say that you might want to stay on here together, with me.

PEDLEY: Yes.

BEESLEY: Yes, I should love to stay on with you, yes, but . . . I mean it's just that it's not precisely what I had in mind, but . . . but it is a thought, then, isn't it? Yes, it certainly *is* a thought—

LIL: She's not serious, Mrs. Beesley. This room's not large enough for two, now is it?

BEESLEY: Why, yes, that's true, Mrs. Pedley, it is a tiny room, in actual fact, now isn't it? I mean it's not like a . . . a train station, not like Waterloo. You wouldn't get lost and miss your train in a room this size, no, surely not. (*At window*) I've been so curious about the view, you don't mind if I have a little bit of a look? I've always been so lucky with my views, you know. I mean where are you, if you can't see a bit of the world from your window, where are you indeed? I must have just a small look-out, if you don't mind? (*Raises the shade; disap-*

pointed) Oh. Yes. (*Pulls shade down halfway*) I see they're quite active in . . . building up the pavements and tearing down the houses in this part of the city, aren't they then?

LIL: Yes, there's a good bit of building up and tearing down here, yes.

BEESLEY: Well, it keeps them off the street, doesn't it, these workmen? At least they're not idle. I've had my fill of idle men, and I can tell you: it's not a day in the country, to be married to an idle man, not on your life! And the worst are the idle young. My son Les, when he was out of work, there was no end of trouble he'd get into. (*Confiding*) You see, there was this neighbor of ours and she had this retarded daughter—diabetic, do you know—and, well, she was not "capable," if you know what I mean?

LIL: Yes, yes, not "capable."

BEESLEY: And every time she'd see Lessy's van parked in front of our flat she'd be over, like a shot, up two flights, and jump right into his bed! Incredible, isn't it? Why, she even jumped into our own bed, once, by mistake, that was how excited she'd get when she knew my Lessy was at home.

LIL: Did your son Lessy—that is, would he, with this girl—

BEESLEY: Well, only at the start, before he knew she wasn't "capable." What can you expect, with a normal growing lad? But after he found out, he'd have nothing to do with her, not a thing. Because *I* wouldn't let him! Not on your life! Terrible, isn't it, to have a daughter like that? (*Noticing the dead plants out the window*) Why, look! You had a small garden, didn't you, Mrs. Pedley?

PEDLEY: I did have, yes. But now, as you can see—

BEESLEY: Plants do such wonders! Cheer the whole place up! Yes, give me my plants. You know where you stand with a growing green plant. I'll certainly do my best to keep them up, start on them tomorrow, first thing. Yes, no end of things you can do—and even though it is down below the level of the pavement, I wouldn't have to stay here all day long, now would I? I could go out, on trips, go to the parks, the public gardens, now couldn't I?

LIL: Of course you could, Mrs. Beesley, yes.

PEDLEY: Yes. A trip to the parks can be a whole day affair, if you've the legs and the fine bright day. I often went—

BEESLEY: Do you know, I've just had an idea!

PEDLEY: (*Hopefully*) An idea? What is it then, Mrs. Beesley?

BEESLEY: (*Decisively, hands on hips*) What this room needs is . . . is an *animal!*

PEDLEY: (*Disappointed*) Oh. An animal?

LIL: (*Perking up; getting interested*) Are you fond of animals, Mrs. Beesley?

BEESLEY: Fond? Let me tell you this: give me my animals! I hate the others, but give me my animals. I don't love 'em or hate 'em, not on your life. You know where you stand with animals, now don't you?

LIL: You most certainly do, yes.

BEESLEY: I should think this room could do well with, say, a cat, or perhaps, a dog. Some animal, to liven up this room.

PEDLEY: I had a cat, a little cat, once.

BEESLEY: Did you really? Now wasn't that a sensible thing to have. But there's nothing like an animal for affection, nothing in this world!

LIL: Have you had animals, Mrs. Beesley?

BEESLEY: Have I had animals? I should say I have! Cats, dogs. There's nothing like a dog. You know where you stand with a dog!

LIL: You do. But you get so attached to them, don't you?

BEESLEY: Well, this is the thing. But you know right where you stand with a dog. Have you ever seen a dog drunk, staggering along the road, singing, picking a fight with anyone who happens to cross him? Not on your life! They're not like men, these dogs, no. My friend used to say: "*They're* not beasts, these dogs, not like men, oh no." And I'll tell you one thing: she was right. She wasn't wrong in saying that, she was right. (*As if telling a secret*) But I'll tell you a peculiar thing—I like the mongrels the best. Yes, give me my mongrel every time. None of them fancy pedigree aristocratic dogs for Mrs. Beesley, not on your life!

LIL: (*Interested, getting involved with Beesley*) That's just the way I feel as well. You see, I had mongrels all my life, but when the last one died, I bought this great pedigree Alsatian. The papers on this dog were a book in themselves, generations and generations—Germany, Italy, them Alps in Switzerland—and you should have seen him. Beautiful? His head was as big as a ten-month old baby's, and his paw was as big as your hand.

BEESLEY: Now that's a good-sized dog, surely.

LIL: And the first night, I'm sitting there with him, his head on my lap, getting to know him, running my hand over him, and I feel a lump. On his shoulder. Oh, it's probably just a cyst, I say to myself, and I take him to the vet. The vet puts him to sleep, and starts working on the lump. (*Pause, getting sadder*) Well, the lump turns out to be a tumor, and the vet cut deeper and deeper and deeper and deeper until finally he saw that . . . that this tumor went right down into the dog's heart.

BEESLEY: Good God, no!

LIL: Right down into his heart. No use, says the vet. Hopeless. Only a matter of time. I nursed him and all, but it didn't do no good, and two months later, he died. (*Pause, bitterly*) It's no use with these pedigrees, no. I'll never forget sitting there, stroking him, him looking up at me with those great brown eyes, never even knowing anything was wrong.

BEESLEY: Horrible! I know what it's like, luv, to care for one that's ill. And then to lose him, too. Yes, I know just what you went through, Lilly, I know just what it's like.

LIL: (*Sincerely, appreciating Beesley's concern*) It's good to hear you say that, Mrs. Beesley. You're a sensitive, understanding woman, and I hope that I shall have a chance to get to know you even better.

BEESLEY: Yes, well, isn't that grand. But I shall have my animals, here. They'll make the place more lively, my animals will. The view isn't so bad, really, though it will be hard to get used to looking up at things, after living high up and looking down. But it's nothing that a few green plants and a dog or a cat won't do wonders for, now is it? Well, then, the room looks larger already. (*Noticing the portrait*) Now there *is* a handsome man! Yes, a handsome man indeed! And is he your son, Mrs. Pedley?

PEDLEY: No, he was my husband, actually.

BEESLEY: Oh, I'm sorry. I didn't know. There is a resemblance, though, don't you think? They say husband and wife grow to look alike, in time—same as they say about animals and their masters as well. A definite resemblance there, yes.

PEDLEY: It's a portrait of him as alderman—the youngest alderman in the country, he was then.

BEESLEY: Was he really? And a fine alderman he must have been. A man like that wouldn't let a case sit in a desk drawer for a year I shouldn't think, no. Not like the alderman we have at home—(*Stops, embarrassed, then saddened*) Oh. I mean the one I used to have, you know, at the Briarly Road. Why, for years there wasn't even a signpost saying Briarly Road. No one could find us . . . (*Pulling herself together, sincerely*) Yes, a good alderman is a rare thing, now. You were a lucky woman, Mrs. Pedley, to have been married to an alderman as grand as that man there. (*Sighing, sadly*) But everything's changed, now hasn't it?

PEDLEY: (*Sensing the sadness, with compassion*) Oh, yes, everything's changed now, yes. Everything. Everything!

BEESLEY: And not for the best, some of it not for the best by a long shot, some of this change we're having, now.

PEDLEY: I should say not, no. It's such a pleasure, Mrs. Beesley, to meet a woman like you, someone who agrees with your own point of view, knows what it's like. A kind person—

LIL: Good God, look at the time! I was so caught up in what you were saying, Mrs. Beesley, I didn't notice the time! Why, you put me in a trance—a bloomin' hypnotist, you are! (*Picking up suitcase*) Oh, I'm late now! By the time I get you settled, Pedley, I'll be ages late! Come. My family will be roaring with hunger by the time I get home.

PEDLEY: Oh, but the portrait! We've forgotten to wrap up the portrait! Yes, I'm afraid to carry it without wrapping it, Lil, with the rain about to come. I'd die if it were to get wet. Wrap it, will you? There's paper and twine about, somewhere.

LIL: All right. But mind you, then we're off. (*She starts to wrap the portrait*)

BEESLEY: (*Unpacking; hanging up a dress, etc.*) Yes, you must come back and see me, yes.

PEDLEY: (*Sensing Beesley's fragility; exploring, firmly*) But I should imagine a woman like you would have many many visitors, coming here. We'd have to book ahead, I'd expect, to come and visit a woman like you, Mrs. Beesley.

BEESLEY: Oh, no, not many would come and visit me, no.

PEDLEY: Your children? Surely they would come—often, I should think, with a mother like you? I'm surprised they didn't help you move in. It's so lonely, moving in by yourself.

BEESLEY: Yes, well there wasn't that much to carry, was there? (*Pause*) Actually, they don't bother much with me, anymore. They're grown, they've got their jobs, their own families. Even the youngest, he's even got a job and a family, now.

PEDLEY: You must see him often, him being the youngest. The youngest is always closest to mother, now isn't that so?

BEESLEY: You'd think that, yes. But they don't have much time for you, when you get a bit older, now do they?

PEDLEY: You must spend your Sundays with him, I expect?

BEESLEY: Well, yes. Actually no. I haven't seen . . . My family usually comes to me, you know, on a Sunday.

PEDLEY: Now isn't that the way to spend a fine Sunday afternoon—the whole family together over a great joint of meat and vegetables you've cooked yourself. This is the thing that makes it all worthwhile, isn't it?

BEESLEY: Worthwhile? And what do you mean by that?

PEDLEY: Why, being a woman—a wife and a mother—giving up your own cares for your family. I know that this is it, isn't it—having your husband and sons and daughters gathered round your table on a Sunday afternoon, with a walk round the park after Sunday dinner if it's fine. This makes it all worthwhile. (*Pause; Beesley is silent, getting upset*) They'll all come to you here now, I suppose?

BEESLEY: Yes. Well, no, there's hardly room, here, is there, for your family to come to you?

PEDLEY: Perhaps not. You might plan to go to them? Why, you must be swamped with their invitations—this week with one, the next with the other—not to mention Christmas and New Year's and Easter and all the rest. Flooded, you must be, a woman like you, with your family alone! Not to mention your friends. Grand, just grand, isn't it?

BEESLEY: What's that?

PEDLEY: It must be a great pleasure for you to have a large warm family to care for you, now that you'll be living here on your own?

BEESLEY: Yes, well, if they're not too busy with their own families. We've all had our children. We all know what it's like, with children. (*Pause; wistfully*) They never come back, do they? But it's their own life, then, isn't it?

PEDLEY: Yes, not to mention your husband himself?

BEESLEY: What?

LIL: There—that will keep it dry. Safe and sound 'til we hang it in your new room, Pedley. Now we're finally ready. I can almost hear the stomachs grumbling: "Where's momma? Where's mum gone?"

PEDLEY: Not to mention your husband himself?

BEESLEY: What's that?

PEDLEY: I said your husband.

BEESLEY: What about him?

PEDLEY: Well, I'll be frank with you, Mrs. Beesley: I'm wondering in my mind about him. I mean, a fine, kind woman like you with fine, grown children as you've told us about must have a prize of a man for a husband, but you haven't told us a thing about him.

BEESLEY: No, that's true enough.

LIL: Perhaps Mrs. Beesley doesn't want to talk about her husband. It's no business of ours, Pedley.

PEDLEY: Yes, yes, I'm sorry it's just that—strange, isn't it?—Already I feel that I've known Mrs. Beesley a long time, and here it is I'm leaving, and leaving this room after so many years, and I'd like to have some idea about you and your family, and about what a fine man your husband must be to have married a woman as honest and kind as you.

BEESLEY: Yes. That's kind . . . kind of you as well . . . He's . . . he's . . . Well, I'll be truthful with you: he's just left me.

PEDLEY: No!

BEESLEY: That he has. Not two months past.

PEDLEY: Oh, you poor woman. Left you!

BEESLEY: (*Enraged, pouring out in a torrent*) That he has! Picked up and left! I think he's mad, moon-mad, born under an ochred moon so they say, and he changes with the moon. He'd go for six weeks without speaking a word to any of us—me or the children—and then the moon would change and he'd be all right. Oh, he was decent enough up until the war—he went out to India, then, and when he came back he forgot about the children, didn't know any of us, really. Never slept in the same bed with him after that, not on your life! Never good enough for him, I wasn't, with all these other women. As if I didn't have no feelings at all! He had a peculiar upbringing, you see—his uncle was his father—it never works out well between brother and sister does it? He had a go at our own girl, once, and even though the doctor said there wasn't any "interference," still it was a court case and—(*Trying to control herself, failing*) Tight? He worships gold! I'd ask him for money for the children, and he'd say: "It's about time they left. When a bird learns to fly, it leaves the nest," says he, "and when rabbits litter," says he, "they leave!" (*Stopping herself, a littler calmer*) I tried everything. Everything! They all said to look after myself, and I tried to do that, yes. I *did* try. Why, I even found myself a gentleman companion, for a time. Imagine that? Me? Mrs. Beesley? I thought it over—why take it, why not leave them all to fend for themselves with their bicycle punctures and mending clothes and cleaning—the more you do the more they take advantage. Horrible man! Why did I stay with him as long as I did? Did I feel sorry for him? Was I afraid? Afraid of what? And now he's left me! Imagine that? *He's* the one who left! (*Pause; surprised at her outburst, more in control*) But you think of your troubles and they just get worse, though, don't they? I get so depressed sometimes, I just sit there with all my questions and no answers, no answers at all. And then I say right, let's do some work—this is the thing— why just this morning before I left the . . . the Briarly Road . . . I cleaned out the chimney itself. (*Pleading for understanding*) Now isn't that a foolish thing to do when you're leaving a place for good?

PEDLEY: All the same, they do need us, these men, don't you think?

BEESLEY: I did think that, yes. And the children, too, needing us. But now I'm not sure, anymore. They make us think they need us, but what about us, then? What about *us*? There's no one, is there, who says to us, now: "We need you. Come visit. Come to Sunday dinner and a bit of a walk round the park if it's fine. " No, they tell us they need us, and make us think that they need us, and then they throw us away when the time comes for it. (*Pause*) That's why I say give me my animals, and my plants, yes, and my view out the window at a bit of the world, and . . . and my dreams.

LIL: Pedley, come, we're off—

BEESLEY: (*Allying herself with Pedley*) Oh, yes—Lil has her family, yet, and she's looking at you and me, Mrs. Pedley, like we're two . . . two casualties, two human disasters, two strange old ladies who made some mistake, and wound up alone. And she's thinking: this won't happen to me, oh, no. I've chosen different, this won't happen to me. Now isn't that what's in your mind, Lil, looking at Mrs. Pedley and myself?

LIL: What does it matter, what's in my mind?

BEESLEY: Isn't it, my pet? Hey?

LIL: All right, then, yes. Yes, it is. I know my man's not perfect—there's no such thing as a perfect man. I'm not looking for miracles, for magic, hell no! (*Pause; softening*) But I know about loving, too, about loving him, and about loving my children—why, even saying that, right now, I get this thrill inside my heart, and there's no thrill like it, no thrill like it in this world!

BEESLEY: (*Excitedly, reassuringly*) Yes! Yes, I know, I know. Best of luck to you, Lilly dear, best of luck! Better luck you'll need than us, though, better luck you'll need than us.

PEDLEY: Mrs. Beesley?

BEESLEY: Yes?

PEDLEY: You're a woman who's had her sorrow, and had her joy, and I feel I can speak to you straight, and tell you what's on my mind.

BEESLEY: Yes, you can. Surely you can, yes.

PEDLEY: I know how sad and lonely it can be here, but I've grown used to it, I have, and I could show you . . . show you ways it might not be so lonely. I could do that, yes.

BEESLEY: I'm sure you could, yes.

PEDLEY: Let me stay here with you, the two of us here, together.

LIL: Oh, Pedley, come on—

PEDLEY: Let me stay here with you, the two of us here—

LIL: OH, BLOODY HELL, PEDLEY! FOR CHRIS-SAKES—

PEDLEY: (*Vicious*) HUSH! YOU HUSH! I've asked Mrs. Beesley a question, and it's up to her, not you, to answer.

LIL: I don't have the time—my family will be—

PEDLEY: THEN GO TO THEM! LEAVE ME! I'll manage. I've learned to manage. These sticks don't keep me back, if I've the will to manage. I'll manage, in spite of you or of anyone else. So go if you want, woman, go! (*To Beesley*) Will you let me stay on here, with you?

BEESLEY: I don't know, really. It is a thought though, really.

PEDLEY: I shan't beg you, Mrs. Beesley. You've got to decide, right now, one way or the other, yes, or no.

BEESLEY: Well, there's no need to put it in those terms, surely.

PEDLEY: You come to a point where there aren't any others, none at all. Yes, or no?

BEESLEY: Well, I . . .

PEDLEY: Yes or no?

BEESLEY: No, but . . . but I don't want you to feel that—

PEDLEY: It's done, and there's no great surprise in it. Even though you are a kind, honest woman, and even though you'll be bursting with grief, when we've left you here, alone. All right, Lilly, we're off.

BEESLEY: But I didn't mean—

PEDLEY: It's all right. I understand. (*Pause*) It was the same when I first came to this room: there was an old woman, leaving as I arrived. I remember she looked all leached out—like a man's shirt washed too many times. She was thin and ugly, worn. She looked dirty, though I'm sure she did her best to look clean. And she didn't want to leave this room, no. She had had her animals, and she had had her plants, her little garden there, out under the railings near the street. But by that time all her plants had died, and by that time all her animals had left for good. Died and left, died and left. And she looked at me and she . . . she asked me if I'd let her stay, the two of us, together. And even though I wanted to say yes, I turned her out, same as you did me. Sad and lonely as I was, I said no, and I turned her out. (*Pause*) She didn't weep, and I wondered at that, then. Sad as she was, she didn't weep, no, and I wondered, at that. And when she'd gone, I sat here, alone, thinking of her and of this room and of the man who'd died and of the children who'd never come here, and I wept and wept, just sat down and wept. But not now, no. I'm too strong now, too strong now, for tears. Always the way, isn't it? The ones we think we hurt don't weep, but hurting them, we do.

(*Crash of thunder*)

BEESLEY: Listen! It'll be pouring down with rain! You'd best stay, at least 'til it clears.

PEDLEY: (*Moving toward the ramp*) No, I'll not stay longer. Lilly, come. Come.

BEESLEY: You'll have to come back and visit.

LIL: Of course. It's not often I've met someone as sympathetic as you, Mrs. Beesley.

BEESLEY: Both of you, yes. You both must come. We might even have a walk out into the parks, if the day is fine.

LIL: Yes, if this weather ever settles.

BEESLEY: Yes, the parks can be a great joy—

PEDLEY: Come, Lilly, we're off.

BEESLEY: And I'll have the room fixed up when you come back—it's amazing what a few green plants will do, isn't it, to a room like this?

LIL: And an animal, yes.

BEESLEY: Yes, brighten the place up. Make it more lively. Yes, you'll see, when you come again.

PEDLEY: Yes, Mrs. Beesley, yes. You'll have your animals, you'll make up your little snatch of green garden, same as the woman before me, and same as me, and same as Lilly will do, when her turn comes.

LIL: That's a cruel thing to say now, Pedley, a cruel thing to say!

PEDLEY: Yes, and a cruel thing it is, Lilly. A cruel thing it is. Goodbye, Mrs. Beesley, goodbye.

LIL: Yes, goodbye, Mrs. Beesley.

BEESLEY: Goodbye. Goodbye to you both. (*Questioning*) And God Bless?

(*With Pedley leading, she and Lil exit slowly on the ramp. Beesley watches them go, and then turns and looks sadly about the room. She begins to unpack her china, and is startled by a loud crash of thunder, followed by rain. Beesley finds a broken saucer, fits the two pieces together, and then sadly puts them down once again. Shading her eyes from the glare, she looks at the bare bulb, and then turns it out. The room is now dimly lit by the light from the streetlamp through the window. Fierce crash of thunder, sheets of rain. Beesley goes to window, raises shade, looks up to the right, to the left, lowers shade, and stands briefly in silhouette. Finally Beesley turns, comes to chair, sits with hands folded and head bowed, very still, as the dim light turns to:*)

Black

Richard France

THE IMAGE OF ELMO DOYLE

Richard France

The Image of Elmo Doyle, a poignant dramatic portrayal of a farm family during the depression, marks the first appearance of author Richard France in *The Best Short Plays* series.

Mr. France was born in Boston, Massachusetts, on May 5, 1938. After living abroad for extended periods, he became a graduate fellow in playwriting at the Yale School of Drama, going on from there to earn a Ph.D. in Theatre History at Carnegie-Mellon University.

The recipient of a Rockefeller Production Grant and a National Endowment for the Arts Creative Writing Fellowship Award, Mr. France served as playwright-in-residence with the Music and Art Institute of San Francisco and with the University of Pittsburgh.

Currently the Chairman of the Department of Theatre and Drama at Lawrence University, he is the author of a number of published and produced plays, including *Feathertop; One Day in the Life of Ivan Denisovich; The First Word and the Last; The Adventures of the Dying Detective; Fathers and Sons;* and *The Magic Shop.*

Mr. France has contributed stage and film-related articles to dozens of periodicals and, in 1977, published *The Theatre of Orson Welles,* an illuminating study of the actor-director's ground-breaking work in the theatre.

Characters:

Scene:

The Doyle place in the San Joaquin Valley of California. It is the late thirties.

A view of the front room, the porch, a bit of yard, perhaps a wall of the garage.

The front room, center of activity for the family, is a room of contrasts. Luxuries such as a radio are side by side with signs of poverty.

A door leads to the porch, others to the interior of the house. The floor is covered with worn linoleum divided by metal strips. There is an oil heater, a pair of matching chairs, a chair and sofa that match, another chair the dog has chewed up, a desk, a sideboard, and an end table. Photos are much in evidence around the room, some have a religious theme. There may even be a statue of Mother and Child. Noticeably absent are such comforts as books and flowers.

Elmo is seated in the front room reading a newspaper. He is an old man whose recent years of inactivity have left him heavy and sluggish. As the result of two strokes, one side of his body—the right side—is nearly useless. He uses a stick to help him in walking. His speech has also been affected, the words often broken and faltering. However, he should not sound like someone who is unfamiliar with the language.

The Narrator enters, regards Elmo for a moment or two, then turns to face the audience.

NARRATOR: Dawn. That grey pause of the day which ends so abruptly with the appearance of the sun . . . that allows us a glimpse of the Doyle family . . . the passing of a morning with them. (*Pointing*) Over there a hard-packed dirt drive connects the house with the main road. It also serves to separate the house from the first of several out-buildings—a garage. All are shabbily built and in some need of repair. (*He moves over to the wall of the garage, and runs his fingers along the boards*) There are spaces between the boards, and the paint is faded and chalky to the touch. (*There is the sound of a car passing in the distance, and, occasionally birds can be heard throughout*) The house . . . What can be said of it? A low, one-level thing that leaves the impression it began like the family it shelters . . . small . . . and was added to as the family grew . . . a family, for the most part, that's long since scattered.

(*Melba enters with a broom and starts sweeping. She is a good twenty years younger than Elmo, with still a trace of attractiveness about her. There is a great deal of hostility between them, all the more so since she has had to take charge of the family. He avoids her by moving outside onto the porch. She continues sweeping*)

MELBA: (*Calling*) Emma Jean!

NARRATOR: Three remain: Elmo, his wife, Melba, and the last of their children—

MELBA: (*Again calling off*) Emma Jean!! (*She sweeps her way out to the porch. The Narrator exits. Elmo is seated. Then to Elmo, as if for the hundredth time*) I see you got the oleo all over you again. (*As if by reflex, he examines his shirt for the spot*) Doesn't do any good at all, my asking you to watch the way you eat. Does it? Not one bit of good.

ELMO: (*Trying to rub it out*) Sssssooorrrreeeeeeee . . .

MELBA: You're not the one who has to wash these things clean again. I am. And every piece by hand, too. Machines cost money . . . the kind of money we don't have comin' in anymore.

ELMO: W-we ha-ve summm . . .

MELBA: The few dollars I've managed to set aside.

ELMO: An' w-we don' owe an-any.

MELBA: (*Sadly, in all seriousness*) Which still leaves us with next to nothing to our names. Dearest Jesus, even the land's only ours three or four months a year!

ELMO: Be-fffore . . I p-put ev'ree-th-thing into th-that land.

MELBA: Yes, yes, I know. Worked yourself right down to the bone, you did. Poor you. Well, what've we got to show for it now? The roof comin' down on our heads and a few precious dollars in our pockets is all.

ELMO: Wh-which you s-s-spend . . .

MELBA: I can remember back a few years. The money you threw away on pool and beer. What I wouldn't give to have some of that in my hand today!

ELMO: (*Gesturing*) One time . . .

MELBA: One time a week, you mean.

ELMO: Sa-sat-tur-day . . .

MELBA: *Every* Saturday. Pool an' beer. And whatever other little pleasure you found in the streets.

ELMO: (*Flaring up*) Wh-what plez-zure? What?

MELBA: Oh, I don't care so much what you did . . . but the money that went out of this house—

ELMO: (*Getting to his feet*) *I* care!

MELBA: I'd rather you'd gone into the fields for two dollars with one of those Filipino women and a bottle of something—

ELMO: (*With convincing indignation*)—No! Nuth-thin' l-like that!

MELBA: I said, I don't care. It's what we got now that matters, and it's so little . . . so very—

ELMO: Mat-ters to me! No, nuth-in' like tha-that. I n-never took a c-cent out of thisss house f-for that.

MELBA: Well, whatever you spent it on, we could sure do with even a half of your Saturday night spendings today.

ELMO: (*A bit defensively*) You . . . the chil-children . . . n-never went with-out. S-still don't.

MELBA: And you know why, too. 'Cause I don't have to come begging to you anymore.

ELMO: (*Resigning from the exchange*) Aw-right, M-Melba . . .

(*There is a very long silence: ten beats or so. She turns sharply and reenters the house. He gazes out across the yard at some undefined distance. The lights create a mood of reverie. Sounds of laughter and a pool room add a wistful quality to it. These are gradually drowned out by the sound of a car approaching the house. And just offstage the dog begins to bark. The reverie ends abruptly. The sound of a car coming to a stop, and its door opening and closing. The Mailman enters)*

MAILMAN: Well, ain't you up early!

ELMO: Mor-mornin' . . .

MAILMAN: (*Hands over a few letters*) Thought I'd bring these on up ta the house. Save you havin' ta trek down to the box later.

ELMO: No n-need. I can do . . . do w-with the exer-sssize.

MAILMAN: Hell, Elmo, you've had plenty of that in your time.

ELMO: I sup-p-ose . . .

MAILMAN: All the crops you put down.

ELMO: (*Agreeing proudly*) An' go-od crops, m-mostly . . .

MAILMAN: Tha's the truth! Matter of fact, I don't recall you ever havin' a bad year.

ELMO: Nine-nineteen eighteen . . .

MAILMAN: It wasn't just you that year. Nosirreebob. The whole San Joaquin Valley had it hard in eighteen. I can't think of one single person who produced much in the way of eatables. How long'd we go without rain, couple a' hundred days?

ELMO: More . . .

MAILMAN: This wuz the awfullest place that year, I hope ta tell you.

ELMO: A s-san' dune . . .

MAILMAN: A sand dune, thas what it wuz, awright. But, after that . . . Well, frankly, Elmo, I never could figure why you didn't buy up more land than ya did. Considerin' your luck with cotton and oranges, and 'specially with the government hollerin' all during the war for every bit of both crops they could get their hands on, you could've really made out awright for yourself.

ELMO: (*Somewhat distractedly*) Es-ter . . .

MAILMAN: Nineteen eighteen: that the year she passed away?

ELMO: Tw-twenty . . .

MAILMAN: (*Very sympathetic*) I guess a time like that in any man's life would be enough to slow him down for good. (*Brief silence*) Been seein' a lot of fruit tramps over Dinuba lately. I reckon the pickin' berths'll be comin' due soon.

ELMO: G-g-grapes an' pee-ches . . .

MAILMAN: Looks like they're gonna be real plentiful this year.

ELMO: Keep the p-prices l-l-low . . .

MAILMAN: It'll do that, awright. An' a whole lot a' people planted 'em, too. If I had ta pick me a money crop, I'd go with cotton an' oranges again. For the life of me, Elmo, I just can't understand why you let the Benedicts pull up all them trees like they did.

ELMO: They r-rent the l-l-land.

MAILMAN: But ta pull up all them trees on the hope the raisin companies'll be payin' high for grapes! Seems kinda silly, if you ask me.

ELMO: Th-they thought it w-would pay.

MAILMAN: Hell! With Napa not two hundred miles north a' here, an' them floodin' us with grapes their wineries don't use up? I tell ya, I can't see how Benedict's gonna be able to pay you the rent on the land, plus the cost of pullin' up all your orange trees, and still be left with enough ta provide for the five of them through plantin' time next year.

ELMO: Work the win-winter f-for one of the c-can-ner-ries.

MAILMAN: Yes, sir, guess that's what he'll have ta do, aw-right.

(*The phone rings in the front room. Melba answers it*)

MELBA: Hello. No, this is her mother. I'll get her. (*Calling*) Emma Jean! (*Emma Jean enters. She is a young girl, still in her teens. Melba hands her the phone*) It's Cora. Now, you make it quick, ya hear? I want to get into that garden before the sun comes up any higher.

EMMA JEAN: Okay, okay . . . (*Into the phone*) H'lo, Cora? Hi . . .

(*She sits down, silently absorbed in her conversation. Melba moves out onto the porch*)

MAILMAN: I bet about now they're wishin' they still had hold a' those trees for next year.

ELMO: They w-w-were good trees.

MELBA: Which trees are those, dear?

MAILMAN: Mornin', Miz Doyle.

ELMO: Ben-ed-dict's . . .

MELBA: (*Nods to the Mailman*) Oh, yes—the Benedicts.

MAILMAN: Me an' Elmo wuz just talkin' about the mistake they made themselves by pullin' up all them trees.

MELBA: (*Leafing through the mail*) That's the truth. They did it against our advise. Well, it's their worry if grapes don't return the kind of money they thought they would. You haven't seen a package for me, have you?

MAILMAN: A package? No, ma'am . . . can't say as I have.

MELBA: It's overdue.

ELMO: Wh-what pac-kage?

MELBA: I've ordered a pair of gloves from the Sears catalog. (*To the Mailman*) Frilly things. The kind that flatter a woman's vanity. Gloves are my weakness. I see a pair that's white and frilly, and I naturally want them.

MAILMAN: I know just what you mean. I gets me a tickle in my stomach every time I come across a clock I don' have. I collect them. Clocks. Got more'n two dozen at home, and none of 'em alike neither. I got one last month that runs four hundred days. Came all the way from Germany.

MELBA: Runs for four hundred days, does it? Isn't that something!

MAILMAN: Then, there's the one where this big ol' bird comes out from behind a door every hour on the hour, an' goes "Cookoo, cookoo!"

MELBA: I think I saw one like that over at Visalia.

MAILMAN: Only trouble with 'em is you gotta work the weights every day or they'll run down on ya.

MELBA: Not like the other one, apparently.

MAILMAN: What other one's that?

MELBA: That goes four hundred days.

MAILMAN: It sure ain't. Once that's wound you can go off and never have to worry about it.

MELBA: Just be back in four hundred days.

MAILMAN: That's a fact! Yes, sirree . . . (*Brief silence*) Well, I best be gettin' along. I'll keep an eye out for your package,

Miz Doyle. But I wouldn't worry none: Sears may be slow but they'll get it to you in the end. Still, I'll keep an eye out.

MELBA: Thank you.

MAILMAN: Yes, ma'am. Be seein' ya, Elmo.

ELMO: Go-od-bye . . .

(The Mailman exits. Emma Jean, still on the phone, laughs. Melba opens a letter. The dog barks as the car drives off)

MELBA: What do you think . . . will the Benedicts get enough for their grapes to pay us what they owe?

ELMO: They sh-should.

MELBA: Well, that's something to be grateful for, anyway.

ELMO: Are y-you going to t-take it?

MELBA: Am I going to take what they owe us?

ELMO: All of it?

MELBA: I most certainly am.

ELMO: They'll . . . h-have noth-thing.

MELBA: And what do you think we'll have if we don't get paid? *(Holds out a letter)* You see this? This is a bill. These people don't care to know our difficulties. It's none of their concern. Their only interest in us is the fourteen dollars we owe them. I don't see why you're so worried 'bout the Benedicts. At least three of them can take jobs this winter, which is more than this family can do. If you've got to worry, worry about *us* . . . how we're going to survive. *(Calling loudly)* Emma Jean! You've been on that phone time enough to talk to ten people! Emma Jean! Do you hear me?

EMMA JEAN: *(Answering, loudly)* All right. I'm coming . . . *(Normal; on the phone)* I know. 'Course I wanna go. Oh, what's the use; she's only gonna say no to it anyway. Okay. Okay, I'll ask her. But you'd better not count on my gettin' ta go. I know what she's gonna say. She's gonna say—

MELBA: *Emma Jean!*

EMMA JEAN: *(On the phone)* I said I would. Yeah. Cora, I gotta . . . Yeah. Okay, I'll let you know tonight. Okay. Bye, bye . . . *(She hangs up and moves out onto the porch)*

MELBA: *(To Elmo; angrily)* Can you work the winter? Can you come up with enough money, aside from the rent on the land, to support this family? Well, can you? Then it's up to me, and I say we need that money—every last dime of it—just to scrape by. (*Noticing Emma Jean*) Now, what was that all about?

EMMA JEAN: I was talkin' to Cora.

MELBA: I answered the phone, remember? Wha'd she want?

EMMA JEAN: She's goin' to Yosemite for the weekend.

MELBA: An' I suppose she wants you along?

EMMA JEAN: Her mother and father's goin' too. An' they're takin' their car, so all I'd really need is food money. A dollar or two . . . (*Her voice trails off*)

MELBA: It seems to me there was somethin' about Ella Swing's family goin' over to Morro Bay.

EMMA JEAN: That was more than a month ago—

MELBA: An' before that a slumber party down at the Fletcher place . . .

EMMA JEAN: (*Faintly pleading*) A weekend away from here once in a while . . . Is that so much to ask?

MELBA: It's every weekend. No, I can't have you runnin' off whenever you want. There's too much to be done around here.

EMMA JEAN: I do my share.

MELBA: I said, no. Now, let that put an end to it. Wait here while I get somethin' ta cover my head.

(*She brushes by them and exits through the interior of the house. Elmo watches her silently, then turns to Emma Jean*)

ELMO: I'll talk . . . to her.

EMMA JEAN: *You'll* talk to her?

ELMO: To-n-night . . . after sup-supper.

EMMA JEAN: What good will that do? She won't listen.

ELMO: Yes . . .

EMMA JEAN: Not to you, not to me . . .

ELMO: We'll g-get her to lis-sen.

(*Melba reenters tying a bandanna around her head*)

MELBA: (*Passing by; to Elmo*) I left the dishes in the sink. You better get to them 'fore the egg hardens and they have ta be soaked and scrubbed.

(*She exits toward the garden. Emma Jean slaps her thighs in resignation and follows. Elmo opens the screen door to the house. The hinge squeaks. He goes into the front room, finds a can of oil, returns to the screen door, and tries to oil the hinges. His coordination fails him, and the frustration registers on his face. He drops the can of oil, and with the aid of his stick, makes his way down the stairs and across the yard to the shade and a bench up against the garage wall. Again the lights create a mood of reverie. The sound of pool balls breaking and a game being played. The Narrator reenters)*

NARRATOR: It was still morning as he shuffled and tapped his way across the sun-baked yard to the wooden bench, the companion piece to the one in the separator room. He let himself down slowly till he felt the touch of the wood beneath him. And there, with his stick handy, his leg extended like a log in front of him, he'd sit till Melba and the girl returned from the garden, and watch the road. (*Elmo gazes out across the yard. The reverie continues*) On weekends, battered pickups would rattle by with young people on their way to Dinuba for the movie matinees. But he wouldn't see them this morning, it being only Wednesday. There'd be others though, all loaded down with crates of peaches and melons and jars of green and ripe olives, and headed for the shipping platforms. (*The sound of another car approaching. Elmo turns his head to look for it*) He'd been sitting there for over an hour, alternately glancing out at the road and up at the starlings which were carrying away every last bit of green that remained of the otherwise bare yard, when he heard behind him the hum of a car. Coming *from* town. Must be someone going further out, he thought. The back road to the river. He waited for it to pass the house and enter his field of vision.

(The reverie concludes. The Narrator exits. Elmo shifts his position on the bench, and in doing so knocks over his stick. Again, the sound of a dog's barking offstage. The car stops, and a door opens and shuts)

RANSOM: (*Off; jovially*) Hello, puppy. Nice puppy. Go on, take a sniff. Go on. Atta pup. Good boy. Girl. Which are you? I know; I don't bite either. As long as you're heard, I know. (*He enters. A man in his thirties, Ransom is obviously a city boy, and too well dressed for the Valley. No jacket, though. A long-sleeved shirt, with a tie and fancy cuff links. He is wearing a pair of sunglasses and carrying an equipment case. He spots Elmo)* Hi, there! Found yourself some shade, I see.

ELMO: *(Surprised)* I . . . I . . .

RANSOM: *(Glancing around)* Home here alone, are you?

ELMO: *(Feeling for his stick)* I . . . my . . .

RANSOM: *(Retrieves it for him)* Lost your stick? Hold on, pops, I'll get it for you. Listen, is . . . uh . . . anybody else at home?

ELMO: *(Pointing off)* Yes . . . yes. Are y-you frum ish-shur-rence?

RANSOM: Ish . . . Insurance, you mean? The case, is that it? Don't let it fool you. I'm a photographer. *(Loud and distinct)* FOE-TOG-RAH-FER!!!!!

ELMO: *(Almost to himself)* Foe-t-tog-rah-fer . . .

RANSOM: That's me. Insurance! No, sir! I'm the world's worst risk, myself.

ELMO: *(As before)* Foe-tog-rah-fer . . .

RANSOM: *(Eager to get on with it)* Right. Say . . . uh . . . do you . . . live with someone?

ELMO: *(Again pointing)* Yes. My cuh . . . cum-ing . . . f-frum the gard-in.

RANSOM: Got a garden, have you?

ELMO: *(Rises to show him)* Bee-hind hen . . . hen house.

RANSOM: I mean, you people look a little short of water hereabouts.

ELMO: Wah-ter in d-dam. Ir-rig-gates the wh-whole val-valley. We grow . . . grow our o-o-o-own veg-tables.

(Ransom does not answer, just nods dutifully and continues to look about him. Finally, Melba and Emma Jean enter from the garden)

MELBA: Morning . . .

RANSOM: *(His old self again)* Good morning.

MELBA: *(Takes off her bandanna)* Sorry I couldn't come any sooner. I've been workin' in the garden.

RANSOM: So your father here's been telling me.

MELBA: *(Matter-of-factly)* He's my husband.

RANSOM: *(Somewhat ruffled)* Oh, I'm . . . sorry!

MELBA: I'm his second wife.

RANSOM: Whatever made me think—

MELBA: He's had a stroke . . . a couple of them, actually.

RANSOM: Well, I don't know what I must have been thinking.

MELBA: You're the new insurance man . . . Mister—

RANSOM: Ransom, ma'am. Jim Ransom. No, as I was explaining to your husband, I'm in the photography business.

EMMA JEAN: You go around takin' people's pictures, do ya?

MELBA: This is our daughter, Emma Jean.

RANSOM: *(Big smile)* Hi!

MELBA: I'm Melba Doyle . . . and you've already met Elmo.

RANSOM: Mrs. Doyle . . .

MELBA: *(Prompting him)* Photography, Mr. Ransom?

RANSOM: Yes, ma'am. I'm traveling for a very well-known San Francisco firm—

MELBA: *(Duly impressed)* Ohhh . . .

RANSOM: The Brewer Company. You've undoubtedly heard of us.

MELBA: The Brewer Company? The name's familiar. You remember, Elmo—the storekeeper. What was his name?

ELMO: Whii . . . White.

MELBA: No, not White. The people before them. Same name as . . . Ford! Their granddaughter, the blonde girl that came down from San Francisco one summer. She married a Brewer.

RANSOM: *(Launching into his pitch)* Yes, well, San Francisco's probably a bit out of the way for you here. Fresno'd be more your center, I imagine. But I can personally assure you that the Brewer Company is known throughout the Bay Area and all of Northern California as the best in the business. Just recently, Don and I . . . Don Brewer . . . I'm also a close friend of his. *(Holds up two fingers)* Our wives are like this. Anyhow, Don and I were discussing the problems that confront you good country people who want to have your pictures taken. *(Melba opens her mouth, but gets no chance to say anything. Emma Jean is transfixed. She sits down)* Now, we realize that you good country people, you who've done so much to keep this great state of ours on its feet during these hard times, you who support us cityites with your farming and agriculture . . . parasites, I guess you could call us—

EMMA JEAN: (*Dazed*) Parasites?

RANSOM: (*Snatching the word back from her*) Yes, parasites. Or . . . uh . . . perhaps the word "fleas" is a better one, like fleas on a dog's back. So, we felt that one way to show our gratitude was to bring the photographer to you, rather than the other way around. And, quite frankly, folks, I think our meeting like this today is particularly auspicious . . . (*They all look puzzled*) Today is . . . uh . . . particularly fortunate? (*Same look*) Lucky? (*They nod knowingly*) Yes, it is, too, because I can see that poor old . . . that . . . uh . . . your good husband here, Mrs. Doyle, would find it impossible to get over to Fresno to have his picture taken. I'm equally certain that, under the circumstances, nothing would be of greater comfort to you than a real live keepsake of this moment. I can tell the sort of wife you are. Believe me, Mrs. Doyle, a man doesn't travel around as much as I do without witnessing life to the fullest and gaining real insight into the nature of people. And I say that nothing would comfort you more than to have a picture taken of your husband here as soon as possible.

(*A long pause. This torrent of words has momentarily numbed everyone*)

EMMA JEAN: (*Finally*) That is the longest—

MELBA: Well, I appreciate your thinkin' of us, Mr. Ransom . . . and Mr. Brewer, too. He must be related to the Brewer that married that Ford girl. Such a nice boy he was. Still, I don't see how we can do with a photograph, I'm sorry ta say.

RANSOM: Five minutes, Mrs. Doyle; that's all I need to make a permanent record of you all as you are today.

ELMO: (*The beginnings of an idea*) Perm-man-nent???

RANSOM: (*To Elmo*) One that'll last forever.

MELBA: No, I don't think so.

RANSOM: (*Turning back to her*) I mightn't be back this way for quite awhile, and . . . by that time your daughter—Irma Jane, is it?—she could be married and off on her own by then. And that'll be too late for any reminder of these happy days of her youth when you were all here in this house together. (*As an afterthought*) And, of course, it might be too late for Mr. Doyle as well.

MELBA: The doctors say he could last another five years yet.

RANSOM: Yes; but on the other hand . . . Well, you never know.

MELBA: (*Only half downcast*) No, you don't. Then, as you say, it's hard enough to get him even as far as Visalia. That's where we usually have our pictures taken.

RANSOM: Do me this much: let me show you samples of our work; we can compare them with what you have here.

MELBA: (*Considers; then:*) Emma Jean, go on in and find that picture you had taken at your confirmation.

(*Emma Jean crosses to the front room and gets it. Ransom opens his case*)

RANSOM: Mark my words: you really owe it to yourselves to at least *see* what we can do. Be it color or black 'n white, there's always that little something extra to our work. Clarity, attention to detail, call it what you will. (*He takes out a sample book. Emma Jean returns with her photograph and hands it to him. He makes a show of studying it*) Very nice. You look very nice in this. All in white, too. Your . . . confirmation? Of course, white—ha, ha! But, my, you've changed so! I'd be willing to bet this wasn't taken recently.

MELBA: No; that goes back . . . How long is it? Four years? Just over four years, because confirmation was—

RANSOM: And the photo, itself. It's . . . presentable. A little on the grainy side, but . . . Well, here, let me hold it up alongside this one of ours. (*Showing them to her*) See what I mean by quality?

MELBA: Oh, will you just look at the expression on that child's face!

RANSOM: (*With Emma Jean peering over his shoulder*) It took me the better part of an hour to get that shot; but there she is, captured for all time.

ELMO: (*Caught up by the idea*) A p-perm-man-nent rec-c-cord.

RANSOM: You got the idea: long as this picture exists, so does the moment. (*Back to Melba*) Four years ago! Young girls what's-her-name's age change quite a bit in four years. They . . . develop, if you know what I mean. Forgive me; of course you'd know that . . . keeping them in clothes and all. Who'd know better? Ha, ha! Yes, I do, Mrs. Doyle. I really feel you owe it to your daughter here to have a new photo taken of her today. And, naturally, one of you alone, dear. And you and your husband together. And no sitting's complete without a family group.

MELBA: (*Somewhat abstractly*) Four years! Yes, we've all changed. Maybe you're right. Maybe we ought to have one taken of Emma Jean, anyway.

ELMO: (*His mind racing ahead*) No! No!

RANSOM: (*Taking out his camera*) Now, you're going to find it a great comfort to have a nice picture of your lovely wife and daughter with you, Mr. Doyle, if you should have to return to the hospital.

ELMO: No! To-ge-gether . . .

MELBA: One picture of the three of us . . . Is that what you want?

ELMO: Take . . . take us to-geth-ther.

RANSOM: Just the family group, you mean?

ELMO: Yes . . . fam-lee . . .

RANSOM: Anything you say.

ELMO: Alllll . . . uv us.

MELBA: About how much is this going ta cost us, Mr. Ransom?

RANSOM: The cost? Believe me, my dear, our rates are more than reasonable.

ELMO: (*Taking her arm*) Mel-ba . . .

MELBA: (*Shrugging him off*) He says they're not expensive.

ELMO: (*Very insistent*) No! No! To-geth-ther . . . ev-'ree-one!

MELBA: But don't you think—

ELMO: Have Ru-Ruby an' the boy-boys . . .

MELBA: (*Increasingly impatient*) How can we, when they're not even here? An' there's no tellin' when Mr. Ransom'll be back this way again.

RANSOM: I'm afraid your wife's right, Mr. Doyle. I've got the whole San Joaquin Valley to cover, and much as I'd like to, I can't be—

ELMO: *(With finality)*—Wait t-til they . . . are.

MELBA: *(Glares at him; then, to Ransom)* He wants a picture of the whole family. Besides the three of us, there's Ruby . . . she's the eldest . . . and our two sons, Ned and Lester.

RANSOM: *(Delighted)* Three, five, six . . . That many?

MELBA: Ruby's over Three Rivers way. She's married to a barber. Lester and his wife, they got themselves a little place the other side of Los Baños. And Ned was just married last—

RANSOM: Do you have any pictures of them here?

MELBA: We've got all their weddin' pictures, all except Ned's. They're still havin' it framed. Emma Jean, go and get—

RANSOM: Tell you what I can do for you, Mr. Doyle: I'll have a look at these pictures and see if I can fit them to the one I'm going to take of you now.

ELMO: *(Starting toward the house)* Aw-right. Yes, th-that's aw-right . . .

MELBA: *(Following after them)* Can you really do that, Mr. Ransom—fit them in?

RANSOM: Simple as one, two, three. It's a bit more expensive, but if that's what you want . . .

(They cross the porch and enter the front room. Elmo gestures to Emma Jean, who searches through the desk, finally finding two framed pictures which she gives to her mother. Ransom goes about the business of setting up his equipment)

MELBA: *(Presenting pictures to Ransom)* This is Ruby's wedding. That's her husband there beside her. You don't want him included, do ya, Elmo? No, I didn't think so. Just the immediate family. Here's our Emma Jean; she was the flower girl. The dresses we made ourselves, even Ruby's. But I suppose they show it . . .

RANSOM: My dear, they look right out of Magnin's window.

MELBA: *(Succumbing to his flattery)* I tell you, the hours we spent. This is Lester's group. He was so nervous . . . in and out that door I don't know how many times. Ned chased around after him to make sure he had everything. Even then, he nearly went off and forgot the ring. The ring, mind you! Left it sittin' inside on the bureau. If he hadn't gone back after a hankie . . . Well, I'm sure I don't know what would've happened.

RANSOM: Unh-hunh. And Ned's . . . you don't have his as yet?

MELBA: No, not yet . . .

RANSOM: Got any others of him, preferably by himself?

MELBA: Well, there's this one we had taken when he turned twenty-one. A flashlight photographer came out from town—

RANSOM: That should do fine. (*By now, his camera should be loaded and mounted on its tripod*) Ready any time you are.

MELBA: (*Suddenly aware of her appearance*) You'd better let me see myself in a mirror first. (*Starting off*) Elmo, you stay where you are; I'll bring in your tie and jacket.

RANSOM: (*To Melba, as she exits*) One thing, though: do you have a sheet I could borrow for the background?

MELBA: (*Calling back*) Emma Jean, go get one for Mr. Ransom.

(*Emma Jean exits after her mother into the interior of the house. Ransom busies himself arranging three chairs against one of the walls. He smiles at Elmo, even pats him on the back, as he moves about. Emma Jean reenters with the sheet*)

RANSOM: (*Taking it from her*) Thank you, honey. Now, all we need are some tacks.

EMMA JEAN: (*Searching through the desk*) There oughta be a couple . . . yes, here they are. (*They climb up on the chairs and tack the sheet behind them. Ransom goes back to his camera and lines up the shot. Elmo and Emma Jean look on*) Are you from San Francisco?

RANSOM: (*Perfunctorily*) Not originally, no . . .

EMMA JEAN: Where are you from . . . originally?

RANSOM: Originally? Pennsylvania . . .

EMMA JEAN: My father's from Arkansas. Ever been there?

RANSOM: Have I ever been where?

EMMA JEAN: In Arkansas.

RANSOM: No. I mean, I've passed through it.

EMMA JEAN: We were all set to go back the summer before last. Even had it arranged with the Filipino family down the road ta plant our cotton seed for us.

RANSOM: What stopped you?

EMMA JEAN: My daddy had his stroke.

RANSOM: That's too bad.

EMMA JEAN: I've been north as far as Modesto, and south to Bakersfield. But I suppose you travel that far every day.

RANSOM: How far?

EMMA JEAN: From Modesto to Bakersfield.

RANSOM: Pretty near.

EMMA JEAN: *(Pauses; then)* Is this gonna cost us more than a couple of dollars?

RANSOM: I wouldn't be surprised.

MELBA: *(Off)* Emma Jean, come get these clothes for your father. *(Emma Jean exits. Elmo takes his place in the center chair. Emma Jean returns with his jacket and tie)* And help him into them. *(Emma Jean does)* I hope I'm not holdin' up anything.

RANSOM: No, no . . .

(He unrolls a length of electric cord, keeping hold of the switch end. The other he extends offstage. Melba reenters. She has changed her dress, added a pair of heels, and perhaps even a touch of make-up)

MELBA: Sorry I took so long.

RANSOM: Nonsense. You weren't gone more than a minute. My dear, how lovely you look!

MELBA: *(Somewhat demurely)* Oh! Well, I've had this dress in my closet more years than I'd like to remember. *(Takes the tie from Emma Jean)* Here, let me finish this. *(Putting it on Elmo)* Did you have any seating arrangements in mind, Mr. Ransom?

RANSOM: Ordinarily, the wife sits to the right of her husband; and since there's only one child involved, she can take the chair to the left.

MELBA: Yes, that sounds proper.

(She finishes dressing Elmo. They take their places. Ransom flicks the switch and light floods the three of them. He approaches with a meter, gets a reading and returns to his camera. Elmo hands his stick to Emma Jean who puts it out of the picture. He straightens up

in his chair and, momentarily, assumes a more commanding and vigorous appearance)

RANSOM: Is everybody ready?

ELMO: Ready.

RANSOM: (*Bends over the camera*) Here goes. Hold it. Hooooold it . . . (*The shutter closes. Lights flash. He winds the film*) Let's do it again to be on the safe side. You can wet your lips, if you like. Okay, eyes straight ahead, now. A little higher. Little higher. Emma Jean, you're not looking up.

MELBA: (*Holding her pose*) Emma Jean . . .

EMMA JEAN: (*Trying not to squint*) It's like lookin' into the sun. (*But she manages*)

RANSOM: (*Again over the camera*) Better. Better. Now, hold it . . . just . . . like . . . that! (*The shutter closes. Lights flash. He switches off all the additional lights, and immediately sets about to dismantle his equipment*) That should do us.

(*Emma Jean returns the stick to her father. He remains in his chair. Melba goes to the desk and rummages around until she locates a packet of photographs*)

MELBA: (*Showing one to Ransom*) Here's the one of Ned.

RANSOM: (*With barely a glance*) Unh-hunh. That looks about the right size. Do you have any of the other two alone? They're both a bit small in their wedding pictures.

MELBA: (*Checking the packet*) I'm . . . not . . . sure.

EMMA JEAN: There's one of Ruby in my room. She's still in her gown, though.

RANSOM: Let's see it, anyway.

MELBA: (*To Emma Jean*) Well, bring it here. (*Still checking*) That leaves only . . . Yes, here he is . . . Lester!

(*Emma Jean exits into the interior of the house. Ransom examines the picture Melba is holding*)

RANSOM: Nothing of him in a shirt and tie?

MELBA: (*Checking further*) I . . . don't . . . think . . . so. Afraid not. No, Lester's the open collar type. Never did like the feel of a tie around his neck. Said he couldn't ever turn his head right ta left when he had one on without cuttin' off his wind.

RANSOM: Well, that's alright; I can fix him up in the shop.

(*Emma Jean reenters with a picture, which she thrusts at her mother*)

EMMA JEAN: Here . . .

RANSOM: (*Giving it a quick look*) This one of what's-her-name . . . ?

MELBA: Ruby.

RANSOM: Right. I think we ought to take her veil off.

MELBA: (*Looks; considers*) Well . . . if you think so.

RANSOM: I do. Absolutely . . .

(*His equipment should be just about packed away by now. Also, about now Melba is beginning to weigh the expense involved in all this*)

EMMA JEAN: You sure can do all sorts o' things . . . to a picture, I mean.

RANSOM: Honey, I can put two heads on you, and a mustache, if you think you'd look better that way.

EMMA JEAN: (*Laughs at the idea*) No, thank you very much.

MELBA: Emma Jean, be a good girl and take down the sheet. That is, if Mr. Ransom's through with it?

RANSOM: Yes, ma'am, all through. Now, do I have everyone's picture?

ELMO: Mel-ba . . .

(*Emma Jean begins removing the sheet*)

RANSOM: (*Anticipating money troubles*) No need for you to go worrying yourself, Mr. Doyle. Your lovely wife and I'll get this all worked out.

ELMO: No . . . no! Mel-ba, the oth-thers!

MELBA: What others? There's the three of us Mr. Ransom just took, an' Ruby's weddin picture, an' that one of Ned, and Lester's twenty-first . . . Oh, you mean the girls?

ELMO: Ev-'ree-one . . .

MELBA: (*Again checking the packet*) He's got two more daughters.

RANSOM: (*Wonderful news*) Ohhh!

MELBA: (*As an afterthought*) By an earlier marriage.

RANSOM: (*To Elmo*) Weren't you the busy one!

MELBA: It'd be a nice thought, I suppose . . . to include them, I mean. But the only ones we have are awful old now.

(*Finds a picture*) Here's Gloria when *she* was confirmed. You'll have to take her veil off, too, won't you?

RANSOM: It would be best . . . in the interest of harmony.

MELBA: Elmo, you don't think this is gettin' ta be more than we meant to spend?

ELMO: I w-want ev-'ree-one.

EMMA JEAN: (*The sheet in hand*) Where do ya want this?

MELBA: (*Annoyed; snaps*) Want what? What is it?

EMMA JEAN: The sheet . . . Where do you—

MELBA: Oh . . . uh . . . just leave it inside for the time bein' . . . on one of the beds. I don' imagine it's hangin' there like it did dirtied it any. (*As Emma Jean exits*) An' fold it. I don' want it left wadded up the way ya have it.

RANSOM: How long ago was this taken?

MELBA: (*Turning it over*) There's the date there. When she was thirteen . . . that's goin' back some thirty-four, thirty-five years now. Should be one of Betty in here . . . someplace. Here she is. When she was . . . (*Turning it over*) Eighteen. The changes that've happened since this was taken. (*Looking at Elmo*) There's nothin' like an old photograph to remind us of what we once were. (*Pauses; then*) Will it matter, Mr. Ransom? I mean, Betty's really younger than Gloria, but she'll look older if we use this picture of her.

RANSOM: Well, as you yourself said, dear, it's the thought that counts. You agree with that, Mr. Doyle?

ELMO: (*Ignoring him*) Mel-ba, I s-said ev-'ree-one.

MELBA: But, that is everyone.

ELMO: (*Rises; starts off*) Es-ter . . . ha-have Es-ter, too.

MELBA: (*As Elmo exits*) Do we have a picture of her? (*To Ransom*) Esther's his first wife. (*Checking still further*) No. No, there's nothin' of her here, Elmo.

(*Elmo reenters with a framed picture which he wipes on his coat*)

ELMO: (*Handing it to Ransom*) Shelf . . . in th-the bed-room. (*He sits*)

MELBA: (*Over his shoulder*) Won't she be smaller than the rest of us?

RANSOM: (*As Emma Jean reenters*) Don't you worry, we'll blow her up to size.

MELBA: Blow her up?

RANSOM: Oh, that's just . . . trade talk. One thing, though: we have to charge double. Respect for the dead. It's a rule in our business.

MELBA: Isn't that interesting? But I suppose we should have her.

RANSOM: Now then, I'll bet you're all wondering how much this amounts to.

MELBA: I think I'll sit down.

(*Ransom laughs and takes out a pad and pen, which he uses to add up the costs as he goes along*)

RANSOM: It's not so bad as that, my dear. Let's see, now. Five dollars for the one we took today. A dollar-fifty to add Ned. Another two-fifty for this one . . . Betty, is it? Three each for your other son and daughter. The same again for Gloria. And three . . . six . . . for the first Mrs. Doyle. We have to take her veil off, too . . . and double it . . . is . . . six. Right. That comes to . . . (*Totaling it inaudibly*) Twenty-three dollars. (*Melba is stunned*) Now, that may seem expensive; but it's really not—not when you consider the work involved. There's one, two, three veils to be removed, and a shirt and tie to be put on what's-his-name . . . Lester. And, of course, you'd expect to pay something for the name, Brewer, on the picture. No, twenty-three dollars is not expensive at all for what you're getting. (*Going for broke*) I imagine you'd like a fairly heavy frame for a family gathering of this size. (*He takes a sample frame out of his case and shows it around*) Something impressive to set it off . . . like this gold frame, for instance. Old stock. Like they used to make it. You won't be able to get anything like it much longer, and we're offering it—despite the demand—for just ten dollars. Ten dollars! How's that for value! Now, I notice some of these pictures are tinted: the one of Betty, for instance, and your first wife's, too. I want to be perfectly frank with you. I don't as a rule recommend tinting pictures. And there are some who don't care for them. But, in this case, my advice would be to tint them *all*. I'll tell you why I say that. The pictures I'll be working with are what we call in the business a wild lot. Some old, some new, some tinted, some not. There's things to be added, things to be removed. A touch of color would go a long way towards smoothing out any of the little—oddities, shall we say—that might appear. Now, usually the charge for coloring is high . . . extremely high. But, since you've been such good customers . . . (*He tears off and crumbles the sheet of paper he has been writing on*) And, as I said before, we *are* out on the road to help all our good country neighbors by bringing big city amenities . . . (*Remembers their vocabulary*) Conveniences? Comforts? Yes, comforts . . . within your reach. So, I feel sure that Don—Don Brewer—would agree with me if I reduce the cost, and make it an even—

(*He marks a big $30 on the pad, and holds it up to them*)

MELBA: Thirty dollars for a photograph?

RANSOM: Oh, but consider, Mrs. Doyle—I'm cutting down on the tinting, and the savings on the frame—

MELBA: Yes, yes, I understand all that. But thirty dollars! I thought five, ten maybe. But *thirty*? No, you'd better try further down the road.

ELMO: (*On his feet*) I w-want it.

MELBA: We can't *afford* thirty dollars! No, Mr. Ransom, I think you'd better look for another family to take your pictures of. (*Elmo goes to the desk, locates her purse, and holds it out to her*) Elmo, it's too much!

ELMO: Here . . .

MELBA: You want to throw thirty dollars away on a photograph?

ELMO: (*A pronouncement*) I w-want us to-geth-ther . . .

(*Melba snatches her purse from him, counts off thirty dollars, and hands it to Ransom*)

MELBA: There! Thirty dollars.

RANSOM: (*Has the paperwork all ready*) Thank you. And your signature here, if you will.

(*She just glares at the receipt, then turns away. Elmo comes forward and signs it. The dog can be heard offstage barking*)

MELBA: Emma Jean, go shut that dog up in the separator shed.

(*Emma Jean crosses to the porch, into the yard, and exits. Ransom hands a copy of the receipt to Elmo*)

RANSOM: This you get . . . (*Pocketing the pad*) This I keep. Notice, I've marked it paid-in-full. That way there won't be any questions upon delivery; you'll have your receipt right in front of you. Incidently, delivery's free of charge. Another little benefit from the Brewer Company. Well, I'd say that about wraps things up, wouldn't you? (*He picks up his case and walks over to Elmo. A big smile on his face. They shake hands*) Mr. Doyle, it's been a pleasure.

ELMO: (*Taking his arm*) How l-l-long?

RANSOM: You mean, before your picture arrives?

ELMO: (*Anxiously*) Yes . . .

RANSOM: Oh, I'd figure on two weeks, if I were you. That's a lot of work you're having done, don't forget; and done properly, it takes time. Remember: the name Brewer goes on nothing but the very best. (*To Melba; defensively*) Now, to get to town, I go down to the end of the drive, and turn—

MELBA: (*Grimly polite*) Left.

RANSOM: (*Crossing to the porch*) Left. And that puts me on Avenue 432.

MELBA: (*Following him*) Anybody can tell ya where ta go from there. (*Ransom exits. Long pause. Elmo stands in the doorway. The sound of a car starting up and driving off. Sound of the birds. Melba calls to offstage*) Emma Jean! (*Turns; to Elmo*) Are those dishes washed yet?

ELMO: (*Withering*) I . . . I'll g-get them d-d-done.

(*Melba exits towards the garden. Elmo reenters the front room, visibly weary, his limp much more pronounced. He turns to a section of the wall, and gazes at it. The Narrator enters*)

NARRATOR: He'd hang it there on the wall. It would be good to have them all together again: Esther and the girls, Melba and their children, and himself, of course, in the middle. They'd be there always now, waiting for him when he returned from his morning watch on the bench and afternoon tour of the sheds. And they'd be quiet, submissive. Even Melba. Surely, they would act in some way as a charm against the terrible decay he sensed within himself.

Curtain

Stanley Richards

Since the publication of his first collection in 1968, Stanley Richards has become one of our leading editors and play anthologists, earning rare encomiums from the nation's press (the *Writers Guild of America News* described him as "easily the best anthologist of plays in America") and the admiration of a multitude of devoted readers.

Mr. Richards has edited the following anthologies: *The Best Short Plays* series, issued annually 1968–1979; *Great Musicals of the American Theatre: Volume One; Great Musicals of the American Theatre: Volume Two; America on Stage: Ten Great Plays of American History; Best Plays of the Sixties; Best Mystery and Suspense Plays of the Modern Theatre; 10 Classic Mystery and Suspense Plays of the Modern Theatre; Great Rock Musicals* (the latter seven books have been The Fireside Theatre–Literary Guild selections); *The Tony Winners; Twenty One-Act Plays; Best Short Plays of the World Theatre: 1968–1973; Best Short Plays of the World Theatre: 1958–1967; Modern Short Comedies from Broadway and London;* and *Canada on Stage.*

An established playwright as well, he has written twenty-five plays, twelve of which (including *Through a Glass, Darkly; Tunnel of Love; August Heat; Sun Deck; O Distant Land;* and *District of Columbia*) were originally published in earlier volumes of *The Best One-Act Plays* and *The Best Short Plays.*

Journey to Bahia, which he adapted from a prize-winning Brazilian play and film, *O Pagador de Promessas,* premiered at the Berkshire Playhouse, Massachusetts, and later was produced in Washington, D.C., under the auspices of the Brazilian Ambassador and the Brazilian American Cultural Institute. The play also had a successful engagement Off-Broadway and subsequently was performed in a Spanish translation at Lincoln Center. During the summer of 1975, the play was presented at the Edinburgh International Festival in Scotland, after a tour of several British cities.

Mr. Richards' plays have been translated for production and publication abroad into Portuguese, Afrikaans, Dutch, Tagalog, French, German, Korean, Italian, and Spanish.

He also has been the New York theatre critic for *Players Magazine* and a frequent contributor to *Playbill, Theatre Arts,*

The Theatre, and *Actors' Equity Magazine,* among many other periodicals. He currently serves as Drama Consultant for *Literary Cavalcade,* published by Scholastic Magazines.

As an American Theatre Specialist, Mr. Richards was awarded three successive grants by the U. S. Department of State's International Cultural Exchange Program to teach playwriting and directing in Chile and Brazil. He taught playwriting in Canada for over ten years and was Visiting Professor of Drama at the University of Guelph, Ontario. He has produced and directed plays and has lectured extensively on theatre at universities in the United States, Canada, and South America.

Mr. Richards, a New York City resident, is now at work on *The Best Short Plays 1980.*

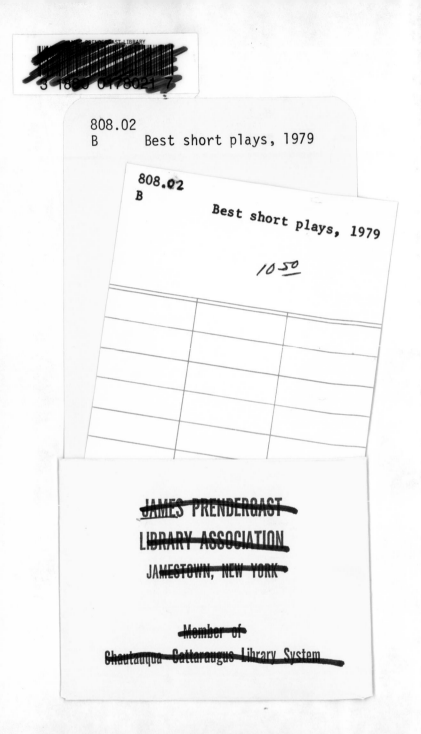
